REVELATION

Tribulation & Triumph

REVELATION

Tribulation & Triumph

A Devotional Commentary Series by

PCF
Practical Christianity
Foundation

L.L. SPEER, FOUNDER

CREATION HOUSE
A STRANG COMPANY

REVELATION—TRIBULATION AND TRIUMPH
by Practical Christianity Foundation
Published by Creation House, A Strang Company
600 Rinehart Road, Lake Mary, Florida 32746
www.strangbookgroup.com

Cover art: The Resource Agency, Franklin, Tennessee

Strang Communications Design Director: Bill Johnson

www.practicalchristianityfoundation.com

Library of Congress Control Number: 2010940896
International Standard Book Number: 978-1-61638-355-8

First Edition

10 11 12 13 14 — 9 8 7 6 5 4 3 2 1
Printed in Canada

CONTENTS

PREFACE

From the conception of the Practical Christianity Foundation (PCF), it has been the goal of the organization to convey the truth in Scripture through verse-by-verse devotional studies such as this one. As part of that goal, we agree in an attempt neither to prove nor to disprove any traditional or alternative interpretations, beliefs, or doctrines but rather to allow the Holy Spirit to reveal the truth contained within the Scriptures. Any interpretations relating to ambiguous passages that are not directly and specifically verifiable by other scriptural references are simply presented in what we believe to be the most likely intention of the message based on those things that we are specifically told. In those instances, our conclusions are noted as interpretive, and such analyses should not be understood as doctrinal positions that we are attempting to champion.

This study is divided into sections, usually between six and eight verses, and each section concludes with a "Notes/Applications" passage, which draws practical insight from the related verses that can be applied to contemporary Christian living. The intent is that the reader will complete one section per day, will gain a greater understanding of the verses within that passage, and will daily be challenged toward a deeper commitment to our Lord and Savior Jesus Christ. Also included at certain points within the text are "Dig Deeper" boxes, which are intended to assist readers who desire to invest additional time to study topics that relate to the section in which these boxes appear. Our prayer is that this study will impact the lives of all believers, regardless of age, ethnicity, or education.

Each of PCF's original projects is a collaborative effort of many writers, content editors, grammatical editors, transcribers, researchers, readers, and other contributors, and as such, we present them only as products of Practical Christianity Foundation as a whole. These works are not for the recognition or acclamation of any particular individual but are written simply as a means to uphold and fulfill the greater purpose of our Mission Statement, which is "to exalt the holy name of God Almighty by declaring the redemptive message of His Son, the Lord Jesus Christ, to the lost global community and equipping the greater Christian community through the communication of the holy Word of God in its entirety through every appropriate means available."

Practical Christianity Foundation
Value Statements

1. We value the Holy Name of God the Father and will strive to exalt Him through godly living, committed service, and effective communication. *"As long as you live, you, your children, and your grandchildren must fear the Lord your God. All of you must obey all his laws and commands that I'm giving you, and you will live a long time" (Deuteronomy 6:2).*

2. We value the redemptive work of the Lord Jesus Christ, God's Holy Son, for a lost world and will strive to communicate His redemptive message to the global community. *"Then Jesus said to them, 'So wherever you go in the world, tell everyone the Good News'" (Mark 16:15).*

3. We value the Holy Spirit through Whose regenerating work sinners are redeemed and the redeemed are convinced of the truth of God's Holy Word. *"He will come to convict the world of sin, to show the world what has God's approval, and to convince the world that God judges it" (John 16:8).*

4. We value the Holy Word of God and will strive to communicate it in its entirety. *"16Every Scripture passage is inspired by God. All of them are useful for teaching, pointing out errors, correcting people, and training them for a life that has God's approval. 17They equip God's servants so that they are completely prepared to do good things" (2 Timothy 3:16–17).*

5. We value spiritual growth in God's people through the equipping ministry of the church of the Lord Jesus Christ and will strive to provide resources for that ministry by the communication of God's Holy Word, encouraging them to be lovers of the truth. *"But grow in the good will and knowledge of our Lord and Savior Jesus Christ. Glory belongs to him now and for that eternal day! Amen" (2 Peter 3:18).*

INTRODUCTION

The word *revelation* is derived from the Greek word *apokalypto*, which means to disclose, uncover, manifest, and reveal that which is hidden.[1] In the entire Bible, there is perhaps no other book that generates more conversation or controversy, none that is more studied yet less understood than this last book in the canon of the Christian Scriptures.

The problems of interpretation are generated from attempts to decipher each detail in such a way as to reflect the current world situation. However, as the world situation changes, so do the interpretations of this book. The first century Church expected Jesus to return in a very short time. It is evident that Jesus' closest disciples began to rethink their position even before the apostolic period ended. Toward the end of his life (around A.D. 68), Simon Peter, the leader of Christ's apostles, wrote a second epistle that seemed to address such concerns. "*8Dear friends, don't ignore this fact: One day with the Lord is like a thousand years, and a thousand years are like one day. 9The Lord isn't slow to do what he promised, as some people think. Rather, he is patient for your sake. He doesn't want to destroy anyone but wants all people to have an opportunity to turn to him and change the way they think and act*" (2 Peter 3:8-9). Ever since that time, Christians have struggled to understand

1

the Book of Revelation in the context of world history as they watch the slow progression of events that impact their lives. In times of terrible persecution, famines, wars, and human atrocities, Christians have concluded that the end was near, wondering when Jesus would return and right all wrongs.

Because of these multiple streams of Christian thought, today's Christians, no matter how sincere and passionate in their pursuit of biblical knowledge, find themselves at a juncture that challenges their best efforts at unraveling the mystery of this marvelous book. In the midst of this noble pursuit, they may discover that there is no other subject that will generate more heated debate than this one. Instead of discovering the glorious Christ of John's Revelation, they often find themselves embroiled in debates that appear to have no satisfactory resolution.

Despite all of the debates, all of the numerous theories and interpretive systems, and all of the controversies that consume the energy of Christ's Church, there is perhaps no more exciting book in all of God's Word. It is the crowning jewel of God's unfailing plan to save for Himself a people that will live with Him and praise His Holy Name for all eternity. From the beginning of Genesis, one overriding, all-consuming theme comes to light in God's Word—*redemption*. Revelation is the consummation of that theme when Christ completely destroys all evil and invites His bride to the marriage feast of the Lamb. We view Christ as high and lifted up. Here we discover the glorious riches of His Kingdom that He has prepared for those who have been invited to share in this feast. Now, at long last, the Lord Jesus Christ ascends His throne that has been preserved for Him from the foundation of the world, and every knee bows at the awesomeness of His unsurpassed majesty, power, dominion, and glory. On this theme—on this revelation—all Christians who love the Word of God will universally and enthusiastically agree.

Generally, there are four positions by which the Book of Revelation is traditionally interpreted: historicist, preterist, futurist, and idealist (sometimes called the spiritual or symbolic view).

- The *historicist* believes that the Book of Revelation is an outline of the history of the church between the first and second comings of Christ.

- A *preterist* believes that a majority of the prophecy in Revelation was fulfilled in the first century and that the main theme of the book points to the destruction of Jerusalem in A.D. 70.

- A *futurist* believes that Revelation contains end-times prophecies and, more specifically, prophecies pertaining to the tribulation and second coming of the Lord Jesus Christ.

- An *idealist* believes that Revelation is largely (in some cases exclusively) symbolic, that it should not be taken literally, and that it merely illustrates the greater cosmic struggle between good and evil.[2]

Obviously, these camps vary greatly in their viewpoints, and the impact and significance of this book depend upon whether one believes that the events depicted within have already occurred, are yet to occur, or have never and will never occur in a physical sense at all. Granted, these positions were created by men, defined by men, and defended by men. If any one of these positions could be shown to be true beyond question or doubt, all other positions would be rendered obsolete. Such is evidently not the case. Each position has certain arguments that seem valid and worthy of consideration, just as each position has certain areas of susceptibility and fallibility. Some verses of the book are more easily understood through the arguments of one position while other verses seem to make more sense as interpreted by an alternate position. This is both the frustration and fascination that surrounds the Book of Revelation.

The dilemma is that as soon as one agrees with a certain interpretation on a specific point, he is quickly dismissed by an opposing view as an advocate for the position that most closely aligns itself with that interpretation. To avoid such labels, some have even adopted new labels, such as "partial preterists," but in doing so perhaps only further cloud the already murky waters.[3]

The point is this: each position has at least some merit or else it would not have gained credibility among the other viewpoints. There is no "safe" way to approach the interpretation of Revelation except to agree neither to fully adopt nor to fully reject any of these positions. Still, such an approach should not be misconstrued as indecisive or uncertain. Rather, it is only with a clear understanding of these and other viewpoints that one could even attempt to interpret this book. There is always a sense of mystery when attempting to explain the ways of God.

For instance, one can scarcely question that the seven churches addressed in chapters one through three were literal, historical churches that existed in Asia Minor, yet one would have great difficulty proving that all of the events depicted in later chapters of Revelation have already occurred. Therefore, one must conclude that the book contains both historical and prophetic elements. Similarly, both symbolic and physical elements coexist. Few can doubt that there is a great deal of symbolism in the book, yet to suggest that its contents in their entirety are merely symbolic illustrations of spiritual realms is to disregard the physical ramifications of its many conditional warnings, such as repent, change your life, return to God (*Revelation 2:5, 2:16, 2:22, 3:3, 3:19*). Indeed, the entire book is imbued with physical judgments, physical conditions, and physical consequences.

Furthermore, a variety of interpretations have been entertained regarding the authorship of Revelation. Most of the early church fathers agree that the book was written by John, the beloved apostle of Jesus. Some critics doubt the apostolic authorship of Revelation because of the inferior style and grammar of the Greek with which the book was written when compared to that of other writings by John the Apostle.[4] However, Acts 4:13 refers to John as someone with "no education or special training," so the use of such unpolished Greek should not be surprising, especially considering the urgency and exhilaration with which he surely felt compelled to record the visions as they were occurring. Some commentators even suggest that John owed the more skillful Greek demonstrated in his Gospel and epistles to an *amanuensis* (or secretary), who was, for obvious reasons, not accessible to the apostle during his banishment on the isle of Patmos.[5] For these and many other reasons, the acceptance of an apostolic authorship is favored.

Even more a subject of debate is the dating of the text. Most preterists insist on an authorship occurring between A.D. 54-68 during the reign of the notorious Roman emperor Nero, which assists an explanation that the events in the book depict the grueling cultural climate of the first-century church, culminating with the destruction of the temple and the city of Jerusalem in A.D. 70.[6] More popular and more convincing are the arguments that the writing occurred between A.D. 90-96 during the reign of the Roman emperor Domitian. The historical recordings of early-church fathers such as Irenaeus, Clement of Alexandria, and Jerome substantiate a later dating of the book.[7] Furthermore, some scholars have suggested that chapters two and three reveal the prominence of certain cities that would only be historically consistent with their conditions in the late first century.[8]

An in-depth study of the varied interpretations regarding the countless symbols, numbers, events, judgments, sequences, and visions presented in Revelation is surely better reserved for those books which endeavor to present a thorough critique. In virtually every book written about Revelation, even the smallest details are credited with having monumental significance. Ultimately, there is far too much controversy over Revelation to be adequately presented in what is intended as a devotional study. With the preceding foundation laid, we approach this commentary on Revelation from the viewpoint that the prophecies within are perhaps telescopic (also called expanded or double-fulfillment prophecy). Whereas, not to dismiss altogether the possibility of an earlier date of authorship and a partial fulfillment of certain prophecies with the destruction of Jerusalem in A.D. 70, we

uphold the tenet that the events described within Revelation pertain
to the final judgment of Almighty God upon the reprobate inhabitants of the earth in the last days. Apart from such an interpretation,
one might find little validity or usefulness to this book in the modern
world.

Almighty God has yet to judge the entire sum of unrepentant
inhabitants on the earth *(Revelation 6:16–17;14:7)*. He has yet to pour
out the full measure of His wrath and indignation *(Revelation 14:10)*.
The world has yet to experience the utter devastation that will come
upon its environment *(Revelation 16)*. The Lord Jesus Christ has yet to
return to the earth in triumphant glory *(Revelation 19:11–16)*, to conquer wholly the world's evil *(Revelation 19:19–21)*, to reign upon the
earth for a thousand years *(Revelation 20:1–5)*, to finish the judgment
of Satan and his followers *(Revelation 20:7–15)*, or to establish and
reign in His eternal Kingdom with those He has redeemed *(Revelation
21, 22)*.

Aside from the wrath and tribulation uniquely depicted in
Revelation, no other book so fully illustrates the magnificent splendor
of the everlasting Kingdom that awaits those who have placed their
faith and hope in Jesus Christ. Indeed, there is much to be gained
by reading this book despite its tendency at times to seem puzzling,
overwhelming, and even frightening.

So, what is the benefit in reading a book whose interpretation is
so difficult to affirm with absolute certainty? God did not give us the
Book of Revelation to frustrate us but to strengthen us, not to confuse us but to encourage us.[9] Instead, we should take confidence both
to persevere in the midst of tribulation and to anticipate the Lord
Jesus Christ's glorious, ultimate triumph. Therefore, we approach this
book with full cognizance of the debates with which the Christian
community struggles, but with full devotion to the Savior Who has
redeemed us, Who is redeeming us, and Who will one day redeem
us when He ushers us into His eternal Kingdom. While we acknowledge that we now *"see a blurred image in a mirror, then we will see very
clearly"* *(1 Corinthians 13:12)* and admit that our understanding has

been obscured by the boundaries of our human limitations. We can perhaps find the simplest benefit written in the first lines of the first chapter: "Blessed is the one who reads, as well as those who hear the words of this prophecy and pay attention to what is written in it because the time is near" *(Revelation 1:3).*

REVELATION

Revelation 1:1–6

1:1–2 *¹This is the revelation of Jesus Christ. God gave it to him to show his servants the things that must happen soon. He sent this revelation through his angel to his servant John. ²John testified about what he saw: God's Word and the testimony about Jesus Christ.*

This is the revelation of Jesus Christ delivered to the apostle John directly by Jesus Himself or through appointed angels or messengers. The prologue declares its chief themes and provides a vantage point from which the reader may rightly interpret the vision that follows.[1] The major theme of the Book of Revelation is to tell the nations that Jesus is the Judge of all creation and the coming King of kings. The mysteries that the Lord unveiled to John further illuminate teachings revealed in other portions of God's Word. The message of this book is meant as an encouragement to believers so that they will not be afraid or deceived about events that will take place in the last days. Furthermore, they will find joy and hope in Christ as the final authority on all things temporal and eternal.

For nearly two thousand years, Christians have asked, "When will these events occur?" Only God knows for certain. In this verse, the word *soon* connotes something happening quickly.[2] However, God's timetable is not our timetable because God is not constrained by time (*2 Peter 3:8*). He is not swayed by man's actions or desires, so He will fulfill these prophesies according to His predetermined plan.

John introduces himself to his readers as a servant of the Lord. As one of the original twelve disciples of Jesus, John was qualified as one who bore witness to "God's Word and the testimony about Jesus Christ" from firsthand experience. John had walked with Jesus, had witnessed and experienced the Lord's ministry personally, and had suffered persecution for proclaiming the Gospel of Jesus Christ. He undoubtedly believed the things he witnessed and recorded in this book. In one of the letters he penned to young, struggling churches, John affirmed the ministry of Jesus in the things he had personally witnessed:

> [1]The Word of life existed from the beginning. We have heard it. We have seen it. We observed and touched it. [2]This life was revealed to us. We have seen it, and we testify about it. We are reporting to you about this eternal life that was in the presence of the Father and was revealed to us. [3]This is the life we have seen and heard. We are reporting about it to you also so that you, too, can have a relationship with us. Our relationship is with the Father and with his Son Jesus Christ. [4]We are writing this so that we can be completely filled with joy. (1 John 1:1–4)

1:3 Blessed is the one who reads, as well as those who hear the words of this prophecy and pay attention to what is written in it because the time is near.

This verse does not simply mean that one who reads and hears this message will be blessed. Rather, the implication is that God bestows peace and happiness only to those who absorb the message and whose lives are impacted by the Truth of God's Word.[3]

John clearly states that this book is prophetic. More specifically, we know from later verses that it reveals events of the last days. Although many of these events have not yet been fulfilled, they will certainly occur at a future time. By studying this book, believers will learn biblical truths that will impact their lives and receive God-given security and confidence about the future.

1:4 *From John to the seven churches in the province of Asia. Good will and peace to you from the one who is, the one who was, and the one who is coming, from the seven spirits who are in front of his throne...*

It is commonly accepted that John wrote to seven literal churches that existed in Western Asia.[4] However, there are also several interpretations regarding the universal symbolism of these churches. Among these, the most persuasive interpretation contends that these churches also represent a general variation found in spiritual conditions still prevalent throughout churches today.[5]

John opened his letter with a familiar salutation, *"Good will and peace to you."* This greeting was extended on behalf of the eternal God. John identified the source of this revelation as the One *"Who is and Who was and Who is to come."* Normally Christians immediately conclude that John was speaking of Jesus. But the following verse makes it clear that John is speaking of the eternal God, the One Who is the Eternal I AM. The Jerusalem Targum (a Jewish commentary) on Deuteronomy 32:29 expanded *"I am who I am"* as *"I am He who is, and who was, and I am He who will be,"* thereby setting forth God as the Lord of all time and eternity.[6] The greeting is also given on behalf of "the seven spirits who are in front of His throne." This will be studied in greater detail in later verses.

1:5 *...and from Jesus Christ, the witness, the trustworthy one, the first to come back to life, and the ruler over the kings*

of the earth. Glory and power forever and ever belong to the
one who loves us and has freed us from our sins by his blood...

Good will and peace were also offered from the Lord and Savior Jesus
Christ, the Son of God. While He was on earth, Christ was the faithful Servant Who fulfilled the Law of God and thereby died as the
perfect sacrifice to atone for the sins of the world (*John 1:29*).

This verse also identifies Jesus as *"the first to come back to life."*
The Bible tells of others who were raised from the dead through
Jesus' power (*Matthew 9:24–25; Luke 7:12–15; John 11:11–44*). When
Jesus brought these people back to life, however, they eventually experienced physical death again. Jesus, the eternal Son of God, did not
relinquish His deity when He came to earth, but, in His role as God's
Passover Lamb gave His life and then took it back again, providing
evidence that He alone is the Lord of both life and death. Death could
never hold the Eternal One.

Finally, John called Jesus "the Ruler over the kings of the earth."
Christ unilaterally appoints all earthly dominions by His sovereign
decree. *"The holy ones have announced this so that every living creature*
will know that the Most High has power over human kingdoms. He gives
them to whomever he wishes. He can place the lowest of people in charge
of them" (*Daniel 4:17*). This title may also allude to Christ's position as
King of kings and Lord of lords. Whatever the interpretation, Jesus
holds this position of sovereign dominion over all aspects of His creation, demonstrating His perfect love, absolute justness, consummate
holiness, and complete supremacy.

The last part of this verse summarizes the place that Jesus holds
at the very center of the splendid Gospel message: Jesus is the One
Who loves us and washes us with His own blood from our otherwise
condemning sins. He willingly laid down His life to redeem us from
the consequence of sin, and opened to us the portals of His eternal
Kingdom.

1:6 ...*and has made us a kingdom, priests for God his Father. Amen.*

Through the atonement of Jesus Christ, our High Priest, God has made His people to be priests in His eternal Kingdom, living their lives in His service. The redeemed of the Lord stand before Him as members of a royal priesthood. When Peter wrote his letter to first century Christians, he said: *"⁹However, you are chosen people, a royal priesthood, a holy nation, people who belong to God. You were chosen to tell about the excellent qualities of God, who called you out of darkness into his marvelous light. ¹⁰Once you were not God's people, but now you are. Once you were not shown mercy, but now you have been shown mercy"* (1 Peter 2:9–10).

John recognized and praised the Lord for His glory and dominion over the earth. Then, the apostle concluded with an "Amen," which means "so be it," thereby affirming that these things he said about Jesus Christ were eternally and unequivocally true.

Notes/Applications

No other book of the Scriptures is more fiercely attacked, defended, debated, and argued by differing Christian perspectives throughout the Christian world. Its mysteries confound the most educated scholars. Its soaring depiction of heavenly scenes in turn causes believers' hearts to soar. Its plagues and godly judgments cause the stoutest of hearts to tremble.

Yet, regardless of any individual's personal opinion and the debate it engenders, one fact is abundantly clear—the author of this book is not John, the beloved apostle. It is the Triune God. At the outset, John reports that he was addressed by the eternal "I AM," the Spirit, and Jesus Christ. Divine authorship is emphatically affirmed like no other book of the Bible.

Because of this authorship, Christians should approach the study of this book with care, discernment, and not a little bit of awe. Those passages that are difficult to understand should be accepted without doubt that this is God's Word. Those passages that are clearly under-stood should give birth to reverent fear for unbelievers and reverent worship for believers.

While we understand that Christ's return was a predominant factor in their Christian lives, we also understand that it was not to *dominate* their daily routines. Christians were called to tell others about Jesus, the One Who had died and come back to life again, assuring them of His full payment for the sins of those the Father has given to Him. Just as they were certain of the risen Lord, Whom they served with full and happy hearts, they could be equally assured that He was coming again.

Like those early believers, Christians today should not major in the study of the last days, but embrace gladly the calling of God in the work of His Kingdom. When looking forward to the return of Jesus Christ, they should likewise remember the Author of this revelation, happy that He will return again to execute both His salvation and His judgment on the people of the world. Suppressing the details of His return that often lead to dissension among God's redeemed people, Christians should instead engage in the work of Christ's Kingdom, rejoicing that their Savior abides with them and within them until that day when He returns in power and glory.

Revelation 1:7–11

1:7 *Look! He is coming in the clouds. Every eye will see him, even those who pierced him. Every tribe on earth will mourn because of him. This is true. Amen.*

Jesus will return in the clouds in a manner similar to that by which He left the earth after His resurrection. Luke, in his history of the early days of the Church, opens with this account:

> *⁹After he had said this, he was taken to heaven. A cloud hid him so that they could no longer see him.¹⁰ They were staring into the sky as he departed. Suddenly, two men in white clothes stood near them. ¹¹They asked, "Why are you men from Galilee standing here looking at the sky? Jesus, who was taken from you to heaven, will come back in the same way that you saw him go to heaven." (Acts 1:9–11)*

When Jesus returns, He will come in unimaginable glory so extraordinary that every eye on earth will see Him, both the redeemed and the lost, including those "who pierced him," which symbolically represents the sum of people who have rejected the Savior.[7] Though all unbelievers will grieve over God's coming judgment, God's chosen people, the Jews, are specifically targeted for their part in their rejection of Christ as their Messiah.[8] In fact, it is clear that John is quoting the prophet Zechariah:

> *And I will pour on the house of David and on the inhabitants of Jerusalem the Spirit of grace and supplication; then they will look on Me whom they pierced. Yes, they will mourn for Him as one mourns for his only son, and grieve for Him as one grieves for a firstborn. (Zechariah 12:10 NKJV)*

However, Zechariah's prophecy also shows that the horrendous crime the Jews committed against their promised Messiah lies within the boundaries of God's measureless grace. This crime was committed under the direction of God Himself, making the crime the unsurpassed fulfillment of God's plan to bring salvation not only to

His chosen people but also to all the nations of the world. The tribes of the earth have similarly been described by many commentators as a reference to an all-encompassing body of unbelievers.[9]

1:8 *"I am the A and the Z," says the Lord God, the one who is, the one who was, and the one who is coming, the Almighty.*

A and Z are respectively the first and last letters of the English alphabet just as *Alpha* and *Omega* are respectively the first and last letters of the Greek alphabet, so in using this imagery, the Lord God emphasized His sovereignty over the past, present, and future. God also described Himself as *"the one who is, the one who was, and the one who is coming,"* showing His timelessness, and also as "the Almighty," a term describing His absolute authority of all aspects of time and space. Jesus has always existed with God the Father and is responsible for the creation of the world *(John 1:1–3)*. Though He is not a created being, He manifested Himself in a temporal human existence to accomplish His divine purposes. He has otherwise never been bound, limited, restricted, or constrained by the time that He created. This appears to be the significance of His declaration. All things live and die within the boundaries He has created.

1:9 *I am John, your brother. I share your suffering, ruling, and endurance because of Jesus. I was exiled on the island of Patmos because of God's word and the testimony about Jesus.*

John referred to himself as a "brother" in suffering, ruling, and endurance. John was able to persevere in his earthly tribulation not with his own patience but by the patience given to him by the Lord Jesus. John could testify from personal experience that Christians will endure hardships, but they will never face trials alone because Jesus never forsakes His own. *"I've told you this so that my peace will be with you. In the world you'll have trouble. But cheer up! I have overcome the world"* (John 16:33). Even during the recording of this vision, the apostle endured isolation and persecution. In the previous verse, John is writing specifically what God was telling Him, identifying the eternal God. Now John immediately describes his personal role in this revelation. John made sure that the reader understood that there was a clear distinction between the divine authorship of this message and his service to the Lord simply as the recorder of his vision.

The Romans had exiled John to the isle of Patmos, a small, rocky island located off the southwest coast of Asia Minor, known today as Turkey. This barren island is approximately ten miles long and six miles wide.[10] John had been banished to this remote location as punishment *"because of God's word and the testimony about Jesus."* Although no man would desire imprisonment, this was all in God's plan as a means to reveal these great visions describing creation's ultimate destination. While in exile, John was alone and not distracted by the world. He was given time to commune with God and to record all that he witnessed. God planned John's isolation to record His message to the inhabitants of the earth and to write the last book of what is the inspired and inerrant Holy Word of God.

1:10 *[10]I came under the Spirit's power on the Lord's day. I heard a loud voice behind me like a trumpet, [11]saying, "Write on a scroll what you see, and send it to the seven churches: Ephesus, Smyrna, Pergamum, Thyatira, Sardis, Philadelphia, and Laodicea."*

The fact that John was aware that it was the Lord's Day indicates that the apostle retained full control of his senses even though he had been exiled to an isolated, deserted island.[11] He had not become disoriented or delusional. John was "under the Spirit's power," captured by the Holy Spirit of God by which he could enjoy a unique, unhindered fellowship with his Lord and, thereby, could be in a condition to receive this divine revelation.[12] As the vision began, he heard a great voice behind him like that of a loud trumpet.

The Lord then told John to record the things he would be shown in the visions and to send the Lord's message to seven specific churches in Asia Minor. The word *churches* is translated from the

Greek word *ekklesia*, which means "a calling out."[13] These churches, therefore, were not buildings or temples of worship as we many times think of this word. The New Testament use of the word signifies the core of believers throughout a particular community. Thus, Christ told John to deliver messages to the believers in seven specific cities: Ephesus, Smyrna, Pergamum, Thyatira, Sardis, Philadelphia, and Laodicea.

Notes/Applications

These words penned around the sixth century by an unknown author mirror Jesus' message when He proclaimed, *"I am the A and the Z ... the one who is, the one who was, and the one who is coming, the Almighty."* Christ is the Almighty—the supreme One. He is the A—no one came before Him, and He is the Z—none will come after Him.

> O, Christ the heavens' eternal King,
> Creator, unto Thee we sing,
> With God the Father ever One,
> Co-equal, co-eternal Son...
> All praise be Thine, O risen Lord,
> From death to endless life restored;
> All praise to God the Father be
> And Holy Ghost eternally.[14]

In the same way, the apostle Paul described the transcendent majesty of Jesus Christ, Who is both Creator and Redeemer (*Colossians 1:15–18*):

> [15]He is the image of the invisible God,
> the firstborn of all creation.
> [16]He created all things in heaven and on earth,
> visible and invisible.
> Whether they are kings or lords,
> rulers or powers—
> everything has been created through him and for him.
> [17]He existed before everything
> and holds everything together.

¹⁸*He is also the head of the church, which is his body.*
He is the beginning,
the first to come back to life
so that he would have first place in everything.

These passages from Revelation and Colossians impact our understanding of Who Jesus is and our acceptance of Him as the one, true, and eternal God! The Lord Jesus Christ transcends all, yet His supremacy does not negate the individual attention He bestows upon each of His children. He is eternally both a transcendent and personal God. Such majesty is difficult for our limited minds to comprehend; nevertheless, the Holy Spirit convicts our hearts of its truth. Such a Savior is trustworthy. Such a Lord is worthy of our sole devotion. Only when the Holy Spirit removes the scales from our eyes do we recognize the supremacy of our risen Lord and understand His love for those He has redeemed.

Revelation 1:12–20

1:12–13 *¹²I turned toward the voice which was talking to me, and when I turned, I saw seven gold lamp stands. ¹³There was someone like the Son of Man among the lamp stands. He was wearing a robe that reached his feet. He wore a gold belt around his waist.*

John turned to see the source of the voice that spoke to him, and he saw seven golden lamp stands. We are told in the interpretation offered at the end of this first chapter that these lamp stands or tall candlesticks correspond to the aforementioned seven churches. References to Jesus as the essence of light are used many times by this same author in his Gospel account (*John 1:6-7; John 8:12*).

Jesus Christ stood in the midst of the seven golden candlesticks. Because of His position in the midst of the seven churches, it seems that John witnessed the significance of Jesus' centrality and authority in everything that the seven churches did. It also appears that this position means that Jesus intends to meet with these churches and give them His evaluation of their witness to Him in each of their communities.

Jesus' appearance made it obvious to John that He was the Son of Man, the true light of the world. John had seen Jesus in His earthly, human form, and he had also seen Him in a glorified form during Christ's transfiguration. *"¹After six days Jesus took Peter, James, and John (the brother of James) and led them up a high mountain where they could be alone. ²Jesus' appearance changed in front of them. His face became as bright as the sun and his clothes as white as light"* (Matthew 17:1–2).

The garment in which Jesus was now clothed was virtually identical to that of the vision of Christ that appeared to the prophet Daniel in the Old Testament. *"⁵When I looked up, I saw a man dressed in linen, and he had a belt made of gold from Uphaz around his waist. ⁶His body was like beryl. His face looked like lightning. His eyes were like flaming* torches. *His arms and legs looked like polished bronze. When he spoke, his voice sounded like the roar of a crowd"* (Daniel 10:5–6).

Outstanding similarities aside, there can be no doubt concerning the identity of this Being that now stood before John, for He had already identified Himself twice as the A and Z, a claim that could have been made only by the eternal Lord and Savior.

1:14 *His head and his hair were white like wool—like snow. His eyes were like flames of fire.*

In this vision, Jesus' white crown of hair did not depict aging, but it instead symbolized His righteousness, purity, and infinite wisdom.[15] In addition, Jesus' eyes blazed with a purifying, refining fire, perhaps signifying His capacity to see not only what is on the surface but also what is in the heart of man.[16]

1:15 *His feet were like glowing bronze refined in a furnace. His voice was like the sound of raging waters.*

Most biblical expositors agree that John's efforts to record the indescribable appearance of Jesus Christ often lends itself to symbolic significance. Interpretations vary widely regarding the meaning of Christ's feet appearing as fine brass, but such imagery is more likely used to convey the magnificence of Jesus' glory as He stood before John.[17]

Furthermore, the Lord's voice resembled the sound of many waters. This depiction parallels descriptions of God's voice in other biblical accounts.

> *I saw the glory of the God of Israel coming from the east. His voice was like the sound of rushing water, and the earth was shining because of his glory.* (Ezekiel 43:2)

By these verses and others, we may ascertain that the Lord's voice can be heard both near and far when He speaks.

1:16 *In his right hand he held seven stars, and out of his mouth came a sharp, two-edged sword. His face was like the sun when it shines in all its brightness.*

We are told in the interpretation that concludes this chapter that these stars represent angels or messengers. We need not explore too deeply the significance of this comparison, yet we should conclude that the stars were under the full control and direction of Jesus Christ, Who held them in His right hand. Their ministry to the seven churches was appointed and empowered by Him Who sent them.

Christ radiated with the light of His glory, and a two-edged sword emerged from His mouth. In other biblical passages, the Word of God is also described as a two-edged sword *(Hebrews 4:12).*

John compared the Word of God that came from Christ's mouth with a sharp, double-edged sword because God's Truth precisely and justly divides soul and spirit, good and evil, truth and lie, thought and motive. He will judge the poor justly. He will make righteous decisions for the humble people on earth. He will strike the earth with a rod from his mouth. He will kill the wicked with the breath from his lips *(Isaiah 11:4).*

1:17–18 *[17]When I saw him, I fell down at his feet like a dead man. Then he laid his right hand on me and said, "Don't be afraid! I am the first and the last, [18]the living one. I was dead, but now I am alive forever. I have the keys of death and hell.*

When John saw the Son of Man, his reaction resembled the responses of Daniel *(Daniel 10:8–9)*, Ezekiel *(Ezekiel 1:28)*, and Manoah *(Judges 13:22)*, when manifestations of God appeared to them. John fell at Christ's feet in paralyzed fright.

John was the Lord's beloved disciple during His earthly sojourn. John had also been present when the Lord was transfigured on the mountaintop and held counsel with Moses and Elijah *(Mark 9:4–5)*. Yet this same John, when he encountered the presence of His Lord in the unveiled revelation of His glory and holiness, experienced paralyzing terror. His response was no voluntary gesture of esteemed regard but a reaction of fear so intense that He was "like a dead man." However, Christ touched him and commanded him not to be afraid. Then, as if to validate this command, the Lord repeated a third time that He is the first and the last, reminding John of their previous moments together and identifying Himself as the same Lord John had always known.

Jesus further identified Himself as the One Who lived, died, and conquered death forevermore by rising from the grave. It seems almost as if God wanted to encourage John by saying in a sense: "John, you know me. I am the same One Who walked with you, Who taught you. I am the one you witnessed on the cross and then watched ascend into heaven."

The Lord's statement, *"I have the keys of death and hell,"* confirmed His supreme authority over life and death in both the physical and spiritual aspects. Christ displayed this power when He raised people from the dead during His earthly ministry as well as when He Himself defeated sin and death for the redemption of mankind. When Jesus appeared to John on Patmos, He had already conquered death at Calvary, finished the atonement, and thereby secured "the keys of death and hell."

1:19 *Therefore, write down what you have seen, what is, and what is going to happen after these things.*

Imagine how exciting this must have been for John! As a disciple, John had known the Christ that walked on earth and had witnessed His transfiguration. Now, Jesus stood before him as the living, eternal God. Even though the sight before John and the visions that would be revealed to him seemed unbelievable, they were, are, and always will be true and certain. Therefore, John was instructed to document all that was about to be revealed to him.

1:20 *The hidden meaning of the seven stars that you saw in my right hand and the seven gold lamp stands is this: The seven stars are the messengers of the seven churches, and the seven lamp stands are the seven churches.*

Jesus interpreted this first vision for John and for believers of all ages. The seven stars mentioned in verse sixteen represent seven angels or messengers, and the seven candlesticks represent the seven aforementioned churches in Asia Minor. The seven messengers, like the rest of the heavenly host, stand in the service of the Lord as His ministering spirits. In this case, they are appointed specifically as the Lord's messengers to deliver the Lord's message to each one of the seven churches.

Notes/Applications

Believers, although redeemed, still struggle to understand the grace of God in Jesus Christ that has saved them. Paul wrote these words in his letter to the Corinthian church: *"[9]Our knowledge is incomplete and our ability to speak what God has revealed is incomplete. [10]But when what is complete comes, then what is incomplete will no longer be used. [12]Now we see a blurred image in a mirror. Then we will see very clearly. Now my knowledge is incomplete. Then I will have complete knowledge as God has complete knowledge of me"* (1 Corinthians 13:9–10, 12).

On the Isle of Patmos on this particular Lord's Day, John witnessed the unparalleled brilliance, majesty, and glory of the eternal God when he saw his risen Lord. The experience was so frightening that John fell to the Lord's feet, trembling in paralyzing terror. Even though this same John had walked with Jesus for three and a half years, even though he knew Jesus as well as any man can know another, even though John had seen Jesus in the blinding light of His transfiguration, he now had a completely different view of Jesus. This new perspective caused him to faint and become like a dead man.

This was no meek and mild Jesus. This was no quiet, prayerful Jesus. This was no kind, compassionate Jesus. This was the incomprehensible Creator of the universe, Who called the worlds into being;

Who placed the stars in the heavens; Who silenced the raging seas; Who called forth light and substance and order in the chaos of human existence.

We must never forget Paul's words. Whatever our particular point of view about Jesus, we must never forget that our perceptions are blurred by the clothing of our sinful flesh. Surely, through the revelation of Jesus Christ given to John, we catch a glimpse of the eternal "I AM." And that glimpse should cause all people to tremble. That glimpse should also cause believers to approach the throne of His glory with fear, cautious respect, and mind-bending awe.

The Seven Churches in Asia Minor
Chapters 1–3

REVELATION 2

Revelation 2:1–7

2:1 *"To the messenger of the church in Ephesus, write: The one who holds the seven stars in his right hand, the one who walks among the seven gold lamp stands, says:*

The first church the Lord addressed was in the city of Ephesus. Ephesus, located on the west coast of what is now Turkey, was the largest city in Asia Minor. It was situated at the junction of many natural trade routes and was on the main road from Rome to the East, so the city's economy was chiefly built around commerce and trade.[1] It was also a very religious city, boasting great temples to gods and goddesses. The temple of Artemis (Diana) was one of the seven wonders of the ancient world.[2] The Gospel message may have been introduced to Ephesus through Aquila and Priscilla, though their efforts were surely advanced with the return of Paul, who lived there for two years[3] *(Acts 18:18–19)*. It is perhaps the apostle John who should be credited most with the discipleship of those Christians in Ephesus since he had committed much of his life to the church there. This may be the reason that this city is listed first among the seven churches.

John was instructed to write this message and to identify the sender of the message as the One Who holds the seven stars and walks among the seven lamp stands. No one could rightfully claim this authority and position except for God's Son, Jesus Christ. Christ's position as the author of this revelation is once again confirmed to John and his readers. John's position as the authorized recorder of these visions is likewise confirmed.

2:2 *I know what you have done—how hard you have worked and how you have endured. I also know that you cannot toler-ate wicked people. You have tested those who call themselves apostles but are not apostles. You have discovered that they are liars.*

Jesus acknowledged the outstanding witness of this church. They had worked hard for Christ and had patiently persisted in their labor. Their works and patience were outward displays of Christ's presence in their lives. It is evident that Jesus Himself had been the central focus of everything they did.

Specifically, this church demonstrated an uncompromising intol-erance for wicked people. They refused to compromise the message of Christ's redemption with the evil influences of their surrounding culture. In the same way, they did not accept every teacher that came to them. Rather, they tested them, making sure that they were faithful interpreters of the doctrine that had been taught by Christ's apostles. In that way, they were able to distinguish between true apostles and false teachers, keeping the church centered on the teaching of Christ, affirming the atoning work of Christ's Cross. As a result, the Ephesian Christians knew that such people were liars.

2:3 *You have endured, suffered trouble because of my name, and have not grown weary.*

The church of Ephesus had patiently endured in Jesus' Name. Jesus not only praised them for their works but also recognized that these acts had been done in Christ's Name. Even though these believers had suffered, they had stood their ground against the ungodliness that was so prevalent in their environment. Amid hardship and hostility, they remained true to the Lord and persevered in their labors.

2:4 *However, I have this against you: The love you had at first is gone.*

Although Jesus commended the Ephesians for their faithfulness, He knew their hearts intimately and admonished them for leaving their first love. Evidently, the Ephesians' love for Christ had waned over time. They still loved God and expressed their commitment to Him through their faithful works and endurance, but the Lord recognized that their passion and enthusiasm needed restoration. They remained obedient to God and labored in His Name, but it appears their works were motivated more by their Christian responsibility than their intimacy with Christ (*Deuteronomy 6:5*).

2:5 *Remember how far you have fallen. Return to me and change the way you think and act, and do what you did at first. I will come to you and take your lamp stand from its place if you don't change.*

Christ told the Christians in Ephesus to recall the time when they walked most closely with the Lord. They were to repent for their waning love and once again embrace their Savior and Lord. In so doing, the Lord would properly redirect their hearts, refocus their priorities, and once again restore their love for Christ. If they did not repent, God would judge them by removing their lamp stand, that is, removing them from His presence.[4]

The word translated as *repent* comes from the Greek word *metanoeo*, which means "to change the mind."[5] When an individual repents, Jesus Himself realigns the heart of the penitent believer with God's will instead of his own. Conviction over sin and confession of sin are important components of repentance, but sincere repentance is best demonstrated through a reformed life.

2:6 *But you have this in your favor—you hate what the Nicolaitans are doing. I also hate what they're doing.*

Jesus again commended the Ephesian church on another point. They agreed with the Lord in their hatred of the Nicolaitans' deeds. Not much is known about the Nicolaitans, but evidently, they were disciples of a false doctrine that was prevalent during that time. They were a Gnostic cult that practiced a heresy, which taught that a person could do anything in the physical realm without experiencing any spiritual consequences.[6] Jesus declared that He did not hate the Nicolaitans, but He despised their depraved practices. What Jesus told this church was consistent with God's message in the Old Testament: "Do I not hate those who hate you, O Lord? And do I not loathe those who rise up against you?" *(Psalm 139:21).*

2:7 *"Let the person who has ears listen to what the Spirit says to the churches. I will give the privilege of eating from the tree of life, which stands in the paradise of God, to everyone who wins the victory."*

Jesus now addressed believers of all times and places, inviting them to discern the message that He has given to the Ephesian church. Jesus, the beginning and ending of creation's history, held out the promise of eating from the tree of life, Christ's gift of eternal life to all those who win the victory—that is, to those who endure all things for Christ's sake. However, in the framework of His message to the Ephesian church, it should be clear that Jesus wants His redeemed people to exalt Him above everything. He alone is the beginning and ending of their salvation. He covets a relationship with His people, even more than He covets their good works. Good works outside of this relationship become simply good works. Rather, those who have been redeemed should love their Lord above all things, clinging to the One Who has won the vic-

tory for them at His Cross, verifying His promise of eternal life by the
evidence of His own bodily resurrection.

Notes/Applications

Maltbie D. Babcock, a nineteenth century pastor and hymnist, once
said, "The Christian life that is joyless is a discredit to God and a dis-
grace to itself."[7] It appears that the believers at Ephesus had lost heart
in their spiritual battle. They still performed notable acts of service but
not with the all-consuming passion they had once possessed. Christ
corrected the Ephesians by commanding them to remember the time
when they cherished their relationship with Him more than anything
else, when they marched closely at His side savoring His presence, and
when their desire to glorify Him motivated their good works.

Jesus here invites believers to return to a warm, loving relationship
with Him. This is the essence of the message to the Ephesian church.
Without this relationship, all work, all worship, all prayer is empty
and vain. Good works without this relationship are meaningless. In
everything believers do, Jesus urges them to stay close to Him, to draw
strength from Him, to find direction from Him. He is the Christian's
Victor. He is the One Who gives to His people victory over sin and joy
in the work of His Kingdom.

Can we identify with these believers? Has our love for our Lord
diminished? Are we simply performing acts of Christian service out of
routine? It is so easy to become consumed in serving the Lord that we
lose focus on the Lord Himself. When this happens, we are easily shot
down by the enemy's schemes, becoming prime targets for the devil's
advances in areas where we never considered ourselves vulnerable..
The principle is simple: we dare not withdraw from the presence of
our Holy Commander. May the Holy Spirit strive within us to maintain a fiery passion for our calling in Christ, Who has rescued us from
life's distractions and empowered us to serve in His Kingdom.

Revelation 2:8-11

2:8 *"To the messenger of the church in Smyrna, write: The first and the last, who was dead and became alive, says:*

Jesus this time identified Himself as "the first and the last" and as He Who "was dead and became alive." Jesus was talking directly to the messenger of the Smyrna church and John was faithfully recording the message. Since Jesus was the only Person to have died and then rise again from the dead, it is clear that He is the only One Who can be considered as the author of this message.

The city of Smyrna was located on the western coast of Asia Minor about forty miles north of Ephesus at the mouth of the Hermus River. Smyrna, too, was a populous and prosperous city, second only to Ephesus in trade and commerce.[8] Culture thrived in this city that featured the largest public theatre in all of Asia. It is also believed by many to be the birthplace of Homer, author of the great epics *The Odyssey* and *The Illiad.*[9] Smyrna gained her notoriety, however, from the bloody campaign that the Roman emperors had waged against the Christians there. It was in this city that Polycarp, John's closest disciple, was appointed bishop of the early church by the apostles and was later martyred and buried.[10] Interestingly, the name Smyrna means "myrrh," which was one of the ingredients used as an embalming ointment by the ancients.[11]

2:9 *I know how you are suffering, how poor you are—but you are rich. I also know that those who claim to be Jews slander you. They are the synagogue of Satan.*

Jesus told the people of the church of Smyrna that He knew their circumstances. He also recognized their many tribulations and persecutions. The Lord Jesus placed a high value on the suffering of this church because He, too, had suffered greatly. The believers at Smyrna were physically and economically poor as a result of their persecution, but Jesus turned their focus upon the eternal wealth and riches prepared for them in heaven. It is important to note that this church's persecution apparently did not result as judgment from God because of some wrongdoing but, rather, for their faithfulness to the Gospel of Jesus Christ.

The believers in this church were viciously attacked by some who claimed to be Jews, who earnestly bolstered the Romans' efforts to kill the Christians.[12] Jesus called these people "a synagogue of Satan" because they rejected Jesus as the Messiah and violently opposed any who followed His teachings. It is important to note that Jews were not included in Christ's harsh rebuke simply because of their ethnicity. Unquestionably, a vast percentage of Jesus' followers at that time were Jews, and it was obviously not these to whom the Lord referred. Rather, this "synagogue of Satan" was comprised of those blasphemers who "claimed to be Jews."

2:10 *Don't be afraid of what you are going to suffer. The devil is going to throw some of you into prison so that you may be tested. Your suffering will go on for ten days. Be faithful until death, and I will give you the crown of life.*

The Lord explained the trials awaiting the faithful believers at Smyrna. Specifically, some of them would be imprisoned for their faith. The direct cause of this suffering, as Jesus clearly revealed, was the devil. Some believers would lose their physical lives for the cause of Christ.

This tribulation, however, would not be without purpose or without end. There are varied explanations that define this period of "ten days." This could, of course, refer to a literal ten-day duration. Some scholars believe these ten days are a reference to ten periods of intense persecution under ten pre-Constantine emperors while others believe this refers to the ten years of persecution at the hands of Diocletian.[13] Whatever the case, God reassured the believers in Smyrna that their suffering would last only for the appointed period of time He had ordained.

Because God had preplanned it, He had also prepared to give these faithful ones the strength and power to endure it. Those found faithful to the very end would be given the "crown of life." Though much has been speculated about the significance of such a crown, specifically in relation to the city of Smyrna, it can be said with reasonable certainty that the "crown of life," at the very least, signifies the unmerited reward of eternal life that these believers would receive.[14]

2:11 *Let the person who has ears listen to what the Spirit says to the churches. Everyone who wins the victory will never be hurt by the second death.*

Again, we are advised to listen to the message that the Holy Spirit gives to this church. The promise of eternal life is again promised to "everyone who wins the victory" (all who have placed their faith in Christ Jesus) and is expressed to this church as exemption from the second death, which will occur after the final judgment when all unbelievers will be cast into the lake of fire. "*[14]Death and hell were thrown into the fiery lake. (The fiery lake is the second death.) [15]Those whose names were not found in the Book of Life were thrown into the fiery lake*" (Revelation 20:14–15).

Notes/Applications

The encouragement directed to the church of Smyrna, and ultimately to all believers, was to endure in the midst of suffering. Sometimes, tribulations occur as an act of judgment, but they may also transpire to refine our faith, to strengthen the testimony of our witness, or to correct us. The rains of suffering fell upon our Lord Jesus during His time on earth, and they will surely fall upon us as His disciples. However, when we feel trampled by hardships, we need to remind ourselves of the inheritance that we have in Christ.

> "*[17]These things I command you, so that you will love one another. [18]If the world hates you, know that it has hated me before it hated you. [19]If you were of the world, the world would love you as its own; but because you are not of the world, but I chose you out of the world, therefore the world hates you. [20]Remember*

the word that I said to you: 'A servant is not greater than his
master.' If they persecuted me, they will also persecute you. If
they kept my word, they will also keep yours." (John 15:17–20)

Many Christians count heaven as their glorious treasure—their
blessed hope. Certainly, assurance of an eternal, heavenly home in
the Father's presence is a fundamental doctrine of our faith that
should move us to grateful anticipation. However, we do not have to
wait until then to enjoy our wealth in Christ—the precious treasure
beyond appraisal. In knowing Him, we can experience abundant life
even now. We may incur financial, physical, and emotional challenges,
but we have acquired indescribable security by the miraculous grace of
Christ, our present and future "hope of glory." As Paul reminded the
believers in Colossae:

> [24]*I am happy to suffer for you now. In my body I am complet-*
> *ing whatever remains of Christ's sufferings. I am doing this on*
> *behalf of his body, the church.* [25]*I became a servant of the church*
> *when God gave me the work of telling you his entire message.*
> [26]*In the past God hid this mystery, but now he has revealed it*
> *to his people.* [27]*God wanted his people throughout the world*
> *to know the glorious riches of this mystery—which is Christ liv-*
> *ing in you, giving you the hope of glory.* (Colossians 1:24–27)

Revelation 2:12–17

2:12 *"To the messenger of the church in Pergamum, write: The one who holds the sharp two-edged sword says:*

Jesus then addressed the third church, Pergamum (also called Pergamos) This message, like the others, was given directly from Jesus, referred to as "the One Who holds the sharp two-edged sword." The two-edged sword identifies Jesus as the One Who dispenses God's judgment.[15]

Pergamum lay inland from the coast of the Aegean Sea about sixty-five miles north of Smyrna and was the provincial capital of Roman Asia.[16] The city boasted many grand Hellenic and Roman temples and was also home to an impressive library second only to the one in Alexandria.[17] Persecution of Christians was rampant in Pergamum, but as with the church of Smyrna, the persecution did not destroy the faith of most Christians there.

2:13 *I know where you live. Satan's throne is there. You hold on to my name and have not denied your belief in me, even in the days of Antipas. He was my faithful witness who was killed in your presence, where Satan lives.*

The Lord told the church in Pergamum that He was well aware of their situation. These Christians lived in the midst of the most dire and challenging of circumstances.

The Lord called Pergamum the home of Satan's throne, indicating that the church was situated in the heart of rampant wickedness and spiritual perversion.[18] Pergamum was a center of heathen worship and practices, and the ungodly influences so prevalent within the city had infiltrated the church. However, even in the midst of Satan's strongest temptations, many were able to hold on to His Name and remain faithful to the Lord. As a result of their faithfulness, these believers were persecuted, and several were martyred. One of them, as mentioned in this verse, was Antipas, whom the Lord called the "faithful witness."

In fact, some scholars credit Antipas as being the pastor of the first church in the city.[19] This historical reference to Antipas verifies that these were actual letters to specific churches and not simply an illustration of distinct periods of the church throughout history.[20]

2:14 *But I have a few things against you: You have among you those who follow what Balaam taught Balak. Balak trapped the people of Israel by encouraging them to eat food sacrificed to idols and to sin sexually.*

Though the Lord commended the overall commitment of this church, there was a minority of believers who had yielded to the influence of false teaching, so Jesus not only rebuked the minority who adhered to the false doctrine but also the majority who tolerated the rebelliousness of a few.[21] One of these sins was that some in the church adhered to the doctrine of Balaam.

In the Old Testament account, the Moabite king, Balak, asked Balaam to curse Israel, but Balaam could not do this because God controlled Balaam's actions. Since God forbade Balaam to speak against the Israelites, Balaam then deviously encouraged the Israelites to ally themselves with the Moabites through intermarriage. Balaam's plan was corrupt, but the Israelite people were also at fault for blindly following his suggestions to intermarry with this pagan nation and to eat its defiled foods. In essence, a stumbling block was cast, and the people faltered because they fell prey to Balaam's false teaching. The Pentateuch clearly shows the error of Balaam's perverse instruction. *"Remember, they were the ones who followed Balaam's advice and caused the Israelites to be unfaithful to the Lord in the incident that took place at Peor. The Lord's community experienced a plague at that time"* (Numbers 31:16).

Peter's warning in his second letter shows that the philosophy of Balaam was prevalent during the first century. *"These false teachers have left the straight path and wandered off to follow the path of Balaam, son of Beor. Balaam loved what his wrongdoing earned him"* (2 Peter 2:15).

The doctrine of Balaam, therefore, describes the seduction of fornication and idolatry. Many others in Pergamum who claimed the Name of Christ tolerated the pagan teachings that embraced worldliness and rejected the absolutes of godly truth.[22] They had succumbed to the temptation that they could simultaneously serve the Lord and remain a part of this world. More importantly, they had forsaken the purity of their godly identity in Jesus Christ.

2:15 *You also have some who follow what the Nicolaitans teach.*

Unlike the church of Ephesus that hated the doctrine of the Nicolaitans as the Lord did, some in Pergamum adopted this philosophy. As we studied before, not much is known about the specific practices of the Nicolaitans, except they believed that their physical actions bore no spiritual consequences. We do know that God hated their heretical teachings, which appear to be very similar to the doctrine of Balaam. Several scholars, in fact, consider these two doctrines essentially one and the same.[23] The meanings of their names (Nicolaitans and Baalam) are virtually identical.[24]

2:16 *So return to me and change the way you think and act, or I will come to you quickly and wage war against them with the sword from my mouth.*

The Lord instructed the church in Pergamum to repent. It can be reasonably assumed that He was addressing those who had adhered to this false doctrine as well as those members who had not indulged themselves in such practices but were tolerant of those who had. If they would not repent, there would be swift judgment as indicated by the term "quickly." The Lord would judge them with the sword of His mouth according to His absolute justice.

2:17 *Let the person who has ears listen to what the Spirit says to the churches. I will give some of the hidden manna to everyone who wins the victory. I will also give each person a white* *stone with a new name written on it, a name that is known only to the person who receives it.*

The Lord once again repeated the admonishment to all those willing to open their spiritual ears to hear "what the Spirit says to the churches." Those believers who were faithful were promised eternal life, expressed to this church by two objects: hidden manna and a white stone bearing a name uniquely assigned to the owner.

When the Israelites wandered in the wilderness, they obtained nourishment from physical manna that fell from heaven. In like manner, those believers that refuse to compromise with false teaching and are able to stand firmly against the temptations of the world will similarly be nourished with a spiritual manna. This manna is hidden, not to Christ's redeemed people, but to those who do not belong to God. When Jesus walked among His disciples, He made the distinction between physical manna and spiritual manna abundantly clear: *"⁴⁸I am the bread of life. ⁴⁹Your ancestors ate the manna in the desert and died. ⁵⁰This is the bread that comes from heaven so that whoever eats it won't die. ⁵¹I am the living bread that came from heaven. Whoever eats this bread will live forever. The bread I will give to bring life to the world is my flesh"* (John 6:48–51).

Patient, persistent believers would also receive a white stone. There are many interpretations regarding the significance of the white stone, though none can be convincingly proven to be anything more than speculation. The specification of a white stone may in some manner symbolize triumph, righteousness, or atonement. Whatever the case may be, the significance of the stone is in the "new name written on it."[25] In some manner, this new name bears the mark of the unique and personal relationship between Almighty God and those who belong to Him.

Notes/Applications

The condition of the church in Pergamum was particularly tenuous, if not frighteningly dangerous. Some of the people in the church had fallen prey to false teaching—Balaam and the Nicolaitans. That was bad enough. But what made this particularly dangerous was the tolerance that other believers offered to this treacherous condition. False teaching, promoted within the protective womb of tolerance, leads the entire body of believers down the pathway to God's cleansing judgment.

Christ's encouragement to the church of Pergamum and to the believers represented by this church's ungodly characteristics was to remain faithful even in the midst of ungodly influences. Christ wants His followers, no matter the hour in history, to penetrate the darkness of human disobedience and its resulting misery that presses upon them with the light of His absolute Truth. *"Use the truth to make them holy. Your words are truth"* (John 17:17).

But how can we remain faithful when we are perplexed under extreme pressures that surround us on every side? How can we discern between biblically reliable doctrine and those teachings that are patently false? Most important of all, how long will the people of God tolerate the seduction of false teaching and surrender the integrity of God's Word to the interpretation of those who oppose our Lord?

Christ's strongly worded rebuke reminds believers to avoid false teaching, and, more importantly, to be inflexibly intolerant of such perversions of the true Gospel. In today's world, that is a big order. When virtually all cultures demand the virtues of tolerance above all else, the rebuke of Christ places God's people squarely in the center of the world's accusatory assault. The Church of Jesus Christ, receiving the blows of the unsaved, tolerant world must lean heavily upon the Spirit's enlightening truth and faithfully proclaim the absolute, unchanging exclusivity of the Gospel message.

The words of an early Puritan prayer offer encouragement to today's believers with a simple reminder of the importance of our relationship with Jesus Christ, which keeps us safe from the world's derision and strong in the face of the world's opposition.

> *May I never dally with this world*
> *and its allurements,*

but walk by thy side,
listen to thy voice,
be clothed with thy grace,
and adorned with thy righteousness.[26]

Revelation 2:18-29

2:18 *"To the messenger of the church in Thyatira, write: The Son of God, whose eyes are like flames of fire and whose feet are like glowing bronze, says:*

Jesus, the Son of God, whose eyes appeared as flames of fire and whose feet resembled refined brass issued the fourth message to the church of Thyatira.

Of the seven churches mentioned in the Book of Revelation, the longest letter was addressed to the church in Thyatira. However, less is known about this city than any of the other six cities. Thyatira was located inland about forty miles east of Pergamum.[27] After the death of Alexander the Great, his empire was divided among four of his generals, two of whom were Seleucus and Lysimachus. These generals often engaged in military excursions against one another. Seleucus I founded Thyatira as a military strategy to guard one of his empire's main routes against Lysimachus.[28] After the death of Alexander the Great, Lysimachus was appointed to govern Asia Minor.[29] Thyatira was perhaps best known for its thriving trade guilds, which included bronze smiths, potters, bakers, tanners, and various garment workers.[30] Lydia, mentioned in the Bible as a seller of purple-dyed garments, was a Jewish citizen of Thyatira (*Acts 16:14*).

2:19 *I know what you do. I know your love, faith, service, and endurance. I also know that what you are doing now is greater than what you did at first.*

The labor of the faithful believers in Thyatira was praiseworthy. Their love for God and their service to Him were motivated by their abiding love for Jesus Christ. With much patience, they remained faithful to Almighty God despite the ungodliness that surrounded them. Furthermore, the mention of their later works being greater than their earlier works indicates that their acts of service progressed in both quantity and quality.[31]

2:20 *But I have something against you: You tolerate that woman Jezebel, who calls herself a prophet. She teaches and misleads my servants to sin sexually and to eat food sacrificed to idols.*

Most scholars agree that the description of "that woman Jezebel" is an allusion to the Old Testament character by that name. Jezebel was a wicked queen who promoted the worship of Baal, the storm god that the Canaanites believed was responsible for rain and fertility.[32] So strong was Jezebel's hatred toward Almighty God that she commanded the execution of His prophets throughout the land and promoted the idolatrous, sensual rituals associated with her pagan religion *(1 Kings 18:1–4)*.

In His address to the church in Thyatira, the Lord exposed an individual whose heretical teachings had apparently been allowed to continue within the church without opposition. Considering the gender reference, it seems likely that this teacher was a woman because other allusions could have been made if such was not the case. Furthermore, this woman must have attained some status within the church, perhaps due to her claim of being a prophetess, since some within the church were eager to follow her teachings.[33] Nevertheless, according to verse twenty-four, there were clearly several who saw through her apostasy.

Some commentators actually attempt to specifically identify this person.[34] While this was obviously a specific person, solid evidence does not exist to corroborate such claims, so we must instead pay attention to the reason this person was singled out, the reason being that she taught and seduced God's servants "to sin sexually and to eat food sacrificed to idols."

2:21 *I gave her time to turn to me and change the way she thinks and acts, but she refuses to turn away from her sexual sins.*

The Lord afforded this woman gracious opportunities to repent of her adulterous ways, but she refused. Her lifestyle was her personal choice and she would be punished for it. However, her effort to get others to join her by disseminating her perversion among the rest of the believers was particularly abhorrent to the Lord. Therefore, because of her lack of repentance, the Lord would no longer permit her obstinacy.

2:22 *Watch me! I'm going to throw her into a sickbed. Those who commit sexual sins with her will also suffer a lot, unless they turn away from what she is doing.*

The judgments explained refer to the physical consequences that could be expected by this woman and all who followed her teachings. The Lord would turn what the woman perceived as a bed of carnal pleasure into a bed of sickness. The woman's promiscuity would probably lead to a debilitating sexual disease that would bring her to the point of death. If this was a sexually transmitted disease, then it is perfectly understandable that her consorts would likely contract the same disease and suffer the consequences of their infidelities.

2:23 *I will kill her children. Then all the churches will know that I am the one who searches hearts and minds. I will reward each of you for what you have done.*

The spiritual consequences awaiting those who indulged themselves in this fornication were severe. Some commentators contend that the phrase "her children" refers to this false teacher's followers.[35] Although this may be the case, the phrase may also allude once again to the Old Testament Queen Jezebel and the violent death that she and her descendants suffered due to the gravity of her transgressions (2 *Kings* 9:7–10). Furthermore, some scholars argue that the phrase "kill her children" refers to the second death spoken of in Revelation chapter twenty.[36] However, as indicated by the common Hebraic use of the phrase, which means "to slay utterly," perhaps it describes an unusually brutal death. Whatever the case, the severity of God's punishment will reveal that God was the source of this judgment. Witnessing God's judgment was motivation enough to alert the rest of the church that

God was not always patient, and that His judgment was swift and sure.[37]

Christ alone possesses the power to search the minds and hearts of every individual and to know the motive behind every deed. Whereas the Lord addressed the entire church in Thyatira, He also offered assurance that every believer within that church would not be condemned for the exploits of a few but would be judged on an individual basis (*Romans 2:5-9*).

2:24–25 *²⁴But the rest of you in Thyatira—all who don't hold on to Jezebel's teaching, who haven't learned what are called the deep things of Satan—I won't burden you with anything else. ²⁵Just hold on to what you have until I come.*

The Son of God spoke more gently to those in Thyatira who had not accepted the doctrine of Jezebel. He promised these believers that they would not encounter any additional burden. This did not mean that they would never experience other struggles or tribulations but that they would not share in the consequences of those who embraced this heretical teaching. The Lord Jesus Christ encouraged those believers who had not known "the deep things of Satan" to persevere until His return. The meaning of "the deep things of Satan" is ambiguous, and its interpretation varies widely, but at the very least, it denotes the difficulty of escaping the snares of Satan's deceiving ways. A particular encouragement to this church is not only to those who overcome but also to those who remain faithful in the midst of the struggle. The Lord encouraged these believers to persist or "hold on" to the faith that had been given to them, looking forward to the glorious return of the Lord (*1 John 3:2-3*).

2:26–28 *²⁶I have received authority from my Father. I will give authority over the nations to everyone who wins the victory and continues to do what I want until the end. ²⁷Those people*

*will rule the nations with iron scepters and shatter them like
pottery. ²⁸I will also give them the morning star.*

These verses are a direct reference to a psalm that proclaims the Messiah's authority. *"⁸Ask me, and I will give you the nations as your inheritance
and the ends of the earth as your own possession. ⁹You will break them with
an iron scepter. You will smash them to pieces like pottery"* (Psalm 2:8–9).
Though this promise is believed to refer to Christ's first advent, it is
also traditionally interpreted to refer to His victorious second coming.[38] It seems that those who receive their victory through Jesus Christ
will also be given some level of authority to rule with Christ.

The concluding promise of "the morning star" has also received
varied explanation. The most defensible interpretation of this phrase
contends that it refers to Jesus Christ Himself.[39] *"I, Jesus, have sent my
angel to give this testimony to you for the churches. I am the root and descendant of David. I am the bright morning star"* (Revelation 22:16). Using this
explanation, this promise parallels the promises to the other churches
in which Christ assured His redeemed people of everlasting life in His
presence in heaven.

2:29 *Let the person who has ears listen to what the Spirit says
to the churches.*

Once again, the Lord Jesus encouraged all believers, all those whose
perceptions have been changed by the transforming work of the Holy
Spirit, to listen to the message of this letter and to heed the warnings
and discern their significance.

Notes/Applications

The church at Thyatira had commendable traits. Jesus spoke well of
the people of the church regarding their deep and abiding love for their
Lord. Their lives openly reflected a living testimony of the transforming power of Jesus Christ. Their conduct displayed "love, faith, service,
and endurance." In fact, the Lord openly testified that the church por-

trayed a greater Christian maturity during their latter years than at the beginning. Such a witness from the mouth of the Lord Himself is an indisputable evidence of the continuing growth of the church. However, Jesus saw a terrible blight within this community of believers. There were chronic compromises within the church resulting in sexual immorality and pervasive debauchery. There was a woman of some importance within the church who was leading some of the flock down the wrong pathway to open contempt. She was much like the woman Jezebel whose story is recorded in 1 Kings.

Baal, the fertility god of the Sidonians, was Jezebel's god. The followers of Baal practiced sexual immorality and other depraved activities in the belief that such rituals would bring fertility to their land. Much like the Jezebel of Israel during the reign of Ahab (1 Kings 16:29-33), the prominent woman in Thyatira, also identified as Jezebel, seduced members of the church to indulge in sexual immorality and in eating food sacrificed to idols.

Jesus indicted the church at Thyatira for tolerating such blatant corruption and for worshiping a false god, forsaking the God Who created them and redeemed them for Himself. Jesus dispensed His judgment, condemning the woman and her followers to a bed of sickness and death. Jesus' swift judgment confirms to all, especially believers, that sin cannot evade judgment because Jesus is the One Who searches the hearts and minds (verse 23).

One wonders how such a growing, maturing, faithful church could tolerate such blatant contempt toward God. However, we do not have to look very far to find the answer to this question. Even though the redeemed continue to live in the security of God's saving grace, the battle between the dying sin nature and the growing new man continues to rage in the heart of God's children. Therefore, the old Adamic nature, still functioning as a source of corruption and contempt in all mortals including believers, continues to exert its subtle influences to undermine the godly predispositions of the believers as well as the entire body of Christ. Like all believers across the ages, the conduct and demeanor of the Christians in Thyatira were profoundly influenced by their sin nature. They failed to discern the error of their ways when they accommodated the ungodly behaviors of those who are divisive as well as those who are apathetic toward God's truth. Such misapplication of Christian love and godly compassion will certainly lead to a life of ungodly tolerance, practically recasting the commitment of the redeemed to a position where they support sin.

Christians, having experienced the salvation that Christ brings into their lives, many times tolerate false gods in their Christian communities who lead them down the path to their own destruction by over-extending their ministry of love and compassion beyond the line of godly care. This passage helps today's Christians understand that Jesus is coming again to judge the wicked and reward His saints. He sees everything, knows everything, and judges everything. His eyes are like "flames of fire" and His feet are like "glowing bronze". Let us not fall prey to the seduction of Jezebel, or worship false gods, or tolerate those in our midst who do.

REVELATION 3

Revelation 3:1-6

3:1 *"To the messenger of the church in Sardis, write: The one who has God's seven spirits and the seven stars says: I know what you have done. You are known for being alive, but you are dead.*

The fifth message was addressed to the church in Sardis. The church would know that the message was given to them directly from the Lord Jesus Christ, described as "The One Who has God's seven spirits and the seven stars."

Sardis lay inland approximately thirty miles south of Thyatira and fifty miles northeast of Ephesus.[1] Early in its history the city was one of the most influential in the ancient world and served as the capital city of Lydia, a province of Asia Minor.[2] It was most noted for the Acropolis, a temple built to Artemis, the Greek name for the goddess Diana.[3] The vertical rock walls of the Acropolis rose nearly fifteen hundred feet above the lower valley, thereby providing the city with an excellent natural defense.[4] Despite numerous attacks on the city throughout history, its fortress was only captured twice, once in the

sixth century B.C. and again in the fourth century B.C.[5] In A.D. 17, a
catastrophic earthquake destroyed the city. Though Sardis was eventually rebuilt, it never regained the prominence and affluence it once
enjoyed, and by the time this letter was written, the city was a pitiful
hub of moral debauchery.[6]

The Lord told the believers in Sardis that He knew their works,
and despite their reputation for being a church that was alive, He knew
that their works were no longer prompted by faithfulness and loyalty
to Him. Within their community, and perhaps throughout surrounding regions, they had gained a good reputation for their Christian
works and vitality. Nevertheless, the Lord knew their hearts and recognized that their works were void of any true commitment to Christ.
As such, Jesus considered them not as merely sick but as utterly lifeless.

During Jesus' three-year ministry, before His crucifixion and
resurrection, He often encountered the religious leaders, recognizing
the hypocrisy that pervaded their religious lives. In one incident, He
strongly chastised them: "[27b]*You are like whitewashed graves that look
beautiful on the outside but inside are full of dead people's bones and every
kind of impurity.* [28]*So on the outside you look as though you have God's
approval, but inside you are full of hypocrisy and lawlessness*" (Matthew
23:27b–28).

3:2 *Be alert, and strengthen the things that are left which
are about to die. I have found that what you are doing has not
been completed in the sight of my God.*

The church of Sardis was far from righteous in God's eyes. If they
did not fortify and rebuild those few remaining qualities still deemed
worthwhile, even those things would be taken away. Most of their
works were motivated by selfish ambition and not with any intention
of glorifying God. Although unclear, Jesus' message seems to indicate
that there was something worth holding on to. It may seem somewhat
insignificant in light of the Lord's overall chastisement of these believers, yet they were warned that if they did not cling to that last shred of
true life worthy of mention, even that would be removed from them.

3:3 *So remember what you received and heard. Obey, and change the way you think and act. If you're not alert, I'll come like a thief. You don't know when I will come.*

Jesus spoke to the believers and told them to hold fast to what they had been taught. If they did not repent of their spiritual indifference and did not cling to the few admirable qualities that they still possessed, the Lord would "come like a thief" and remove those things. Some commentators insist upon an eschatological rendering of "come like a thief" simply because this description resembles those found in "end-times" references, such as 1 Thessalonians 5:2 and 2 Peter 3:10. However, the phrase as used in this passage seems to express the sudden and unexpected manner with which the Lord will act.[7] Failure to repent would result in swift judgment.

3:4 *But you have a few people in Sardis who have kept their clothes clean. They will walk with me in white clothes because they deserve it.*

This verse clearly reveals that the Lord deals with the body of Christ, the Church, as individuals. Jesus knows every person's heart and motivations and deals with them accordingly. Though He condemned most in Sardis, a few people in this church had not defiled themselves but had remained strong in their faith and lived obediently. The description "kept their clothes clean" does not mean that they were sinless but that they did not compromise their beliefs by succumbing to the lures of worldliness. These few had been found worthy in the eyes of the Lord, and He promised them that they would walk with Him "in white clothes."

3:5 *Everyone who wins the victory this way will wear white clothes. I will never erase their names from the Book of Life.*

I will acknowledge them in the presence of my Father and his angels.

True and faithful believers of this church were assured eternal life. In heaven, these people would be dressed in white garments, displaying the righteousness received only through the grace of the Lord Jesus Christ.

Those whose names are found written within the Book of Life are those who have been redeemed unto Almighty God by the atoning sacrifice of God's Son, Jesus Christ. Those whose names are not found within the book are those who have been condemned to eternal damnation because of their unrepentant hearts. Later in Christ's revelation to John, the punishment imposed on those who have rejected Jesus' sacrifice is very clear: *"Those whose names were not found in the Book of Life were thrown into the fiery lake"* (Revelation 20:15). *"Nothing unclean, no one who does anything detestable, and no liars will ever enter it. Only those whose names are written in the lamb's Book of Life will enter it"* (Revelation 21:27). In addition, according to this verse, the Lord Jesus will vouch for each and every believer before God the Father and His angels.

3:6 *Let the person who has ears listen to what the Spirit says to the churches.*

For a fifth time, we are told to listen, learn, and apply the Holy Spirit's message to the churches. Jesus said that this church was virtually dead and encouraged those few faithful disciples to hold fast to the faith that had been imparted to them. Implied in this command is a call for obedience. Believers should listen to what Jesus said to these churches, carefully applying these evaluations to their lives, and obeying them by making the necessary improvements as the Holy Spirit prompts.

Notes/Applications

Christ admonished the church of Sardis to repent of spiritual lifelessness. Why was this church dead? Was it their lack of passion for ministry, their worldliness, their attitudes, or their craving for self-glory? Any of these reasons would be detrimental to the growth of believers, but we are not told what specific area was amiss among this body. The passage simply states that the members of this church externally appeared to be spiritual, yet they were internally empty and used up.

Even today, churches throughout the world have enjoyed commendable beginnings only to eventually lose their zeal, grow stale, and become ineffective in their Christian witness. The Lord instructs those believers that have lost fervor and vision for their calling to tear down the façade and to reexamine their position in Christ.

God's Holy Word instructs us not to be indifferent people who dutifully complete the work of the church. This work can only be accomplished within the embrace of our Savior, closely aligned through the Spirit with His every thought, word, and deed. Then, every endeavor reflects genuine joy and enthusiasm when serving Him as we, in turn, serve others as He has served us and given Himself for us.

Thus, on our knees, broken-hearted for our lifeless faith, we pray like David did:

> [10]*Create a clean heart in me, O God,*
> *and renew a faithful spirit within me.*
> [11]*Do not force me away from your presence,*
> *and do not take your Holy Spirit from me.*
> [12]*Restore the joy of your salvation to me,*
> *and provide me with a spirit of willing obedience.*
> [13]*Then I will teach your ways to those who are rebellious,*
> *and sinners will return to you. (Psalm 51:10–13)*

Revelation 3:7–13

3:7 *"To the messenger of the church in Philadelphia, write: The one who is holy, who is true, who has the key of David, who opens a door that no one can shut, and who shuts a door that no one can open, says:*

This is the message of the sixth angel to the church at Philadelphia. The Lord identified Himself to this church, as "The One Who is holy, Who is true." He further confirmed His identity by distinguishing Himself as the fulfillment of messianic prophecy. *"I will place the key of the house of David around his neck. What he opens no one will shut. What he shuts no one will open"* (Isaiah 22:22). Such phrases demonstrate the absolute sovereignty of Almighty God even as they demonstrate the reliability of the biblical narrative. The Old Testament foretells the promise of God's Messiah, and the New Testament affirms Jesus Christ as the completed fulfillment of those Old Testament prophecies.

Philadelphia was located about twenty-five miles southeast of Sardis. It was situated along a major thoroughfare, and as a result, it became a prominent city for both commercial and military purposes.[8] The same great earthquake that leveled Sardis in A.D. 17 also destroyed Philadelphia, which was prone to suffering the aftermath of earthquakes.[9]

3:8 *I know what you have done. See, I have opened a door in front of you that no one can shut. You only have a little strength, but you have paid attention to my word and have not denied my name.*

The Lord prefaced the message to this church in the same manner as He had addressed all of the churches. The Lord always addressed the churches for the purpose of improving the church's relationship to Him, whether in commendation or admonition.

Although Philadelphia was among the smallest of the seven churches addressed in Revelation, it was only the second one (Smyrna being the first) that did not provoke any measure of condemnation from the Lord. These believers were not perfect, but they were true to the Word of God, and they did not deny Christ.

The meaning of the open door seems most likely to refer to Christ as the Doorkeeper of the Kingdom. Despite the Jews' insistence that they alone would inherit the kingdom of David, the Lord assured these believers that their participation lay in His hands.[10] Those to whom the Lord opens the door are guaranteed entrance, and such was the case with these Philadelphians who had kept His Holy Word and boldly proclaimed His Name. In context, such an interpretation seems preferable to those which identify this open door as an opportunity to service, as is familiar imagery used in other biblical references[11] (1 Corinthians 16:9; Colossians 4:3).   *eternal security.*

3:9 *I will make those who are in Satan's synagogue come and bow at your feet and realize that I have loved you. They claim that they are Jewish, but they are lying.*

As with the church in Smyrna, the Christians in Philadelphia faced persecution from devout Jews that rejected Jesus as the Messiah. Christ again referred to these Jews as the synagogue of Satan. In the Lord's eyes, the ones who were Jews by birthright yet rejected Jesus were the enemies of His Kingdom. In contrast to these people, those who accepted Christ regardless of their ethnic heritage had become His people and received the benefits outlined in His covenant. *"[6b]Clearly, not everyone descended from Israel is part of Israel [7]or a descendant of Abraham. However, as Scripture says, 'Through Isaac your descendants will carry on your name.' [8]This means that children born by natural descent from Abraham are not necessarily God's children. Instead, children born by the promise are considered Abraham's descendants"* (Romans 9:6b–8).

Jesus called the Jewish assembly "the synagogue of Satan". As the Jews prided themselves on being God's chosen people with whom He had made a covenant, Jesus implied that they had forfeited the right to be called His people. They became instruments in the hands of Satan, who as their ruler used them to undermine and, if it were possible, to destroy the church. They rejected not only Jesus but also all His followers and, thus, indirectly acknowledged Satan as lord. Therefore, Jesus characterized them as liars because they no longer could claim to be God's people.[12]

The Lord promised the faithful of this city that the liars who were of Satan's synagogue would one day bow at the feet of the faithful believers as evidence of how much the Lord had loved them. The tables would be turned on those Jews who had persecuted God's faithful and challenging the believers' rightful inheritance into the Kingdom.[13]

3:10 *Because you have obeyed my command to endure, I will keep you safe during the time of testing which is coming to the whole world to test those living on earth.*

This verse has been widely used to explain the sequence of "end times" events. The interpretation of this verse is primarily dependent upon one's perception of "the time of testing." Some scholars uphold this verse in defense of a pre-tribulation rapture. Others dismiss a literal interpretation of "the whole world," thereby nullifying the message's universal impact. Whereas valid arguments can be made asserting that the message of this letter applies to more than just those in the church of Philadelphia at that time, it should never be presumed that the message was not initially intended for that church. It is best to refrain from defining "time of testing" as any singular event.[14] Doing so negates this message's relevance to the first-century church in Philadelphia to whom this letter was addressed.

Furthermore, the phrase "I will keep you safe," as rendered from the Greek, seems less to imply a physical removal from the world than to suggest that God will always uphold His faithful in the midst of their struggles. Jesus, the author of this book, also prayed for His disciples the night before He died, saying: "I'm not asking you to take them out of the world but to protect them from the evil one" *(John 17:15)*. As such, it is best to adhere to the conclusion of Matthew Henry, a renowned eighteenth-century biblical scholar, who stated: "Those who keep the Gospel in a time of peace shall be kept by Christ in an hour of temptation. By keeping the Gospel they are prepared for the trial; and the same divine grace that has made them fruitful in times of peace will make them faithful in times of persecution."[16]

3:11 *I am coming soon! Hold on to what you have so that no one takes your crown.* *not eternal security*

This should not be construed as a biblical error in which Christ promised that His return would occur shortly after He had addressed this church. The Lord was only promising that He would return and that His return would come upon man without delay according to His timing. He intended, it seems, to keep His followers expectant of His glorious return so that their perseverance would be strengthened and encouraged by this promise.

Peter, the chief of the apostles, was profoundly aware of this misinterpretation of God's perception of time. The timeless One, the One Who created both space and time, is not subject to the same time constraints as those whom God has created. *"Dear friends, don't ignore this fact: One day with the Lord is like a thousand years, and a thousand years are like one day"* (2 Peter 3:8).

There are several similarities between the churches in Philadelphia and Smyrna. Both received commendation without admonition, both contended against the synagogue of Satan, and both persevered for a period of intense persecution and tribulation. Jesus further reminded the believers in Philadelphia to hold firmly to their faith so that nothing could steal their crown, similar to the challenge He had given those in Smyrna. *"Be faithful until death, and I will give you the crown of life"* (Revelation 2:10b).

3:12 *I will make everyone who wins the victory a pillar in the temple of my God. They will never leave it again. I will write on them the name of my God, the name of the city of my God* *(the New Jerusalem coming down out of heaven from my God), and my new name.*

The Lord repeated His promise of eternal life, which He expressed to this church as a twofold reward. First, He would make them as a pillar in the heavenly temple, an eternal home from which they would never have to depart. As already stated, Philadelphia had endured more than its fair share of catastrophic earthquakes, so the promise of being made a permanent pillar in God's temple would have been received as a promise of God's reliability in a very unstable environment.

Second, the Name of God would be written upon each believer thereby declaring the Lord's ownership. *"His name will be on their foreheads"* (Revelation 22:4b). The name of the holy city would also be written upon the believers, and this city, the New Jerusalem, would serve as their new eternal address. These names would be the physical marks by which their inclusion in the Kingdom of Heaven was declared and authenticated. This promise provides a tremendous sense of security to those who have trusted Christ unto salvation.

3:13 *Let the person who has ears listen to what the Spirit says to the churches.*

Once again, Jesus Christ encouraged the believers in Philadelphia to remain faithful even though they were suffering the opposition of those "Jews" who vehemently opposed Jesus Christ as their promised Messiah and also persecuted those who witnessed to God's saving message. However, Jesus' encouragement to the Philadelphia church is here applied to His Church in all times and places.

Notes/Applications

Unlike His warnings to most of the other churches, Christ commended the believers at Philadelphia because they had patiently endured tribulation and temptation, had kept His Word, and had not denied His Name. But the Lord's commendation contains predictions of an ominous future: a time of terrible testing was on the horizon. Nevertheless, the Philadelphia Christians should not be afraid of this future. The Lord promised that He would reward them for their fidelity with eternal, pillar-like strength. Even in the midst of this future persecution, they would be a monument inscribed with a testament to the One they served as Master (the Name of God), the place of their ultimate dwelling (the New Jerusalem), and the One they trusted as their Redeemer (the new Name). Sixteenth-century hymnist John Newton eloquently paraphrases the Lord's glorious intent for this church in the hymn "Thus saith the Holy One, and True."

> *A pillar there, no more to move,*
> *Inscribed with all my names of love;*
> *A monument of mighty grace,*
> *Thou shalt forever have a place.*
> *Such is the conqueror's reward,*
> *Prepared and promised by the Lord![17]*

Believers of every age can take Jesus' promise to the Christians in Philadelphia as His faithful promise for them as well. Whatever the circumstances, whatever the trial, whatever the persecution, Jesus will keep His people strong, making them pillars of faithful testimony to His salvation and abiding love.

Statture

Revelation 3:14–22

3:14 *"To the messenger of the church in Laodicea, write: The amen, the witness who is faithful and true, the source of God's creation, says:*

This is the message to the seventh and final church, the church at Laodicea. As with each of the previous six churches, the believers in Laodicea should know that this message was sent directly from the Lord Jesus Christ, Who identified Himself as "The amen, the witness Who is faithful and true." Jesus Christ, Son of God, is the fulfillment of all messianic promise. He is the "amen." When there is nothing else, Jesus still remains. He is the beginning and the ending of all things. Jesus also referred to Himself as "the source of God's creation." John, the recorder of this book authored by Jesus Christ, also saw Jesus in this light. As John began his Gospel, he stated: *"¹In the beginning the Word already existed. The Word was with God, and the Word was God. ²He was already with God in the beginning"* (John 1:1–2).

The city of Laodicea was located approximately forty-five miles southeast of Philadelphia.[18] It was founded by Antiochus II in the middle of the third-century B.C. and was named after his wife Laodice.[19] At the time of this letter, the city was among the wealthiest in the region. It was a renowned banking center and had made a name for itself in the production of black wool products.[20] The city was also recognized worldwide for its medical school, especially noted for its development of renowned ear ointment and eye salve.[21] Despite the difficulties posed by its lack of a convenient water source, Laodicea had become a city of great agricultural and commercial prosperity.[22]

3:15 *I know what you have done, that you are neither cold nor hot. I wish you were cold or hot.*

As with each of the other churches, the Lord told the church of Laodicea that He knew what they had done. Laodicea received much of its water supply from Hierapolis, a town about six miles north. Hot

springs from this region found their way to this city, cooling significantly along the way. This metaphor to the problematic Laodicean
water supply seems evident. Like their water supply, Laodicea was neither hot nor cold. In comparison, Colossae, eleven miles away, had
refreshing cold-water springs.[23] The Lord told these middle-of-the-road
Christians that He wished they were either cold or hot. If these people
were hot, it would have shown in their passion for following Christ
and their testimony of His Word. If they were cold, their spiritual de-
ficiency would at least be unmistakable. The Lord told them that He
would rather they be one or the other than to be Christians who were
spiritually indistinguishable from the culture in which they lived.

This verse should not be taken as indicating that the Lord prefers
an atheist or a fanatical religious zealot to a tepid Christian. The issue
is the possession of genuine life in Christ by those who profess the
Christian faith, not the way they hold it.[24]

3:16 *But since you are lukewarm and not hot or cold, I'm
going to spit you out of my mouth.*

Christ would rather people express their faith in a biblically consistent manner than to be ambiguous in their faith and ineffective in
their service. Those who are lukewarm are complacent and fruitless.
To the naked eye, there may be no difference between a believer in this
position and an unbeliever. Unlike those who are hot or cold, those
who are lukewarm are entirely useless to either side. God cannot use
those who are lukewarm and as such, like the distastefulness of a tepid
drink, Christ says He will spit them out of His mouth.

3:17 *You say, 'I'm rich. I'm wealthy. I don't need anything.'
Yet, you do not realize that you are miserable, pitiful, poor,
blind, and naked.*

The church of Laodicea was not burdened by a lack of material goods
but by the abundance of them. Their excess of material provisions
caused them to believe that they could confront any problem, resolve

any conflict, and care for the needs of their people by themselves, so they no longer relied upon God to meet their needs. This church neglected the need to strive for spiritual riches in Christ Jesus. Perhaps they assumed that their wealth was an indication of God's favor toward them and blessings upon them.[25]

The Lord further warned these people that their reliance upon their own physical riches had blinded them of their spiritual destitution, and as a result, they were unable to recognize their deplorable, apathetic condition. God exposed their true spiritual condition to be exactly opposite of what they perceived it to be. Rather than prosperous, they were poor and naked; rather than content, they were wretched and miserable; and rather than enlightened, they were spiritually blind. Their earthly wealth gave them a false sense of security, but in the end, they would be left without direction and be found in desperate need. They thought that they were everything that they were not.

3:18 *I advise you: Buy gold purified in fire from me so that you may be rich. Buy white clothes from me. Wear them so that you may keep your shameful, naked body from showing. Buy ointment to put on your eyes so that you may see.*

Jesus Christ offered the Laodicean Christians the only remedy to their spiritual ambiguity: "Buy gold purified in fire." Refined gold is pure gold without blemish. Here, it signifies the righteousness of Christ.[26] This is not meant to suggest that we can "buy" salvation through any amount of works. The incentive to buy this refined gold from Christ is to obtain the true spiritual riches available only through Him.

In addition, Christ also admonished the Laodicean believers to cover the shame of their spiritual nakedness by dressing in the beautiful white garments that He provided them, which again symbolizes the righteousness they received from Jesus Christ by His atoning sacrifice on the Cross.

Finally, these believers were to seek healing from their spiritual blindness through Christ's anointing. The Lord used this illustration of blindness to show the people their spiritual condition, which fell far short of God's Truth revealed only through the work of the Holy Spirit. The lies of the world had blinded many believers within this church, but Jesus promised that those who sought after Him would have their spiritual eyes opened, and His truths would be revealed to them (*Matthew 6:33*).

3:19 *I correct and discipline everyone I love. Take this seriously, and change the way you think and act.*

Christ corrects and disciplines those He loves. Those that belong to Christ will be redirected by the Word of God. The principle of the Lord's discipline is consistent throughout the entire biblical narrative. Proverbs summarizes this principle effectively: "*¹¹Do not reject the discipline of the Lord, my son, and do not resent his warning, ¹²because the Lord warns the one he loves, even as a father warns a son with whom he is pleased*" (*Proverbs 3:11–12*). The writer of Hebrews echoes both the Old Testament and Jesus' reminder in this verse:

> "*⁶The Lord disciplines everyone he loves. He severely disciplines everyone he accepts as his child.*" *⁷Endure your discipline. God corrects you as a father corrects his children. All children are disciplined by their fathers. ⁸If you aren't disciplined like the other children, you aren't part of the family.* (*Hebrews 12:6–8*)

Through His rebuke and correction, the Lord shapes His faithful into the people He wants them to become.

As with the previous churches, Christ urged the believers at Laodicea to be enthusiastic and passionate about their faith and to repent for their idleness. He wanted them to change their ways and do away with their indifference and apathy.

3:20 *Look, I'm standing at the door and knocking. If anyone listens to my voice and opens the door, I'll come in and we'll eat together.*

Many pastors and teachers are quick to cite this verse as an open invitation to any and all unbelievers to come to Christ. We must remember, though, that Christ was still addressing the "lukewarm" people in the church of Laodicea who had grown apathetic toward their relationship with Christ within the complacence of self-sufficiency.[27] Though this verse well serves as a convenient tool for evangelism, for the purposes of commentary, we must remain true to its context and leave comment on its evangelistic appeal to other discussions.

Christ announced to the believers in Laodicea that He stood knocking outside the doors of their hearts. His presence, at one time, permeated throughout the church. Passion for Him motivated their good works, but now, He was excluded—He was standing outside the door. Eating is frequently used in the Bible, as a metaphor describing a close relationship. The Lord used the illustration of dining as a gentle reminder that He waited patiently for those who had neglected their relationship with God to again welcome Him in and to restore the warm and personal fellowship that was once shared.

3:21 *I will allow everyone who wins the victory to sit with me on my throne, as I have won the victory and have sat down with my Father on his throne.*

Similar promises of an eternal inheritance were offered at the conclusion of each of the messages given to the previous six churches. Eternal life is expressed in this verse as Christ's unfailing promise to sit with Him on His throne. Jesus then states clearly that He has already won the victory and sits with His Father on His throne. Believers, even lukewarm believers, simply need to unlock the door and invite Christ in to dine with Him, that is, to live in a close relationship with the One Who has already overcome Satan and destroyed death with His own resurrection. When the believer unlocks the door, the action is performed in obedience to the Lord's invitation.

3:22 *Let the person who has ears listen to what the Spirit says to the churches. "*

Again, the warning was sounded. This declaration at the end of each of the seven messages to the individual churches stresses its importance. In each instance, this command to hear suggests a response of obedience. Those who overcome—those faithful believers that respond to the prompting of the Holy Spirit and remain obedient to His will—are certain to receive the reward of fellowship with their Lord and Savior Jesus Christ in His presence forevermore.

Notes/Applications

Jesus Christ opened His letter to the church of the Laodiceans by reminding them that He is "the Amen, the faithful and true witness, the beginning of the creation of God". That is, Jesus Christ is the ultimate Authority in and over all things. He is the personification of Who God is and the only true witness of all things pertaining to God. He is the beginning and the end of every thing done by God from the beginning of creation to the end of time.

Jesus' opening words to the Laodiceans did not represent an attempt to reintroduce Himself to an assembly of believers, who had forgotten Him. It was a reminder that the One Who is pronouncing commendations, criticisms, and counsel possesses unquestionable authority to declare His decrees and, as such, possesses God's perfect knowledge of the conditions of each of the churches. Thus, His analyses and declarations are likewise perfectly accurate and absolutely truthful. Indeed, the Laodiceans may have forgotten that they have been redeemed for God by the precious blood of the Lamb of God, and as such, that they belonged to God. But the letter from Jesus Christ was not simply a reminder to jog their memory. It was a word of warning from their risen Savior, demanding that they listen to the One Who had redeemed them.

The Laodicean Christians were spiritually impoverished. Jesus reminded them that He knew everything about them. They could not deceive or fool the One Who had created and saved them. They could not hoodwink the "Amen, the faithful and true witness, and the beginning of the creation of God." Simply, Jesus Christ exposed their apathetic and indifferent ways.

Jesus Christ did not stop at pronouncing His indictment against the Laodicean church. He exposed their apathy, spiritual stagnancy, and sustained immaturity and offered them the cure for their desperate spiritual condition. Jesus invited the Laodiceans to come to Him and get everything they needed for their restoration. More significantly, Jesus Christ offered Himself to the Laodiceans—this time not in salvation, but in restoration of their waning faith. He invited them to fellowship, to dine with Him. Jesus called the Laodiceans to rise from a life of mediocrity and urged them to commit themselves to a life of continued spiritual growth built upon the solid foundation of their faith in the Lord Jesus Christ.

Likewise, Jesus continues to offer His sustaining power to the redeemed of all ages and encourages believers to rely on His nurturing care for strength and perseverance.

REVELATION 4

Revelation 4:1–5

4:1 *After these things I saw a door standing open in heaven. I heard the first voice like a trumpet speaking to me. It said, "Come up here, and I will show you what must happen after this."*

John was then summoned to heaven to be shown "what must happen after this." The text provides the transition from the challenges given to the seven churches in chapters two and three to the apocalyptic portion of this book.

A sense of ambiguity regarding the identity of the speaker exists, but on the basis of the description in this verse and Revelation 1:10, we may reasonably conclude that Jesus Christ issued these words as well. Another indication that there has been no alteration in the speaker's identity is that John does not notify readers of any change, and such disclosure seems to be his common practice when a shift occurs (*Revelation 7:2; 8:3; 10:1; 14:6–18; 18:1*). Though red-letter Bible versions do not render these as Christ's words, this claim seems more feasible since another source has not been introduced to the reader, and many commentaries from both pre- and post-red-letter Bible eras agree with this conclusion.[1]

After John had received the messages from the Lord Jesus Christ to the seven churches of Asia Minor, the apostle peered upward and saw a door open in heaven. Then, a voice like the sound of a trumpet called for him to ascend into heaven and to witness visions of future events. Jesus Christ stood at heaven's door and invited John to enter so that he could be shown "what must happen after this."

Many believers go to great lengths to explain this verse as a symbolic illustration of the rapture of God's elect.[2] Though they extract references from this verse with loose parallels from more traditional "rapture" passages, the effort seems, at best, supposition. Apart from distinguishing John as a symbol of the church, for which there is no justifiable cause or purpose, there is little evidence to suggest anything other than what we are told.[3] Accordingly, any such interpretations as applied to this verse seem too speculative to be defended with biblical certainty.

4:2 *Instantly, I came under the Spirit's power. I saw a throne in heaven, and someone was sitting on it.*

God called John up into heaven "under the Spirit's power." The speaker is now John. There are two main interpretations regarding the meaning of this experience. The first contends that John was physically transported via the Spirit from Patmos into heaven to witness the things he was to be shown.[4] This condition is likely the same state that the apostle Paul once tried to describe. *"³I know that this person ⁴was snatched away to paradise where he heard things that can't be expressed in words, things that humans cannot put into words. I don't know whether this happened to him physically or spiritually. Only God knows"* (2 Corinthians 12:3–4). The second interpretation suggests that John merely witnessed the events which follow as a vision, whereby his consciousness was the only thing altered.[5] Both interpretations attempt to understand an event that is unique to the human experience. As such, they try to understand specifically how this event occurred, speculating on various possibilities. However, it is best to understand that John's invitation to the gates of heaven was unparalleled and is probably best left to a simple acceptance of John's statement.

When John arrived in heaven, he was welcomed with a beautiful sight of a Person sitting on a throne. This glorious Being is soon identified as Almighty God, the Father.

4:3 *The one sitting there looked like gray quartz and red quartz. There was a rainbow around the throne which looked like an emerald.*

Though certainly God's magnificent presence is indefinable, John attempted to explain God's glorious appearance to the beauty of precious gems. Gray quartz is a brilliant, transparent stone, and red quartz is a reddish gem similar to a ruby. The grandeur of this scene is further magnified by the description of "a rainbow around the throne," which is described as an emerald. Surely, the magnificence of this spectacle surpassed any human comprehension, but nevertheless, John, limited to earthly physical comparisons and inadequate human words, attempted to illustrate verbally the indescribable scene before him by drawing comparisons to the most beautiful gems that he knew.

4:4 *Around that throne were 24 other thrones, and on these thrones sat 24 leaders wearing white clothes. They had gold crowns on their heads.*

These twenty-four "leaders" gathered around God's throne seem to have been granted some special authority or distinction from the other heavenly beings. Though some commentators have defined them as angels, they were singled out from the host of heaven as having white robes and golden crowns, so they were evidently unique beings. Scholars have speculated a variety of theories regarding their identity. Among a few of the more prevalent interpretations are these: 1) their number symbolizes the twelve tribes of Israel and the twelve apostles, and therefore, they represent the entire sum of God's redeemed, both

of Old Testament and New Testament saints;[6] 2) they are the heavenly model of the twenty-four priests who served in the earthly temple[7]
(*1 Chronicles 24; 25*); and, 3) they represent only New Testament saints.[8]
It cannot be defended with any certainty that these twenty-four leaders
seated on thrones of distinction have any symbolic implication at all.
More important than who or what they might represent is what we
are specifically told about them within these chapters. They serve the
King's purposes and worship Him without ceasing.[9]

4:5 *Lightning, noise, and thunder came from the throne.
Seven flaming torches were burning in front of the throne.
These are the seven spirits of God.*

Scholars differ in their theories regarding the significance of this description of "lightning, noise, and thunder." Some claim that this is
the voice of God forewarning judgment.[10] However, this same statement is also made when the Lord God descends to meet with Moses
on Mt. Sinai. Thus, this spectacle might better be understood as representative of the awesome, even frightening presence of God.

> [16]*On the morning of the second day, there was thunder and
> lightning with a heavy cloud over the mountain, and a very
> loud blast from a ram's horn [was heard]. All the people in
> the camp shook with fear.* [17]*Then Moses led the people out
> of the camp to meet with God, and they stood at the foot
> of the mountain.* [18]*All of Mount Sinai was covered with
> smoke because the Lord had come down on it in fire. Smoke
> rose from the mountain like the smoke from a kiln, and
> the whole mountain shook violently."* (*Exodus 19:16–18*)

Near the Father's throne were seven lamps representing "the seven
spirits of God." There are no corroborating biblical references outside
of Revelation to suggest that this pictures seven individual spirits of
God. This depiction is difficult to understand, and it might be best to
simply leave it as a description of what John saw and avoid interpreting
something that we really do not understand.

Notes/Applications

The eternal, Almighty God in His awesome graciousness opened the door of heaven and called a mere mortal, John, to enter and witness the indescribable beauty, majesty, and glory of His Presence. John was not given the opportunity to refuse the invitation, but was immediately transported into the presence of the eternal Creator and Judge.

John discovered that human language was amazingly useless when trying to describe what he saw. The beauty seen in the multitude of colors present at sunset, which are seen by the people of this world, will never begin to describe what John witnessed. With stunted and stumbling language, John spoke of grey quartz, red quartz, and emeralds in his feeble attempt to tell his readers what it was like to be in the presence of the eternal God.

At times, despite the hopelessness of the task, people attempt to describe the indescribable glory of God. Nevertheless, God did not withhold the glory of His presence from His ordained prophets. Isaiah likewise saw of vision of the Lord seated upon His throne: *"[1]In the year that King Uzziah died I saw the Lord sitting upon a throne, high and lifted up; and the train of his robe filled the temple. [2]Above him stood the seraphim. Each had six wings: with two he covered his face, and with two he covered his feet, and with two he flew. [3]And one called to another and said: 'Holy, holy, holy is the Lord of hosts; the whole earth is full of his glory!' [4]And the foundations of the thresholds shook at the voice of him who called, and the house was filled with smoke"* (Isaiah 6:1-4).

We can only imagine the striking beauty of Almighty God arrayed in a spectrum of His heavenly glory, for we have yet to behold Him.

Nevertheless, the day approaches when we, too, will behold the kaleidoscopic vision of Almighty God ruling in majestic beauty and strength. We will then bow before Him, overtaken by the light of His gloriousness as we eternally honor Him with multitudes upon multitudes of the redeemed in Christ.

Revelation 4:6–11

4:6 *In front of the throne, there was something like a sea of glass as clear as crystal. In the center near the throne and around the throne were four living creatures covered with eyes in front and in back.*

The throne of God must have been the most beautiful sight in all of heaven! The floor surrounding the throne appeared as a crystal sea, a transparent sheet that was as wide and deep as the eye could see. Evidently, it was completely void of darkness, shadows, and flaws.

Seated all around the throne were four creatures that had many eyes in front and in back. The Greek word for *creatures* here is *zoa*, which means "a living being."[11] These beings, therefore, probably did not appear to be abhorrent monsters but magnificent heavenly creatures. As with the aforementioned leaders, much speculation has been made about a greater symbolic relevance of these creatures and their many eyes, but it seems difficult to reconcile dogmatically any of these interpretations with certainty. Surely, such an arrangement of eyes is unfamiliar to our human experience and clearly depicts some manner of heavenly uniqueness. There is no reason to conclude that the heavenly scene before John was intended to compel any comparisons to earthly things.

4:7 *The first living creature was like a lion, the second was like a young bull, the third had a face like a human, and the fourth was like a flying eagle.*

John described these four creatures surrounding the throne in further detail. These descriptions bear striking similarities to a vision described by the prophet Ezekiel. "*Their faces looked like this: From the front, each creature had the face of a human. From the right, each one had the face of a lion. From the left, each one had the face of a bull. And from the back, each one had the face of an eagle*" (Ezekiel 1:10). Comparisons have also been drawn between the characteristics of the animals described in this verse with the attributes of God.[12] Others have attempted to equate these four animals with the four Gospels.[13] Any such efforts appear unnecessary since they lend no assistance in the interpretation of the Revelation. John merely observed four dynamic, complicated, magnificent beings that worshiped and attended Almighty God on His throne.

4:8 *Each of the four living creatures had six wings and were covered with eyes, inside and out. Without stopping day or night they were singing, "Holy, holy, holy is the Lord God Almighty, who was, who is, and who is coming."*

Each creature had six wings, which perhaps enabled the creatures to fly as well as to cover their form in the Lord's presence. Again, similarities are evident between the four creatures described here and the four creatures in Ezekiel's vision. *"Under the dome, each creature had two wings that were stretched out straight, touching one another. Each creature had two wings that covered its body" (Ezekiel 1:23).* In addition, the creatures were "full of eyes around and within." The beings praised the eternal existence of God Almighty, Who is forever past, present, and future, and their worship of Him never ceased.

4:9–10 *⁹Whenever the living creatures give glory, honor, and thanks to the one who sits on the throne, to the one who lives forever and ever, ¹⁰the 24 leaders bow in front of the one who sits on the throne and worship the one who lives forever and ever. They place their crowns in front of the throne and say,*

These unique heavenly beings evidently served one primary purpose: to offer their worship to God on His throne. Whenever the four creatures gave glory to Almighty God—which, as explained by the previous verse, is unending—they were joined in praise by the twenty-four leaders. The whole environment of heaven is filled with the sound of praise. Though speculation about the significance of the leaders is perhaps best deferred, some good arguments have been made, specifically that these leaders represent in some form redeemed man due to the white garments that the leaders wore and the crowns that they cast before the throne.[14]

4:11 *"Our Lord and God, you deserve to receive glory, honor, and power because you created everything. Everything came into existence and was created because of your will."*

After the leaders cast down their crowns before the Father, they cried aloud declaring that God alone was worthy to receive glory, honor, and power. The leaders had acknowledged God as the Creator of all things. Paul, in his letter to the Colossians, by the inspiration of the Holy Spirit, also expressed his praise to God in similar terms:

> [16]*He created all things in heaven and on earth, visible and invisible. Whether they are kings or lords, rulers or powers—everything has been created through him and for him.* [17]*He existed before everything and holds everything together. (Colossians 1:16–17)*

It is evident that the worship of Almighty God will also be our primary if not sole activity in heaven. The redeemed of the Lord will focus their praise, like these beings, on the awesomeness of His role as Creator and Sustainer.

Notes/Applications

These four beings, along with the twenty-four leaders, gathered around God's throne and continually proclaimed His worthiness as the powerful Creator and Sustainer of all life.

We easily forget our frailty. We forget that we are created by God's immutable will, and by God's grace, we are redeemed by the sacrifice of His Son, Jesus Christ. With so many technological and medical advances in recent years, we may subconsciously rely upon man's ability to extend life. However, just as our Lord spoke creation into being with supreme utterance, He has determined our days with loving authority, and His Word is perfect.

²*Give to the Lord the glory his name deserves.*
Worship the Lord in his holy splendor.
³*The voice of the Lord rolls over the water.*
The God of glory thunders.
The Lord shouts over raging water.
⁴*The voice of the Lord is powerful.*
The voice of the Lord is majestic.
⁵*The voice of the Lord breaks the cedars.*
The Lord splinters the cedars of Lebanon.
⁷*The voice of the Lord strikes with flashes of lightning.*
⁸*The voice of the Lord makes the wilderness tremble. . . .*
⁹*The voice of the Lord splits the oaks*
and strips the trees of the forests bare.
Everyone in his temple is saying, "Glory!"
¹⁰*The Lord sat enthroned over the flood.*
The Lord sits enthroned as king forever.
(Psalm 29:2–5, 7–8a, 9–10)

Some may deny God's mastery as Creator and Sustainer of every facet of creation, but His character remains unchanged. He is complete; He does not need our adoration. Still, His Word tells us that He desires praise from those He has created. When the redeemed meet their Redeemer in the courts of heaven, they will worship Him in their immortal bodies, no longer hindered by their sinful flesh. How our hearts and burdened souls are transformed by such a glimpse of heaven as we worship Him in the beauty and wonder of His eternal Being (Psalm 29:1–5).

REVELATION 5

Revelation 5:1–7

5:1 *I saw a scroll in the right hand of the one who sits on the throne. It had writing both on the inside and on the outside. It was sealed with seven seals.*

This verse is a continuation of the vision of heaven that began in the previous chapter. The heavenly Father held in His right hand a sealed scroll with writing on both sides, likely an indication of the content's length and gravity. Interpretations regarding the scroll range from it representing the redemptive history of mankind to the consequential destiny of the world.[1] Whatever the symbolism intended, it is safe to conclude by the evidence of the subsequent chapters that the scroll represents "the mystery of God's purpose for the world."[2]

Historically, it was not uncommon for a message to be bound with a clay or wax seal in order to bear the mark of the sender and to ensure the privacy of the letter.[3] This particular scroll, however, bore seven seals, and many commentators attribute this to the document's importance and to the guarantee of its secrecy.[4] Some Bible versions render the object in God's hand as a book, not in form but in length.

This leads a few commentators to speculate that this book was actually comprised of seven scrolls, each affixed with a seal and each serving as a volume or portion of the sum of the contents.[5] Regardless, each individual seal bears unique consequence, and the judgments ensue after each seal is broken, as described in subsequent verses.

> **DIG DEEPER:** *Seal*
>
> Seals were a vital component of the ancient Middle East. These artifacts have been found dating more than several thousand years before the birth of Christ. The purpose of these seals varied depending upon the application, but they always provided evidence of ownership. Seals were never to be broken by anyone except those having the proper authority, either the owner or the person to whom the document was addressed. Seals were so important that they were often attached to a man's garment so that it could be used at any given moment when authenticity was required. In this case, Jesus alone had the authority to open the seals of this scroll, indicating His unique position as the Lamb of God, thus ensuring the certainty of the unchangeable decrees that were written within the document.

5:2 *I saw a powerful angel calling out in a loud voice, "Who deserves to open the scroll and break the seals on it?"*

Some expositors believe this powerful angel is asserting a public challenge to any who might come forth and attempt to unlock this scroll and disclose its contents.[6] However, it seems more appropriate to assume that this utterance was made more for the benefit of the human observers, both John at that moment and his readers thereafter. Surely, as evidenced by the lack of response in the verse that follows, all other created beings already knew that there was none among them able to reply satisfactorily. Therefore, this appears to be a rhetorical question, one made for the purpose of proclamation. Although this angel was mighty, he, too, was unable to break the seals because it was not a question of strength but of worthiness. The seals could only be broken by one worthy to do so.

5:3–4 *³No one in heaven, on earth, or under the earth could open the scroll or look inside it. ⁴I cried bitterly because no one was found who deserved to open the scroll or look inside it.*

No created being existed that was worthy to break the seals, so the contents of the scroll could not be read. John wept openly at this, though we can only speculate why he did so. Some have suggested that this disappointment was generated by unanswered questions.[7] Perhaps, however, John feared that he might not be shown "what must happen after this" as promised (*Revelation 4:1*).[8]

5:5 *Then one of the leaders said to me, "Stop crying! The Lion from the tribe of Judah, the Root of David, has won the victory. He can open the scroll and the seven seals on it."*

One of the twenty-four elders comforted John by assuring him that there was indeed One Who was worthy to break the seven seals and to look at the contents of the scroll. He called this One the "Lion from the tribe of Judah," a reference to an Old Testament passage considered to be messianic prophecy.[9]

> *⁸Judah, your brothers will praise you. Your hand will be on the neck of your enemies. Your father's sons will bow down to you. ⁹Judah, you are a lion cub. You have come back from the kill, my son. He lies down and rests like a lion. He is like a lioness. Who dares to disturb him? ¹⁰A scepter will never depart from Judah nor a ruler's staff from between his feet until Shiloh comes and the people obey him. (Genesis 49:8–10)*

The line of royal kingship was given to Judah. As evidenced in the genealogy of Matthew chapter one, Christ is of that royal bloodline. Jesus fulfilled prophecy by being born in the line of David. As Paul says in his letter to the Romans: *"²(God had already promised this Good News through his prophets in the Holy Scriptures. ³This Good News is about* his Son, our Lord Jesus Christ. In his human nature he was a descendant of David" (Romans 1:2–3). However, this Lion is also called the "Root of David," indicating that He was not only a descendent of David but also preceded David as the Root of that bloodline. Jesus Himself told His opponents of His eternal precedence: *"Jesus told them, 'I can guarantee this truth: Before Abraham was ever born, I am'"* (John 8:58). That He was born of the line of David confirms His absolute humanness, that He is from the tribe of Judah, and that He is the Root of David, verifying that He alone is the fulfillment of Old Testament prophecy.

5:6 *I saw a lamb standing in the center near the throne with the four living creatures and the leaders. The lamb looked like he had been slaughtered. He had seven horns and seven eyes, which are the seven spirits of God sent all over the world.*

Ironically, this "Lion" (of the tribe of Judah), the Lord Jesus Christ, appeared in the midst of the throne as a lamb—the perfect Lamb sacrificed for the sins of all men. This same John, the recorder of this vision, also saw Jesus as the Lamb of God, when Jesus walked among men during His earthly ministry: *"John [the Baptizer] saw Jesus coming toward him the next day and said, 'Look! This is the Lamb of God who takes away the sin of the world'"* (John 1:29). Although the Lamb bore the marks of having been slain, He, nevertheless, stood in the midst of the throne.

The Lamb had seven horns and seven eyes, which some scholars suggest illustrate Christ's strength, dominion, and omniscience.[10] Whereas some good arguments have been made that the seven horns and eyes are symbolic of Christ's attributes, this verse specifically states that they represent the seven spirits of God, comparable to the lamps of fire mentioned in chapter four. *"Seven flaming torches were burning in front of the throne. These are the seven spirits of God"* (Revelation 4:5). In the first three chapters of Revelation, the seven spirits spoke to the seven churches in Asia Minor as God's appointed messengers, and in this verse, the ministry of the seven spirits appears to have expanded to the extent that they addressed the entire earth.

5:7 *He took the scroll from the right hand of the one who sits on the throne.*

In a gesture which both asserted His supreme authority and answered earlier concerns that the contents of the scroll might not be revealed, the Lamb removed the scroll from the right hand of Almighty God. Jesus, the Lamb of God, was the only one worthy and able to do this. Though Jesus is God and is of God as one person of the divine Trinity, this action illustrates that Christ is worthy by virtue of what He accomplished at Calvary. God became man in the Person of Jesus Christ, Who came to earth, lived the sinless life, died for the atonement of mankind's sins, and rose again, thereby defeating sin and death forevermore.

Notes/Applications

This passage identifies the Lamb, the Lord Jesus Christ, to be the only one worthy to open the seals of the scroll. Why is Christ esteemed worthy? He is the Son of God, the likeness and essence of God, yet with perfect humility, He yielded Himself to become the sacrificial Lamb through a sinless life, an undeserving death, and a glorious, redemptive resurrection. *"[16]God loved the world this way: He gave his only Son so that everyone who believes in him will not die but will have eternal life. [17]God sent his Son into the world, not to condemn the world, but to save the world"* (John 3:16–17).

Christ is what we could not become. *"If someone obeys all of God's laws except one, that person is guilty of breaking all of them"* (James 2:10). *"Christ paid the price to free us from the curse that God's laws bring by becoming cursed instead of us"* (Galatians 3:13a). The spotless Lamb willingly shed His blood for our corrupt souls. Such determination overwhelms our feeble ponderings. Such divinity pierces our hearts with its saving intents. Such demonstration requires our zealous response:

> *[5]He was wounded for our rebellious acts.*
> *He was crushed for our sins.*
> *He was punished so that we could have peace,*

and we received healing from his wounds.
⁶We have all strayed like sheep.
Each one of us has turned to go his own way,
and the Lord has laid all our sins on him.
⁷He was abused and punished,
but he didn't open his mouth.
He was led like a lamb to the slaughter.
He was like a sheep that is silent
when its wool is cut off.
He didn't open his mouth. . . .
¹⁰Yet, it was the Lord's will to crush him with suffering.
When the Lord has made his life a sacrifice for our
wrongdoings,
he will see his descendants for many days.
The will of the Lord will succeed through him.
¹¹He will see and be satisfied
because of his suffering. (Isaiah 53:5–7, 10–11a)

Revelation 5:8–14

5:8 *When the lamb had taken the scroll, the four living creatures and the 24 leaders bowed in front of him. Each held a harp and a gold bowl full of incense, the prayers of God's holy people.*

In response to the Lamb of God receiving the scroll from the Father, the four beings and the twenty-four leaders fell prostrate before the Lamb to exalt and worship Him. In addition, each of the leaders and each of the four creatures strummed their harps and expressed their worship through music. They also had golden vials that contained incense, which is described as "the prayers of God's holy people." Later in this same revelation, John witnessed a similar event: *"Another angel came with a gold incense burner and stood at the altar. He was given a lot of incense to offer on the gold altar in front of the throne. He offered it with the prayers of all of God's people" (Revelation 8:3).* This particular allusion likely serves to illustrate how the prayers of believers flow upward to God like smoke that rises from incense.

5:9–10 *⁹Then they sang a new song, "You deserve to take the scroll and open the seals on it, because you were slaughtered. You bought people with your blood to be God's own. They are from every tribe, language, people, and nation. ¹⁰You made them a kingdom and priests for our God. They will rule as kings on the earth."*

These twenty-four leaders and four creatures sang a new song unto the Lamb for being worthy of opening the seals of the scroll. The twenty-four leaders and four creatures worshiped Him for Who He is and the things He had done that make Him worthy to open the scroll. The perfect cleansing power of Christ's blood has made redemption available to every person of every nation, tribe, or language.

The Lord Jesus Christ, Redeemer of all believers, made His followers kings and priests unto God. This vision affirmed what John had

witnessed earlier: "*And has made us a kingdom, priests for God his Father.*
Amen" (*Revelation 1:6*). The redeemed of the Lord are described as
"kings" and "priests," generally suggesting two aspects of their relationship with God resulting from their redemption through Jesus Christ:
1) the redeemed have direct access to God through Jesus Christ, their
High Priest; and, 2) the redeemed will reign with Him on the earth in
His future Kingdom[11] (*Revelation 20:6*).

5:11–12 *11Then I heard the voices of many angels, the four*
living creatures, and the leaders surrounding the throne. They
numbered ten thousand times ten thousand and thousands
times thousands. *12In a loud voice they were singing, "The*
lamb who was slain deserves to receive power, wealth, wisdom,
strength, honor, glory, and praise."

A choir of innumerable angels then joined in song with the four creatures, and the twenty-four leaders gathered around the throne. This
multitude of heavenly beings loudly proclaimed that the Lamb slain
from the foundation of the world was worthy of all exaltation because
He is the only One Who deserves to receive all power, wealth, wisdom,
strength, honor, glory, and praise. This massive choir of angels joined
in song to celebrate the fulfillment of prophecy in Jesus Christ, the
sacrificial Lamb of God, slain on the Cross of Calvary.

5:13 *I heard every creature in heaven, on earth, under the*
earth, and on the sea. Every creature in those places was sing-
ing, "To the one who sits on the throne and to the lamb be
praise, honor, glory, and power forever and ever."

Every living being in heaven and on earth then joined this countless
and magnificent choir. John witnessed all creation giving blessing,
honor, glory, and power unto God the Father and unto the Lord Jesus
Christ. All creatures of God, both angelic and human, sang one glorious "Alleluia" in praise of God as their Creator and to Jesus Christ as
their Redeemer.

5:14 *The four living creatures said, "Amen!" Then the leaders bowed and worshiped.*

The four beings declared, "Amen," thereby affirming the worthiness of the praise and worship that had been offered unto God the Father and the Lamb. The twenty-four leaders then bowed again and poured out their worship to Him Who is worthy.

Many have foolishly tried to explain the identity of those represented in this passage. However, it is far better to focus on the One to Whom their worship was offered. The emphasis of these verses redirect the believer's attention on the worthiness of the Lamb Who, as stated in this new song of praise, has bought a special people for Himself with His blood (*v. 9*).

Notes/Applications

Whereas the first passage revealed the Lamb, the Lord Jesus Christ, to be the only one worthy to open the seals of the scroll, this passage reveals Him to be the only one worthy to receive praise and glory.

He is worthy to receive all power, for He will never misuse it. He is worthy of all of the world's riches, for His riches are incorruptible. He is worthy of all wisdom, for all true wisdom comes from Him. He is worthy of all strength, for He is the source of strength and power. How can mortal words express due adoration to such a great Lord and Savior? Our most eloquent whispers or shouts fail in expressing the praise and glory due His name, for He Who is great has done great things. Isaac Watts, named the father of hymnody, has expressed the blessed dilemma of our loss for words when glimpsing Jesus:

> *What equal honors shall we bring*
> *to Thee, O Lord our God, the Lamb,*
> *When all the notes that angels sing*
> *are far inferior to Thy Name?*
>
> *Worthy is He that once was slain,*
> *the Prince of Peace that groaned and died;*

Worthy to rise, and live, and reign
at His Almighty Father's side.

Power and dominion are His due
Who stood condemned at Pilate's bar;
Wisdom belongs to Jesus too,
though He was charged with madness here.

All riches are His native right,
yet He sustained amazing loss;
To him ascribe eternal might,
Who left His weakness on the cross.

Honor immortal must be paid,
instead of scandal and of scorn;
While glory shines around His head,
and a bright crown without a thorn.

Blessings forever on the Lamb
Who bore the curse for wretched men;
Let angels sound His sacred Name,
 and every creature say, Amen.[12]

REVELATION

6

Revelation 6:1–8

6:1 *I watched as the lamb opened the first of the seven seals. I heard one of the four living creatures say with a voice like thunder, "Go!"*

John witnessed Jesus opening the first seal, and a great, thunderous voice resounded. The opening of these seals signaled the beginning of the final judgments upon the earth and all of its inhabitants, a time unlike any creation would ever know.[1] When Jesus was with His disciples, He outlined some of the events that would occur at some future time: *"There will be a lot of misery at that time, a kind of misery that has not happened from the beginning of the world until now and will certainly never happen again"* (Matthew 24:21).

Greek linguists struggle to determine the best interpretation of this verse. Some Greek texts contain only the word *ercou* and most contemporary translations express this word as *come* rather than *go*. Other texts employ the phrase *come and see,* *"ercou kai blepe."* A brief review of these translations shows a preference for interpreting this command as an invitation for John to come closer and witness

87

the events about to take place. Throughout the following verses, the translations consistently repeat the command as they have translated it in this verse. Jesus alone opened the seal, one of the four beings (*Revelation 4:6*) bellowed the command, and the events ordained from the throne of God immediately followed.

6:2 *Then I looked, and there was a white horse, and its rider had a bow. He was given a crown and rode off as a warrior to win battles.*

Immediately following the command of one of the four beasts, John saw a man carrying a bow and sitting upon a white horse. Some commentators ascribe this rider's identity as Jesus Christ in some veiled reference to His second coming as described in chapter nineteen.[2] This comparison, however, seems unlikely since it was the Lamb Himself Who opened the seal which brought forth this rider. Furthermore, this rider's authority, represented by the crown, was given to him, signifying the sovereignty of a higher authority over this figure. The Lord would not need such permission since there is no higher authority than His own. Still other interpreters say this rider's identity is that of the antichrist, acknowledging that this being cannot be Christ yet contending that the similarities (primarily that of the white horse) cannot be ignored.[3]

Wisdom is perhaps best exercised while interpreting this verse by not requiring that the identity of the rider be established since this cannot be done with any certainty. Doing so, in fact, may assign more implication and consequence to this rider than was intended by the text. On the other hand, it can be said that this horse and rider symbolize simply that which we are told—a valiant warrior prepared for battle.

6:3–4 [3]*When the lamb opened the second seal, I heard the second living creature say, "Go!"* [4]*A second horse went out. It was fiery red. Its rider was given the power to take peace away* *from the earth and to make people slaughter one another. So he was given a large sword.*

Jesus opened the second seal, and another of the four creatures exclaimed, "Go!" whereupon John witnessed a second horse and rider. The color of the horse was red, which some commentators theorize signifies the color of blood and slaughter.[4] With the power given to him by the sovereign God, this rider instigated war all around the world. God's authority also gave this rider the power to remove all peace from it. He did not directly battle with the inhabitants of the earth, but it was the source of world-wide strife and conflict.

6:5 *[5]When the lamb opened the third seal, I heard the third living creature say, "Go!" I looked, and there was a black horse, and its rider held a scale. [6]I heard what sounded like a voice from among the four living creatures, saying, "A quart of wheat for a day's pay or three quarts of barley for a day's pay. But do not damage the olive oil and the wine."*

The Lord opened the third seal, and the third creature like the others before it called out "Go!" John observed a third rider sitting upon a black horse, gripping a set of balances in his hand. Balances weigh the exchange of merchandise and possibly serve as a symbol of the economy.

John heard a voice emerge from amidst the four creatures seated around the throne, indicating that this was the Lamb's voice. The prevailing interpretation advocates that the black horse and its rider symbolize famine and economic destitution.[5] Most would also agree that the measurements mentioned in this verse show that one day's wages were only sufficient to attain one day's sustenance.[6]

Scholars agree less, however, on the interpretation of the command, "Do not harm the oil and the wine." Some argue that this emphasizes the economic and social inequality affecting the earth during this period of the final judgment.[7] It seems faithful to the text to maintain that the oil and wine symbolize the excessive availability of luxury items in contrast to the shortage of necessities.[8] In A.D. 92, shortly before the writing of Revelation, an acute shortage of cereals, together with an abundance of wine in the empire, caused Domitian to order the restriction of wine cultivation and an increase of corn growing; the order created such a furor it had to be abandoned. The text may have such a situation in mind.[9]

6:7–8 ⁷*When the lamb opened the fourth seal, I heard the voice of the fourth living creature say, "Go!" ⁸I looked, and there was a pale horse, and its rider's name was Death. Hell followed him. They were given power over one-fourth of the earth to kill people using wars, famines, plagues, and the wild animals on the earth.*

Jesus opened the fourth seal, and the last of the four creatures said, "Go." The fourth and final horseman appeared riding a pale horse. This is the first and only of the horsemen whose name we are told—Death. Unlike the other riders before him, Death was accompanied by another figure identified as Hell. The mention of these two together suggests that Death was given the power to destroy one quarter of the world's population, and Hell followed closely behind to gather the victims.

Death was given power to kill one fourth of the world's population by four means: the sword, which describes man-made military weapons; hunger, which includes famine and perhaps a deliberate rationing of food supplies by those in authority; plagues, which denotes disease and pestilence having far-reaching effects; and finally, wild animals, which apparently become desperate for new food sources in a world devastated by war and famine. This description seems to be the fulfillment of a prophecy foretold by Ezekiel: "*This is what the Almighty Lord says: I will surely send four terrible punishments against Jerusalem. I will send wars, famines, wild animals, and plagues. They will destroy people and animals*" (Ezekiel 14:21).

Notes/Applications

The events that John witnessed when he was invited to come and see what the Lord had planned for the future must have frightened him immensely. When he was invited to the gates of heaven, he had no idea what to expect. The revelation of chapters four and five were exhilarating, showing the hosts of heaven praising God for His glory in creation and His overarching love in His redeeming Lamb.

When the seals were broken, that exhilarating experience before the throne of God and the Lamb was quickly dispelled, only to be replaced by the most horrific predictions of war, famine, pestilence, and death imaginable.

Because God is holy, He must judge sin. He cannot, He will not tolerate rebellion and disobedience. He is a jealous God and demands His rightful place of praise and devotion. He will faithfully execute His justice on all those who have reviled Him and refused His offer of salvation. What John witnesses is the unleashing of God's fury on a world that has rebelled against both His creation and His redemption. The time for repentance is gone. The time for judgment has arrived.

God has been patient with the human race for thousands of years. Now, at last, His salvation is withdrawn and His anger boils over. The four horses bring a time of terrible suffering on all humanity, a suffering that is as painful to endure even as it is perfectly just. There will be wars, famine, economic chaos, disease, pestilence, and death, followed closely by Hell itself which gleefully gathers the victims into his eager arms.

Be wary, O man, of God's just condemnation and the fury of His anger. Flee to Him while there is still time, and His arms are open to receive and forgive. Otherwise, be forewarned! He will not always strive with man, and He will surely execute His judgment on those who refuse His gracious offer of salvation and restoration.

Revelation 6:9–17

6:9 *When the lamb opened the fifth seal, I saw under the altar the souls of those who had been slaughtered because of God's word and the testimony they had given about him.*

The Lord opened the fifth seal, and there appeared under the heavenly altar the souls of those who were martyred for their resolute faith in Jesus Christ. This was the only time that the opening of a seal did not prompt a specific act of judgment upon the world. Rather, when this seal was opened John saw those who had been martyred for the cause of Christ. Perhaps he saw his brother James who had been killed by Herod Antipas just fifteen years after Jesus' ascension. Perhaps he saw Peter and Paul. John had been invited into heaven to witness and record the events that the Lord wanted to show him. This must have provided assurance that God's saints who had died for witnessing to the truth of His Word, were still praising the Lord within the heavenly realm. This group should not be understood to include all of God's elect because these saints have been specifically identified as martyrs. An altar is a place designated for sacrifice and here, under this altar in heaven, it seems that the sacrifice offered to the Lord is the blood of those who never turned their back on Christ even to the point of death. Obviously, all Christians should uphold the faithful testimony that confirms the truth of God's Word, yet certainly not all Christians are put to death because of it.

However, not all questions about this verse are answered by this conclusion. Some commentators believe that this group will consist only of those who are martyred between Christ's ascension and an expected pre-tribulation rapture, while others suppose these to be tribulation martyrs only.[10] No part of this description suggests that this group is limited to anything less than *all* of those killed "because of God's Word and the testimony they had given about Him."

6:10 *They cried out in a loud voice, "Holy and true Master, how long before you judge and take revenge on those living on earth who shed our blood?"*

The souls of these martyred believers that gathered beneath the altar wondered how long it would be before the Almighty dispensed His justice. Their souls cried out to God for revenge. Even in the safety of heaven's refuge, it appears that they were still able to remember the earthly horrors they had endured at the hands of those who opposed their faith. Naturally, they wanted justice. They petitioned the Lord, Who is holy and true, to "judge and take revenge" upon the ungodly for their sacrifice.

6:11 *Each of the souls was given a white robe. They were told to rest a little longer until all their coworkers, the other Christians, would be killed as they had been killed.*

White robes were presented to each of these souls that were under the altar, just as all those who have received the righteousness of Christ will one day be clothed. The white robes worn by the redeemed are a consistent theme of this book. *"Everyone who wins the victory this way will wear white clothes. I will never erase their names from the Book of Life. I will acknowledge them in the presence of my Father and his angels" (Revelation 3:5). "After these things I saw a large crowd from every nation, tribe, people, and language. No one was able to count how many people there were. They were standing in front of the throne and the lamb. They were wearing white robes, holding palm branches in their hands" (Revelation 7:9).*

These souls were told to "rest a little longer," which appears to be the only answer God provided to their question regarding how long it would be until the Lord avenged their deaths *(v. 10)*. In a simple manner, it seems the response urged patience, for that time had not yet come. The timing of God's vengeance, as in all things in heaven and earth, is subject to the Lord's determination as held within His own divine counsel. Even the souls of the martyrs needed to be reminded of this.

6:12 *I watched as the lamb opened the sixth seal. A powerful earthquake struck. The sun turned as black as sackcloth made of hair. The full moon turned as red as blood.*

The Lord Jesus Christ opened the sixth seal, and the whole earth felt the result. There was an earthquake so sizeable and so violent that it affected the entire planet. It seems this earthquake disrupted the normal atmosphere thereby influencing the climate and making the moon appear as the color of blood.

The biblical narrative has numerous references to such cataclysmic events. Joel is the earliest prophet who clearly tells about the Day of the Lord, a day of judgment that shakes the universe to its core. *"¹⁰The earth quakes in their presence, and the sky shakes. The sun and the moon turn dark, and the stars no longer shine. ¹¹The Lord shouts out orders to his army. His forces are very large. The troops that carry out his commands are mighty. The day of the Lord is extremely terrifying. Who can endure it?" (Joel 2:10–11).* Other passages speak to this horrific event *(Ezekiel 38:19; Joel 2:31; Isaiah 13:10; Isaiah 34:4).*

John was very familiar with these passages, and he also remembered the words of Jesus when He told them of this same violent event *(Matthew 24:29; Mark 13:24).* On the one hand, these events should not be received literally. On the other hand, the events are so dramatic that even the stars of heaven are shaken from their orbits. It is probably best to understand that the darkening of the sun and moon is not simply the result of some huge earthquake, but rather signifies the end of their giving and reflecting light. Not light but darkness ruled at the beginning of creation *(Genesis 1:2),* and so it will be for unbelievers when the judgment comes.[11] Sackcloth is a material woven from goat or camel hair, generally very dark in color, and it is used here to describe the totality and depth of the darkness that covered the entire earth.[12]

6:13–14 *¹³The stars fell from the sky to the earth like figs dropping from a fig tree when it is shaken by a strong wind.*

¹⁴The sky vanished like a scroll being rolled up. Every mountain and island was moved from its place.

The stars of heaven fell to earth, resembling a tree losing its leaves in a strong wind. The heavens rolled up as a scroll, and every mass of land shook from its foundation. All of the events described in these verses would occur in a God-directed, God-ordained series of reactions resulting in universal catastrophe. Jesus told His disciples when they looked across the Kidron Valley and marveled at the beauty of the temple: *"²⁵Miraculous signs will occur in the sun, moon, and stars. The nations of the earth will be deeply troubled and confused because of the roaring and tossing of the sea. ²⁶People will faint as they fearfully wait for what will happen to the world. Indeed, the powers of the universe will be shaken"* (Luke 21:25–26).

When the dust settled, the landmasses of the earth would look nothing like they did before. Mountain ranges would be leveled, and islands would be moved miles from where they once rested.

6:15–17 *¹⁵Then the kings of the earth, the important people, the generals, the rich, the powerful, and all the slaves and free people hid themselves in caves and among the rocks in the mountains. ¹⁶They said to the mountains and rocks, "Fall on us, and hide us from the face of the one who sits on the throne and from the anger of the lamb, ¹⁷because the frightening day of their anger has come, and who is able to endure it?"*

The sixth seal, unlike the five preceding it, affected all of mankind. This list generally accounts for every person on earth, both rich and poor, the heads of governments, and the general populace. Position, wealth, power, poverty, free, or slave are insignificant when these calamities fall upon the earth. The Lord levels these distinctions that exist among the human race. No one will be untouched by these events.

People tried to hide themselves in the dens, caves, and crevasses of the mountains to escape the oncoming destruction. However, the widespread devastation left no safe hiding place. Again, Jesus said,

"Then people will say to the mountains, 'Fall on us!' and to the hills, 'Cover us!'" (Luke 23:30). As a result, the earth's inhabitants could neither deny Who had caused this upheaval nor deny why these calamities had befallen them. The events which followed the breaking of these six seals would serve as indicators that God's judgment was being executed, not only upon the people, but also upon the entire fallen universe.

As dreadful as these first six seals would be, they served only as the precursors to the coming judgment that John would witness. Declarations such as this were not a response to the devastation that had come upon the earth but rather were an acknowledgment that the worst was yet to come (Zephaniah 1:14–8).

DIG DEEPER: *The Day of Wrath*

The Day of the Lord is revealed as a day of terrible judgment when God's wrath will be poured out on His rebellious creation. This theme permeates the literature of the prophets and is found most often in the short book of Joel. Joel also saw this day as a time when all of the elements of the universe would tremble at the voice of God's anger. Nothing can stand in the face of such fury, for *"who will be able to endure the day He comes? Who will be able to survive on the day He appears? He is like a purifying fire and like a cleansing soap"* (Malachi 3:2).

Notes/Applications

The fifth seal offers a reprieve from the previous visions of wars, famine, disease, pestilence, death, and hell. There John sees a vision of those who had been killed for their faithfulness to the Gospel of God's saving grace and to the One Who purchased their salvation by the blood of the Lamb. These saints cried out, pleading with God to take vengeance against those who had killed them. But the Lord told these saints to rest. Even though they were great saints of the faith, they needed to remember that the timing of events was in the hand of God, not in their petition for revenge. God's plan was much larger in scope than the revenge that these saints asked for.

When the sixth seal was opened, John witnessed events more ter-rifying than anything he had seen before. Now, the whole universe was shaken out of its formerly reliable courses. The people of the earth witnessed these events and, howling in fear, tried to find refuge in caves. God now poured out His wrath on the whole of His creation. Nothing and no one would escape His penetrating sentence of death and destruction.

Jesus Christ, the same, yesterday, today, and forever, Redeemer and eternal Judge, has faithfully and consistently told all people that He will not tolerate sin. Either a person will be clothed in the righ-teousness given by the redeeming work of Christ by the witness of the Holy Spirit or will be the unhappy recipient of His just anger. The revelation of Jesus Christ that John recorded concludes the biblical narrative that consistently tells people of God's judgment. Thus the Word of God is absolutely consistent throughout the entire biblical narrative. Look at the similarity of the prophecy of Zephaniah, written nearly seven hundred years before John recorded the revelation given to him by Jesus:

> *People will go into caves in the rocks and into holes in the ground because of the Lord's terrifying presence and the honor of his majesty when he rises to terrify the earth." (Isaiah 2:19)*

> *¹⁴The frightening day of the Lord is near.*
> *It is near and coming very quickly.*
> *Listen! Warriors will cry out bitterly on the day of the Lord.*
> *¹⁵That day will be a day of overflowing fury,*
> *a day of trouble and distress,*
> *a day of devastation and desolation,*
> *a day of darkness and gloom,*
> *a day of clouds and overcast skies,*
> *¹⁶a day of rams' horns and battle cries*
> *against the fortified cities*

and against the high corner towers.
[17]*"I will bring such distress on humans that they will walk like
they are blind,
because they have sinned against the Lord."
Their blood will be poured out like dust
and their intestines like manure.*
[18]*Their silver and their gold will not be able to rescue them
on the day of the Lord's overflowing fury.
The whole earth will be consumed by his fiery anger,
because he will put an end, a frightening end,
to those who live on earth. (Zephaniah 1:14–18)*

REVELATION 7

Revelation 7:1–8

7:1 *After this I saw four angels standing at the four corners of the earth. They were holding back the four winds of the earth to keep them from blowing on the land, the sea, or any tree.*

Sometime after the sixth seal had been opened and worldwide catastrophes had begun, John saw an angel standing at each of the four corners of the earth. These angels kept the winds from blowing anywhere over the lands or seas. For the time being, all motion stopped, and not even a breeze fell upon a single tree. These four angels accomplished this at the command and by the will of Almighty God and the Lamb. In a sense, it was the calm before the storm.

7:2–3 *²I saw another angel coming from the east with the seal of the living God. He cried out in a loud voice to the four angels who had been allowed to harm the land and sea,*

3 "Don't harm the land, the sea, or the trees until we have put the seal on the foreheads of the servants of our God."

The purpose for this momentary calm was revealed. John saw an angel approaching from the east, and the angel had "the seal of the living God" with him. This seal was to be used to mark the foreheads of a specific people, "servants of our God," whose identity will be explained in later verses. We cannot be sure about the form of this seal, but it was clearly the method by which Almighty God distinguished this group from all others.

This angel commanded the other four angels not to hurt the earth or sea until God's servants had been sealed with this distinctive mark. The implication is that all people on the earth would be hurt when these angels were allowed to proceed, but God's servants were to be marked for protection.

7:4 *I heard how many were sealed: 144,000. Those who were sealed were from every tribe of the people of Israel:*

Unlike occasions where John was shown a multitude of countless beings described as *"ten thousand times ten thousand and thousands times thousands" (Revelation 5:11)* and *"a large crowd from every nation, tribe, people, and language. No one was able to count how many people there were" (Revelation 7:9)*, in this case, John heard an exact number of people who would have this seal of God on their foreheads. The number was 144,000, which was comprised of twelve thousand members from each of the twelve tribes of Israel. During this period of tribulation, these 144,000 would be sealed by God, so the entire world would know to Whom they belonged, and no one would be able to harm them *(Revelation 9:4)*.

There are some commentators who reject a literal interpretation of this group as being specifically 144,000 in number or Jewish in identity, and they instead consider this group to include the entire sum of believers on the earth during this time of judgment.[1] However, rarely is the Book of Revelation so clear and precise in its wording as it is in this passage, so it seems most logical in such cases to adhere to a literal interpretation.[2] Furthermore, most commentators tend to speculate about the significance of this group even though the Bible has very little to say about it. In reality, once the sealing has taken place, no more mention of this group is made until chapter fourteen, where we are given a little more detail about the character of those who comprised this group but are still told little about why they were ultimately singled out.

7:5-8 *[5]12,000 from the tribe of Judah were sealed, 12,000 from the tribe of Reuben, 12,000 from the tribe of Gad, [6]12,000 from the tribe of Asher, 12,000 from the tribe of Naphtali, 12,000 from the tribe of Manasseh, [7]12,000 from the tribe of Simeon, 12,000 from the tribe of Levi, 12,000 from the tribe of Issachar, [8]12,000 from the tribe of Zebulun, 12,000 from the tribe of Joseph, 12,000 from the tribe of Benjamin were sealed.*

The individual tribes were named, which further supports the Jewish ethnicity of these 144,000.[3] Much conjecture arises from the difference in the order by which these tribes are listed in this passage as compared to the Old Testament (*Exodus 1:1–5*). Again, wisdom is probably exercised by refraining from speculating about what we are not told.

The name *Judah* means "He shall be praised."[4] This tribe might be mentioned first because it is the one through which the Messiah came. The second tribe mentioned was *Reuben*, which means "See ye, a son," and the third tribe mentioned was *Gad*, which means "an invader."[5] Reuben and Gad fought alongside the other tribes on the western side of the Jordan until they conquered the land of Canaan, and they then returned to live on the eastern side (*Numbers 32*).

The fourth tribe named was *Asher*, which means "happy." The fifth tribe was *Naphtali*, which means "my wrestling."[6] These were some of the original tribes to settle in the land of Canaan (*Numbers 34*). The sixth tribe was *Manasseh*, which means "causing to forget."[7]

Manasseh was one of two sons of Joseph to be named a tribe and to receive a territorial allotment *(Numbers 34:23–24)*. Half of this very large tribe settled on the eastern side of the Jordan River with the tribes of Reuben and Gad, and the other half remained to occupy the western side of the Jordan River *(Numbers 34:14–15)*. From each of these three tribes, God sealed the foreheads of twelve thousand people.

The seventh tribe named was *Simeon*, which means "hearkening."[8] This tribe was also among Canaan's original settlers. The tribe of Levi was listed eighth. *Levi* means "joined."[9] This tribe did not receive any territory in the land of Canaan because it was appointed as the tribe of priests, and as such, the Lord was its inheritance. *"The Lord said to Aaron, 'You will have no land or property of your own as the other Israelites will have. I am your possession and your property among the Israelites'"* *(Numbers 18:20)*. The ninth tribe was *Issachar*, which means "there is a reward" or "he will bring reward."[10]

The last three tribes listed were *Zebulun*, which means "dwelling;" *Joseph*, which means "let him add;" and *Benjamin*, which means "son of my right hand."[11] Joseph was listed instead of Ephraim because Ephraim was Joseph's second son. His first son was Manasseh, and Joseph's inheritance was divided between the two sons *(Numbers 34:23–24)*. From each of these three tribes, God sealed the foreheads of twelve thousand people. Each of the twelve tribes had equal representation.

DIG DEEPER: *Where's Dan?*

The tribe of Dan is not among the tribes listed in Revelation even though it was one of the original twelve tribes of Israel *(Numbers 1–2; 10:25)*. One possible reason for this omission is that they despised their appointed heritage and pursued false gods *(Judges 18)*. Others believe that the antichrist will arise from the tribe of Dan because of certain biblical prophecies *(Genesis 49:17; Jeremiah 8:16)*.

Notes/Applications

John witnessed a vision, which was dramatically different from the sixth seal, which preceded it and the seventh seal, which followed it. Whereas the sixth and the seventh seals unveiled calamitous judgment upon the earth and its inhabitants, the vision in this passage reveals God's incontestable authority and definitive purpose in the dispensation of His measureless mercy as well as His judgment. This passage unmistakably shows God's absolute control in administering His judgment on those who have rebelled against Him and simultaneously showering His mercy on those Whom He has set apart for Himself.

Following the catastrophic events of the sixth seal, God directed the four angels to withhold His judgment upon the earth by restraining the four winds coming from the earth's four corners. God held the four angels back while a select few received a seal of God's protection in the same way that He protected the children of Israel during the tenth plague upon Egypt's firstborn sons (Exodus 12:12). One hundred forty-four thousand people out of the twelve tribes of Israel were sealed with the mark of God upon their foreheads. God's mark upon the foreheads of the chosen represented the seal of His protection. It also served as the means by which the angels were instructed when executing God's judgment in the same way the blood of the lamb guided the angel of death to pass over the homes of the children of Israel in Egypt (Exodus 12:13).

The Scriptures unequivocally declare that God is both merciful and just. He dispenses His mercy upon those whom He favors and executes His judgment toward those who rebel against Him. God's attributes work together and simultaneously. God's mercy is poured out upon His favored while at the same time His judgment unleashes His wrath upon the condemned. Those who receive God's mercy should not fear His judgment. Those who are judged cannot escape His wrath. God's protection of His people is absolutely certain. Jesus prayed that God would protect the redeemed while they served Him in this world. God's children should continue to serve Him with the assurance of their safety in His mercy while acknowledging the awesomeness of His fury upon whom it is unleashed.

Revelation 7:9–17

7:9–10 *⁹After these things I saw a large crowd from every nation, tribe, people, and language. No one was able to count how many people there were. They were standing in front of the throne and the lamb. They were wearing white robes, holding palm branches in their hands, ¹⁰and crying out in a loud voice, "Salvation belongs to our God, who sits on the throne, and to the lamb!"*

After these things is an important introduction to the event that follows the sealing of the 144,000. It provides a clear separation between the two events, preventing some false assumption that the two events belong together. This is simply a record of what John witnessed, many times without any explanation about the meaning of the events. Nevertheless, one thing is abundantly evident. If anyone would conclude that there are only 144,000 saved, this scene puts that error to rest. There was a countless host of people who wore the white robes given to them by the Lamb. These people were redeemed from every nation, tribe, people, and language.

These believers were in their resurrected bodies, as seen by their situation before the throne, clothed in white robes, which represents the righteousness they had received through salvation in Christ Jesus. The palm fronds in their hands appear to be symbolic of Christ's royalty and victory.[12] They waved their palm branches much like those who celebrated Jesus' arrival in Jerusalem just a few days before His crucifixion. They offered their praise to God. This multitude had been rescued from the consequences of sin and from the clutches of the curse. They praised the eternal Lord, Who sits upon His heavenly throne, and the Lamb, Who bought their salvation with His blood at Calvary.

7:11–12 *¹¹All the angels stood around the throne with the leaders and the four living creatures. They bowed in front of the throne with their faces touching the ground, worshiped*

God, [12]*and said, "Amen! Praise, glory, wisdom, thanks, honor, power, and strength be to our God forever and ever! Amen!"*

The angels, the leaders, and the four creatures were also gathered around the throne and joined the multitude in worship. The angels began and concluded their worship by declaring, "Amen." They demonstrated their submission to their eternal Creator and Redeemer by bowing down so low that their faces touched the ground. In this humbled position, they thanked God for salvation and acknowledged His power and authority in all matters pertaining to time and eternity. Because of Who He is and what He has done, God alone is worthy of all blessing, glory, wisdom, thanksgiving, honor, power, and might.

7:13 *One of the leaders asked me, "Who are these people wearing white robes, and where did they come from?"*

One of the leaders inquired about the identity and origin of those wearing the white robes. Perhaps it was a rhetorical question posed to John, the witness to this vision, so that the answers to this question could be verbally explained to remove any doubt and speculation about the identity of this group arrayed in white.[13]

7:14 *I answered him, "Sir, you know." Then he told me, "These are the people who are coming out of the terrible suffering. They have washed their robes and made them white in the blood of the lamb.*

John replied to the elder, "Sir, you know," which allowed the elder to answer his own question and, in turn, explain the scene to John.

The elder informed John that the ones dressed in the white robes were those who "are coming out of the terrible suffering." Despite the use of the definite article *the* before terrible suffering, some commentators insist that this multitude included all believers saved throughout history by Jesus Christ's atonement at Calvary.[14] Others contend that this group consists of the same martyrs mentioned in chapter six, including the "coworkers" for whom they were waiting.

Notwithstanding the elder's account of this group, it remains uncertain just which and how many of heaven's host this countless multitude comprised.

It is also helpful to note the tense of the verb in relation to the people described here. This is a present participle best translated *These are the ones coming*.[15] While some hold that these are believers from all ages and others hold that this refers to the last great tribulation, it is clear that the event is not over. Saints are still being added to this number even as John records what he witnessed. Couched between the sixth and seventh seals as God dispenses His judgment on the ungodly, it may indicate that the redeemed of the Lord are still suffering persecution and dying rather than giving in to the hellish opposition they faced.

7:15 *That is why they are in front of the throne of God. They serve him day and night in his temple. The one who sits on the throne will spread his tent over them.*

Only because this multitude had the righteousness of Christ were they even able to stand before the throne day and night to worship God without ceasing. With indescribable joy and peace they worshiped their redeeming Lord. These saints remained faithful and loyal to God while in their earthly bodies, and they now received their reward of eternal life in His presence. In turn, the Lord spreads His tent over them, protecting them from any further conflicts.

7:16–17 *[16]They will never be hungry or thirsty again. Neither the sun nor any burning heat will ever overcome them. [17]The lamb in the center near the throne will be their shepherd. He will lead them to springs filled with the water of life, and God will wipe every tear from their eyes."*

These worshipers would never again feel the pains of hunger and thirst as they had in their mortal bodies. There are two reasonable interpretations. First, they would no longer experience physical hunger or thirst for the food and water that sustained the lives of their earthly bodies. The implication is that believers will never want for sustenance in heaven because it is simply not required. Their lives are no longer physical, and therefore, they will not need physical nourishment.[15] Second, the multitude no longer hungered or thirsted spiritually as they had in their physical lives on earth because they were in the presence of the Lord. In their mortal bodies, they craved a closer fellowship with their Creator, but in heaven, this desire would be fulfilled by perfect communion with God Almighty. These believers were secure in the care of the Good Shepherd. It is also possible that the redeemed will never hunger and thirst, because the supply of these necessities will be abundantly provided in heaven.

Also, the sun's light no longer shined upon the inhabitants in heaven because the light in heaven was God Himself. He is the source of all light and is Light; therefore, in heaven, the sun will not be necessary. *"The city doesn't need any sun or moon to give it light because the glory of God gave it light. The lamb was its lamp"* (Revelation 21:23).

The Lamb would lead them to the living fountains of water. *"But those who drink the water that I will give them will never become thirsty again. In fact, the water I will give them will become in them a spring that gushes up to eternal life"* (John 4:14). *"The Spirit and the bride say, 'Come!' Let those who hear this say, 'Come!' Let those who are thirsty come! Let those who want the water of life take it as a gift"* (Revelation 22:17). God would also wipe away the tears from their eyes. *"He will wipe every tear from their eyes. There won't be any more death. There won't be any grief, crying, or pain, because the first things have disappeared"* (Revelation 21:4).

Notes/Applications

Chapter seven is often described as an intermission inserted between the judgments of the sixth and seventh seal. Here John sees the saints of God, those whose robes are washed in the blood of the Lamb, thus receiving a reprieve from the terror invoked as he witnessed God's judgment when the previous six seals were opened. In those scenes

John saw what was happening to God's enemies. Now John saw what was happening to God's saints.

What precisely does John see? Is it the bliss of heaven as opposed to the terror of God's righteous judgment? Not at all! What John sees is a countless host of people! A host so large that its number cannot be measured! But even the size of the host is not the most important aspect of John's recorded testimony. Rather it is the description of what they wear and, more importantly, what they do!

First, John sees these people wearing white robes. These robes are white, not because they just came from some super heavenly laundry, but because they were made white in the blood of the Lamb. All the redeemed have only one unified profession of their position before the throne of their holy and terrifying God. They stand there without fear, because the blood of the Lamb, Jesus Christ, was applied to their filthy lives. As their own clothes disintegrate from the filth of their sin, Jesus Himself clothes them in His Own righteousness, saving them from their deserved punishment.

Then in the light of Jesus' righteousness, this tremendous crowd of redeemed people joins with the four beasts, the twenty-four leaders, and the entire angelic host of heaven in praise of the One Who has purchased their pardon, secured their salvation, and clothed them in His righteousness.

Is this not the proper occupation for God's redeemed people? Whether in heaven or on earth, there is only one eternal shout of praise: *"Salvation belongs to our God, who sits on the throne, and to the Lamb! Amen! Praise, glory, wisdom, thanks, honor, power, and strength be to our God forever and ever! Amen!" (Revelation 7:10b, 12).*

REVELATION 8

Revelation 8:1–6

8:1 *When he opened the seventh seal, there was silence in heaven for about half an hour.*

Chapter seven reads somewhat like an intermission. It explains an event (the sealing of the 144,000) that had to take place before God's judgment would continue. The Lamb had opened six seals (chapters 5–6), and now, at last, He opened the final seal whereupon there was a pause in heaven. It is not clear whether this silence, lasting about half an hour, was noticeable upon the earth. If so, it served as a dramatic pause, a brief respite between the destruction of the first six seals and the calamities that would follow the opening of the seventh.[1] Despite the intensity of the calamities of the earlier judgment, this silence may mislead the earth's inhabitants into thinking that the worst was over. The tempest of the earlier judgments frightened people to death. But like the eye of a hurricane, this period of quiet may have contained eerie elements, which likewise made people wonder what was coming next.

Some scholars propose that the seven seals, seven trumpets, and

seven bowls are concurrent judgments of God.[2] It appears more prob-
able that these sets of seven would occur consecutively and follows a
chronological progression of increasing intensity.[3] The opening of five
of the first six seals would result in devastation, and the opening of the
seventh seal would usher in the trumpet judgments.

8:2 *Then I saw the seven angels who stand in God's presence,
and they were given seven trumpets.*

Upon the opening of the seventh seal, John observed seven angels
who stood before the Lord with seven trumpets. These trumpets announced God's impending judgment.

8:3 *Another angel came with a gold incense burner and stood
at the altar. He was given a lot of incense to offer on the gold
altar in front of the throne. He offered it with the prayers of
all of God's people.*

Another angel, not one of the seven angels with trumpets, came with a
golden incense burner before God's altar in heaven. The angel's role in
this scene should be understood merely as offering the prayers to the
Lord and not as making the prayers acceptable to Him. Our prayers
need no such intervention.[4] *"The Lord's eyes are on those who do what he
approves. His ears hear their prayer"* (1 Peter 3:12). The emphasis on a large
volume of incense given to the angel may be indicative of the volume
of prayers rising toward God. These prayers are the cumulative sum of
the prayers that God's people have offered to Him, both those under
the altar whose robes have been washed in the blood of the Lamb as
well as those still enduring persecution on the earth.

Throughout the Scriptures, altars always represent a place of sacrifice and prayer. Here, the altar is situated, not on the earth, but in
front of the throne of God in heaven. Here, in front of the Lamb Who
was sacrificed for the sin of the world, the only purpose of this altar is
to carry the prayers of all God's people to the eternal God Who had
redeemed them. Heaven is immeasurably more than angels floating on

clouds. It is a place of physical substance, where God is worshiped by
the innumerable host that have been redeemed by His Son's sacrifice
on the Cross of Calvary.

8:4 *The smoke from the incense went up from the angel's
hand to God along with the prayers of God's people.*

This indicates that God's throne was positioned significantly higher
than the altar and higher than the leaders, the four creatures, the angels, and the multitude of God's redeemed people gathered around
His throne.

8:5 *The angel took the incense burner, filled it with fire from
the altar, and threw it on the earth. Then there was thunder,
noise, lightning, and an earthquake.*

The angel filled the incense burner with fire from the altar in heaven,
cast the fire to earth, and brought an end to the silence that followed
the opening of the seventh seal. This action resulted in thunder and
lightning and another great earthquake, yet all of this was only prepa-
ration for what was yet to come. The atmosphere was charged with
the anticipation of impending catastrophe at the hand of God's anger.
The same incense burner that carried the prayers of the saints to the
throne of God is the same incense burner the angel used to hurl God's
judgment to the earth!

8:6 *The seven angels who had the seven trumpets got ready
to blow them.*

God's seven angels with the seven trumpets assembled together and
readied themselves to sound their trumpets one by one at His command. With that, the next series of judgments was ready to begin.

Notes/Applications

This passage reveals that heaven is the center of God's abode. It is the
place from which He determines everything that happens within the

boundaries of heaven, throughout His entire creation, and even controls the gates of hell.

Now, according to God's inscrutable plan, silence reigns supreme for about one half hour. That silence causes the inhabitants of the earth no small amount of anxiety. They have no way of knowing if the silence is the end of God's judgment or the calm before the storm. However, after this period of silence a remarkable scene takes place. An angel takes a golden incense burner and offers the incense to God along with the prayers of God's redeemed people.

The picture presents a calming effect in the midst of impending doom. It offers assurance to believers that their prayers are important to God, making them the vehicle by which they understand the mind and heart of God. Amazingly, the angel takes that same incense burner, scoops fire off the same altar, and throws it to the earth. It seems as though God is answering the prayers of His saints: *"Holy and true Master, how long before you judge and take revenge on those living on earth who shed our blood?" (Revelation 6:10)*.

What follows removes all questions from those on earth who continue to oppose God's unchangeable will and do so by persecuting His saints. God's justice is unleashed in unrestrained violence, yet saving, protecting, and preserving His saints, even as He obliterates His enemies.

Revelation 8:7–13

8:7 *When the first angel blew his trumpet, hail and fire were mixed with blood, and were thrown on the earth. One-third of the earth was burned up, one-third of the trees were burned up, and all the green grass was burned up.*

The sounding of the first angel's trumpet unleashed hail and fire that was mingled with blood falling from the sky. This hail-and-fire storm destroyed one third of the world's vegetation, including fruits and vegetables. Such an occurrence would surely affect the subsistence of all living beings. Perhaps this occurred simultaneously with the violent thunderstorms and devastating earthquake that were already ravaging the earth. These afflictions were evidently heaped one upon the other as the soundings of the trumpets progressed.[5]

The description of these elements as being "mixed with blood" has roused many diverse theories. Though men often go to great lengths to account for divine experiences with rational, physical explanations, there is no reason to disregard the possibility that there could be literal blood falling from above with hail and fire. Such terrifying signs would surely attest that these events would be direct judgments from the hand of Almighty God. *"I will work miracles in the sky and on the earth: blood, fire, and clouds of smoke"* (Joel 2:30).

8:8 *When the second angel blew his trumpet, something like a huge mountain burning with fire was thrown into the sea. One-third of the sea turned into blood,*

When the second angel sounded his trumpet, a "huge mountain burning with fire" was cast into the sea. Opinions differ among scholars as to what this might mean. Some believe it to be an active volcano erupting and casting unimaginable amounts of lava into the seas.[6] Others believe that this describes an asteroid or comet breaking through the atmosphere and falling into the sea.[7] Whereas the latter interpretation is preferred, it again should be understood that this would not be some rare natural phenomenon but a specific medium created by God for judgment. This mass of fire would upset the world's bodies of saltwater, and upon impact, one third of the sea would turn to blood.

8:9 *one-third of the creatures that were living in the sea died, and one-third of the ships were destroyed.*

One third of all marine life perished in the world's oceans, though this seems unlikely to be the cause for the seas turning to blood. Rather, it is evidence of divine judgment, similar to that experienced by Pharaoh at the hands of Moses as recorded in the Old Testament. *"The Lord said to Moses, 'Tell Aaron, "Take your staff and stretch out your hand over the waters of Egypt—its rivers, canals, ponds, and all its reservoirs—so that they turn into blood"''* (Exodus 7:19). Also, a third of the world's sailing vessels were destroyed, adversely affecting travel, commerce, and naval defenses worldwide.

8:10 *When the third angel blew his trumpet, a huge star flaming like a torch fell from the sky. It fell on one-third of the rivers and on the springs.*

When the third angel sounded his trumpet, a great star fell from the sky upon one third of the earth's fresh water sources, such as rivers, lakes, and streams. A third of the earth's saltwater bodies had just been destroyed with the second trumpet judgment, and now a third of the freshwater bodies were also destroyed. Mankind could manage for a while without food, but could not last very long without water.

8:11 *That star was named Wormwood. One-third of the water turned into wormwood, and many people died from this water because it had turned bitter.*

Wormwood is a poisonous plant, and it is used figuratively to name this star of destruction.[8] The impact of this star on the planet was only the beginning of its devastating influence on the water. The water contamination caused by this event prolonged its effect and many people died as a result of consuming water that they assumed to be safe.

8:12 *When the fourth angel blew his trumpet, one-third of the sun, one-third of the moon, and one-third of the stars were struck so that one-third of them turned dark. There was no light for one-third of the day and one-third of the night.*

The fourth angel blew his trumpet, and celestial bodies were changed, thereby affecting the earth. A third of the sun, moon, and stars were impacted. Seasons and tides were likely altered because of the lunar changes. As a result, days would only be two-thirds as bright as before, and nights would become a third darker as well. Some have interpreted this passage to mean that one-third more of the day and one-third more of the night would be shrouded in total darkness.[9]

8:13 *I saw an eagle flying overhead, and I heard it say in a loud voice, "Catastrophe, catastrophe, catastrophe for those living on earth, because of the remaining trumpet blasts which the three angels are about to blow."*

The Greek word accurately translated in this verse as *eagle* appears in some translations as *angel*.[10] However, neither interpretation changes the meaning of the verse.

This being flew around heaven and loudly proclaimed that the people of the earth were doomed not by those calamities that had already come upon them but by those that were still appointed for them. As horrific as these catastrophes that had befallen the earth were, this dreadful pronouncement warned that the judgments yet to occur would be far worse. Once again, it seems that such a declaration was made more for the benefit of John and his readers than for those inhabitants of the earth during this period of judgment.[11]

DIG DEEPER: *Catastrophe!*

"Woe" is the ancient cry of Israel's prophets. Here, it is translated, "catastrophe" but the meaning is basically the same. *Woe* is the lament of the prophet because of what is to come. *Catastrophe* is the actual event that produces the cry of *woe*. It is the cry of judgment against those who have disobeyed God. It occurs sixty-three times in the Bible, from Isaiah through Zechariah. Jesus Himself warned of impending judgment throughout the Gospels. There are thirty-one occurrences in which Jesus pronounced "Woe," or "How horrible." This one exclamation is the most consistent theme of judgment throughout the Bible and culminates here in Revelation as final judgment is pronounced on unbelievers.

Notes/Applications

God's holy judgment will fall upon the earth as justice for man's disobedience and rebellion. However, despite catastrophic events that should motivate mankind to seek God's forgiveness, people still will refuse to submit to Him in repentance. Instead, they will harden their hearts with hatred toward Him. As a consequence, God's wrath will continue to visit them. When the time of this tribulation comes, people will realize that the destruction befalling them is the judgment of the Almighty, but they will still not turn from their wicked ways. *"[20]The people who survived these plagues still did not turn to me and change the way they were thinking and acting. If they had, they would have stopped worshiping demons and idols made of gold, silver, bronze, stone, and wood, which cannot see, hear, or walk. [21]They did not turn away from committing murder, practicing witchcraft, sinning sexually, or stealing"* (Revelation 9:20–21).

This passage serves as a sober reminder that today is the day of salvation. *"Listen, now is God's acceptable time! Now is the day of salvation!"* (2 Corinthians 6:2) The time for responding to the Lord's call upon our lives is now. When we are confronted by the truth of the Gospel, whether that call is unto salvation or a deeper commitment, we should yield to the Spirit without expecting another opportunity.

Future opportunities may or may not come, for we ourselves do not control the Spirit's power. *"The wind blows wherever it pleases. You hear its sound, but you don't know where the wind comes from or where it's going. That's the way it is with everyone born of the Spirit"* (John 3:8).

The present moment is the only time God has given to us to repent and turn to Him. Yesterday is past! Tomorrow never comes! We only have the eternal present. Failure to answer God's call today will inevitably cast us into the cauldron of God's wrath. When God withdraws His offering of salvation, there is no longer any hope or reprieve. God's judgment is certain.

REVELATION 9

Revelation 9:1–12

9:1 *When the fifth angel blew his trumpet, I saw a star that had fallen to earth from the sky. The star was given the key to the shaft of the bottomless pit.*

When the fifth angel sounded his trumpet, the first of the three catastrophes began as predicted at the end of the previous chapter *(Revelation 8:13).* Unlike the star that fell from heaven after the third trumpet sounded *(Revelation 8:10),* it is commonly agreed that this star depicts an angel. Since the angel is described as "fallen to earth," some believe that this angel is Satan or another fallen angel.[1] However, it is also possible that this angel is one of God's own because the key was given to him presumably by the One Who holds the keys and has the authority to delegate such responsibilities[2] *(Revelation 20:1–3).* Once the fallen star receives the key, he proceeds to open the bottomless pit, fulfilling the task that was assigned to him.

9:2 *It opened the shaft of the bottomless pit, and smoke came out of the shaft like the smoke from a large furnace. The smoke darkened the sun and the air.*

When the fallen star opens the bottomless pit, a huge cloud of smoke erupts and bellows out of the abyss. This massive cloud of smoke will choke out the already diminished sunlight of day, causing the skies to become darker from its magnitude. It is as though an enormous furnace will be opened, which releases smoke that envelops the entire earth and swallows up more of its light.

9:3 *Locusts came out of the smoke onto the earth, and they were given power like the power of earthly scorpions.*

An enormous swarm of locusts will emerge from this immense cloud of smoke. It is likely that John witnessed a multitude of locusts so dense and so vast that they appeared as a great cloud of smoke.

In the past, God sent a plague of locusts upon Egypt to judge Pharaoh for not releasing the Israelites from captivity (*Exodus 10:3-6*). These locusts, however, are dramatically different than those in Moses' day. The locusts described in this verse are given the ability to inflict painful stings like that of a scorpion. The description of these creatures, given in verses seven through ten, further supports the idea that these are not some mutant variety evolved from common locusts but a specific creation well suited to fulfill this purpose of judgment.

9:4 *They were told not to harm any grass, green plant, or tree on the earth. They could harm only the people who do not have the seal of God on their foreheads.*

These locusts are commanded not to consume any of the earth's vegetation, which would normally be their natural diet. God created this cloud of locusts to execute His judgment—to afflict mankind. However, they will be told not to hurt those bearing the seal of God on their foreheads.

Some speculate that the specific habitation (bottomless pit) and task (torment) of these creatures suggests that they could be demonic in nature. Nevertheless, they will be controlled by Almighty God, Who alone holds the sovereign authority both to empower them with the capacity to cause anguish and also to limit the scope of their attack.[3]

9:5 *They were not allowed to kill them. They were only allowed to torture them for five months. Their torture was like the pain of a scorpion's sting.*

These locusts are further commanded not to kill unbelievers but rather only to torment and torture them. Their stings will cause painful, severe welts from which there will be no relief for five months. This means these creatures will be released upon the earth for five months and that their venom will also cause pain and illness to the victim for five months. The hardship upon mankind would be overwhelming and nearly unbearable during this period. God has appointed a very specific duration of suffering in which these locusts will swarm the earth and afflict the entire population of unbelievers. The advance of medical science will not be equipped to deal with this unexpected malady. The pain and torment will not be stopped.

9:6 *At that time people will look for death and never find it. They will long to die, but death will escape them.*

The pain and agony caused by these locusts would be so intense that people will yearn to die to obtain relief from their torment. They will envision death as an escape from the pain of the world, but God will not allow any to escape His judgment before the duration of its appointed time is over. It appears that many will even consider taking their own lives, though such attempts would also be futile since life and death are under the sovereign control of Almighty God.

> *See, I am the only God. There are no others. I kill, and I make alive. I wound, and I heal, and no one can rescue you from my power. (Deuteronomy 32:39)*

9:7–8 *⁷The locusts looked like horses prepared for battle. They seemed to have crowns that looked like gold on their heads. Their faces were like human faces. ⁸They had hair like women's hair and teeth like lions' teeth.*

Whether or not this is a physical description of these creatures, one point is clear: these locusts are more than ready to perform the task assigned to them. Like horses, they are prepared to go into battle. On their heads are crowns that look like gold. Their faces have human features. Their hair is like that of a woman. Like a lion they have teeth prepared for ripping and tearing. Whatever these creatures look like, their appearance is terribly frightening to their intended victims. But that appearance will be nothing compared to that moment when they sting their victim with their tail.

9:9–10 *⁹They had breastplates like iron. The noise from their wings was like the roar of chariots with many horses rushing into battle. ¹⁰They had tails and stingers like scorpions. They had the power to hurt people with their tails for five months.*

These strange creatures are fully armed for battle. They are dressed in breastplates that are as strong as iron. The noise of their wings, unlike the chirping song of a common locust, is so loud that it sounds like a galloping stampede of horses charging into battle.

As explained in verse five, their main weapons are their tails with which they hurt mankind for five months. People will be unable to escape this suffering and will not even be able find relief through death.

9:11 *The king who ruled them was the angel from the bottomless pit. In Hebrew he is called Abaddon, and in Greek he is called Apollyon.*

The locusts have a leader, the "angel from the bottomless pit." The name for the king of these creatures in Hebrew is Abaddon, which means "destruction," and in Greek, Apollyon, which means "destroyer."[4] Here John makes a special effort to ensure that his readers understand exactly who the leader of the locusts is. He gives the leader's name in both Hebrew and Greek, helping both Jew and Gentile understand that this angel has only one specific purpose—to destroy.

9:12 *The first catastrophe is over. After these things there are two more catastrophes yet to come.*

The first of the final three catastrophes is completed, and two more are still to come. These judgments will grow progressively worse, each one more intense and horrific than the last.

Notes/Applications

During this tribulation, God will seal a remnant of 144,000 with His mark on their foreheads (*Revelation 7:2–3*). Christians are likewise sealed with the Holy Spirit. *"You heard and believed the message of truth, the Good News that he has saved you. In him you were sealed with the Holy Spirit whom he promised" (Ephesians 1:13).* God will not lose any of His own because His sealing remains permanently secure in this life and throughout eternity. Neither human hands nor spiritual beings can break the King's signet upon the souls of His heirs. Jesus told His followers: *"My Father, who gave them to me, is greater than everyone else, and no one can tear them away from my Father" (John 10:29).* Paul was also convinced of God's unfailing promise. *"For this reason I also suffer these things; nevertheless I am not ashamed, for I know whom I have believed and am persuaded that He is able to keep what I have committed to Him until that Day" (2 Timothy 1:12).*

The impact of this judgment is directed toward those people who had rebelled against God and refused to accept the salvation offered to them through the sacrifice of Jesus Christ, His Son. Here the seal of God placed on the foreheads of those who belong to Him is not the seal of God's salvation, but the seal of His protection. When the horde of locusts rises from the shaft of the bottomless pit, they are told to harm only those who do not have the seal of God.

As the storm of God's anger escalates among the people of the earth, He visits His judgment on those He condemns and protects those He has saved. His punishment is frightening in its unrelenting torment. The only good thing that people can draw from this portrayal comes from the time limitation of five months. Nevertheless, the torment visited on those who are disobedient, ungrateful despisers of God's salvation is severe enough that people will beg to die rather than endure the pain inflicted on them. But even death will not relieve their suffering. Instead, God will refuse to let them die, and, instead, condemns them to live through this hellish torment.

Even as the months pass, God will place His seal of protection around those who are His. When those who have been redeemed witness the torment of those who have not been saved, their hearts will at the same time shrink in fear of God's punishment and rise to bless the Name of Him Who has saved them not only from this horrible moment, but also saved them from the pit of hell.

Revelation 9:13–21

9:13–14 [13]*When the sixth angel blew his trumpet, I heard a voice from the four horns of the gold altar in front of God.* [14]*The voice said to the sixth angel who had the trumpet, "Release the four angels who are held at the great Euphrates River."*

When the sixth angel sounds his trumpet, the second catastrophe predicted in Revelation 8:13 begins. As the trumpet sounds, a voice echoes from the four horns of the golden altar. The voice tells the angel that blew the sixth trumpet to release the four angels that were bound at the River Euphrates. These were apparently angels that had been bound and restrained from causing destruction until this very moment of judgment.[5] We observe again that the commands given were authoritative, and so we must conclude that this voice belonged to the Lord Jesus Christ, Who is sovereign over all judgments in occurrence, timing, and intensity.

> **DIG DEEPER:** *Euphrates River*
>
> The Euphrates River plays a major role in several biblical events. It was one of the four original rivers that flowed through the Garden of Eden (*Genesis 2:10, 14*). Abraham was living in the area of the Euphrates when he was called to be the father of God's people (*Genesis 15:18*). God spoke to the prophet Jeremiah by the Euphrates River (*Jeremiah 51:60–64*). This river has been fruitful both in blessings and in curses, depending on God's purposes.

9:15 *The four angels who were ready for that hour, day, month, and year were released to kill one-third of humanity.*

The four angels released from the Euphrates River had been prepared for this specific moment in time (*Isaiah 54:16*). Each element of God's judgment always begins exactly at its preordained time and only lasts for its determined duration. This sixth trumpet judgment would be far worse than any that preceded it. These four angels were commanded to kill one third of mankind.

The verse does not indicate that one third of humanity was killed as a result of any military conflict. Rather, it seems that these angels were given a command to execute a large segment of the human population. In the context of the earlier verses in this chapter, it is reasonable to conclude that the targeted population consisted of those who had rejected God's offer of salvation and, therefore, did not have the seal of God on their foreheads, which protected God's redeemed from the horror of this slaughter at the hand of God. However, wars are a natural consequence of a sinful world, and the judgments described in this passage reveal events of a supernatural magnitude and an outcome that greatly transcend the extent of any historical event.[6]

9:16 *The soldiers on horses numbered 20,000 times 10,000. I heard how many there were.*

The four angels brought with them an army of two hundred million soldiers mounted on horses. Some commentators insist that this number is to be taken figuratively and serves only to illustrate the enormity of the group.[7] The content of this verse, though, seems to dispute such suppositions. Rather, John informs his readers that he "heard how many there were," putting to rest any speculation that he exaggerated the scale of this army. This would be the largest army ever assembled in the history of the world, though it has been debated whether this army would be comprised of human forces or spiritual agents.[8] Nevertheless, the size of the army produces an ominous foreboding of the magnitude of the judgment about to descend on the earth.

9:17 *In the vision that I had, the horses and their riders looked like this: The riders had breastplates that were fiery red,*

pale blue, and yellow. The horses had heads like lions. Fire, smoke, and sulfur came out of their mouths.

Most commentators agree that the descriptions given in the previous verses depict an army of demons and not of actual men.[9] The riders wore breastplates of red, blue, and yellow. The heads of the horses resembled lions, which again indicates that these were not mutations of actual animals but were creatures created specifically for this particular judgment. They may or may not be demon-like creatures, but the reason for their existence is clear. They were creations not of this world, and their purpose was strictly and solely to destroy.

9:18 *These three plagues—the fire, smoke, and sulfur which came out of their mouths—killed one-third of humanity.*

Whereas the first catastrophe will bring anguish upon the world's inhabitants, this second one will bring death. While the specific details related to this catastrophe are not clearly described, the horror in the wake of their destruction staggers the mind. Fire, smoke, and sulphur will kill one third of all the people on the earth. Many people will be burned to death. Some will die as a result of smoke inhalation. Others will die by the absorption of sulphur into their lungs. It appears that the horse-like creatures do the actual killing and not the riders themselves.

The task assigned to these demon-like creatures involved the execution of one third of the human population. It should be clearly understood that these creatures were not performing this task under the authority of any human agency, but directly at the command of God Himself.

One quarter of the world's population would be killed by "Death and Hell" during the judgment of the fourth seal (*Revelation 6:7–8*), and one third of the remaining population would be killed by this vast army during the judgment of the sixth seal. Regardless of the size of the world's population at the time of these events, the mathematical equation yields staggering results—the death of one half of the world's total population as a result of these two judgments.

9:19 *The power of these horses is in their mouths and their tails. (Their tails have heads like snakes which they use to hurt people.)*

These creatures are given power to destroy with their mouths and hurt with their serpent-like tails. Although they were able to inflict injury with their tails, their ability to kill came from the fire, smoke, and brimstone spewing from their mouths. We can assume that, though all humanity will not be wiped out, these creatures would succeed in executing their task and one third of the earth's population would be dealt the final death blow as decreed by God. Those who survive will be profoundly affected by what they have observed. They will see the terror that has wrecked havoc throughout the land. They will be deathly fearful for their own lives. But still they will not repent!

9:20–21 *20The people who survived these plagues still did not turn to me and change the way they were thinking and acting. If they had, they would have stopped worshiping demons and idols made of gold, silver, bronze, stone, and wood, which cannot see, hear, or walk. 21They did not turn away from committing murder, practicing witchcraft, sinning sexually, or stealing.*

Despite the unimaginable death and destruction caused by these first two catastrophes, those who are not killed by these creatures still did not repent of their wicked ways and seek the Lord. In fact, their hearts were further hardened against God. They continued to worship false idols made of gold, silver, brass, stone, and wood—idols that could not respond to their worshippers. When they seek help from these gods, none will be found. Likewise, they refuse to repent of their murder, sorcery, immorality, and thievery, which only serve as further evidence of their utterly corrupt hearts.

Some speculate that this lack of repentance shows that these judgments did not generate the anticipated response.[10] To believe this, however, suggests that God's extensive display of His power fails to have the desired effect. Nevertheless, time and again, man's response is often a similar lack of repentance (*Revelation 9:20–21; 16:9, 11*). Are we, then, to believe that this culmination of God's judgment upon His reprobate creation would be in some way ineffectual? No! We must understand that the purpose of God's judgment is to carry out justice, not to evoke repentance.

> *⁵Therefore, put to death whatever is worldly in you: your sexual sin, perversion, passion, lust, and greed (which is the same thing as worshiping wealth). ⁶It is because of these sins that God's anger comes on those who refuse to obey him. (Colossians 3:5–6)*

> *Since you are stubborn and don't want to change the way you think and act, you are adding to the anger that God will have against you on that day when God vents his anger. At that time God will reveal that his decisions are fair. (Romans 2:5)*

Therefore, it seems more accurate to conclude that at the time of God's judgment on the inhabitants of the earth, the opportunity for repentance has passed.

DIG DEEPER: *Repent*

Repentance is a fundamental tenet of Christian doctrine. Without repentance, man cannot be reconciled to God. The summation of Jesus' proclamation to the masses centered on this theme of repentance (*Matthew 4:17*). In the Book of Revelation, the consequences of continued rebellion against the Creator and Redeemer are fully described—failure to repent evokes inescapable judgment. This is God's holy justice.

Notes/Applications

When we read the above passages, it is hard to imagine the immensity of God's anger and the intensity of His judgment. As a result of the "pale horse" and its rider, known as Death, one fourth of the world's population will be destroyed. Now, one third of the remaining population is to be wiped out by the word of God's wrath. The math demonstrates that more than one half of the world's population will be destroyed.

Yet, John still sees a world of people so callused against God that they refuse to repent even when confronted with the reality that their punishment has ensued because of their rebellion. John Milton, a sixteenth century poet, in his epic poem *Samson Agonistes* said it well:

> So fond are mortal men
> Fall'n into wrath divine,
> As their own ruin upon themselves to invite.[11]

Such presumptuous attitudes are the undercurrents carrying our society from the distant shores of truth. Sinful lifestyles have become tolerable and even acceptable within every aspect of modern culture. Consider the boldness of evil—widespread violence, thoughtless and spontaneous murders, countless abortions, increasing acceptability of euthanasia, rampant sexual perversity, and reckless disregard for others' lives and property. Such indifference for human life has become so commonplace that we do not even blink when we hear of such trespasses against the Creator's original design. Even Christians have become desensitized to such acts and adopt the worldly attitude of "live and let live" rather than stand against sin.

We must never allow society's moral decay to become our standard for living or to become a release from our responsibilities as Christians. The Lord remains the same yesterday, today, and forever, and so, too, His commission remains unaltered. Regardless of the moral state of the world around us and of the overwhelming nature of the task, we must boldly testify to the love and grace of the Lord Jesus Christ, even as we consider the frightening power of His judgment.

REVELATION 10

Revelation 10:1–7

10:1 *I saw another powerful angel come down from heaven. He was dressed in a cloud, and there was a rainbow over his head. His face was like the sun, and his feet were like columns of fire.*

A mighty angel descended from heaven to earth. Commentators disagree about this angel's identity. Some of them offer evidence to suggest that this being is Gabriel or another heavenly archangel.[1] Others see him as just another angel, such as appears in previous chapters[2] *(Revelation 7:2; 8:3)*. However, all indications given in this passage suggest that this was not a typical angel or any other created being but that this was an appearance of the Lord Jesus Christ Himself.[3] That the Lord should be described as an angel and not specifically identified as Jesus Christ should no more forbid such an interpretation than His being called *"someone like the Son of Man" (Revelation 1:13)* or a Lamb *(Revelation 5)*. Neither should His making an oath to *"Him who lives forever and ever" (v. 6)* be considered something inappropriate or out of character.[4] Furthermore, in reading the continuation of this passage in the next chapter, we observe the angel declaring, *"I will give power to my two witnesses" (Revelation 11:3, nkjv)*, thereby revealing this same Being as a source of both authoritative empowerment and divine association.

The description further supports the conclusion that this angel is the Lord Jesus Christ.[5] He is *"clothed with a cloud" (Exodus 13:21; Luke 21:27; Revelation 14:14–15)*; His head is encircled by a rainbow, symbolizing the covenant between God and His creation (*Ezekiel 1:28; Revelation 4:3*); His face is bright as the sun, another familiar description of Christ in Scripture (*Matthew 17:1–2; Acts 26:13*); and His feet are dazzling in radiance like bronze (*Daniel 10:6; Revelation 1:15*). Throughout the rest of this chapter, we will take the position that this Angel is Jesus Christ.

10:2 *He held a small, opened scroll in his hand. He set his right foot on the sea and his left on the land.*

This Angel will stand upon the earth with one foot upon land and the other upon the sea, which demonstrates the Lord's sovereignty over the entire earth, including all land masses and all bodies of water as great as the oceans and as small as brooks and streams. *"⁵I know that the Lord is great, that our Lord is greater than all the false gods. ⁶The Lord does whatever he wants in heaven or on earth, on the seas or in all the depths of the oceans" (Psalm 135:5–6).* He holds a small, opened book in His hand. As we will see later in this chapter, there were prophecies in this book that were to be revealed.

10:3 *Then he shouted in a loud voice as a lion roars. When he shouted, the seven thunders spoke with voices of their own.*

The Angel called out with a loud voice like that of a roaring lion, which again draws parallels to other scriptural references that depict the voice of the Lord (*Jeremiah 25:30; Hosea 11:10; Amos 3:8; Joel 3:16*). As the Angel cried out, John heard seven distinct "thunders" speak, possibly a part of the loud roar of the Angel's voice. It is possible that these seven thunders, like the seven seals and six of the seven trumpets that preceded them, were elements of judgment ordained by God.[6]

10:4 *When the seven thunders spoke, I was going to write it down. I heard a voice from heaven say, "Seal up what the seven thunders have said, and don't write it down."*

John apparently understood the message uttered by the seven thunders because he was prepared to record them like he did everything else he had seen and heard to that point. However, a voice from heaven instructed John not to write down what the thunders had revealed. Rather, the voice told John to seal up those things that he had heard the thunders disclose and not to include them as part of his message.

It cannot be determined with any certainty why John would even mention a situation about which he was not permitted to elaborate. It is possible that what he heard was so sacred or so dreadful that it would be beyond our ability to comprehend.[7] It should suffice, though, to recognize that God is under no obligation to disclose everything that He will bring to pass but only those things that He wants us to know.[8] Even from ancient times, God has always revealed only what people need to understand, and He has always withheld what He does not want people to know. *"Some things are hidden. They belong to the Lord our God. But the things that have been revealed in these teachings belong to us and to our children forever"* (Deuteronomy 29:29).

10:5–6 *[5]The angel whom I saw standing on the sea and on the land raised his right hand to heaven. [6]He swore an oath by the one who lives forever and ever, who created heaven and everything in it, the earth and everything in it, and the sea and everything in it. He said, "There will be no more delay.*

As He stands across the land and sea, the Angel lifts up His hand to heaven and vows that all John sees and hears is true and certain. The Angel declares this oath before the eternal Creator of the heavens, the earth, the seas, and everything living within them. As stated earlier, it should not be presumed by this act that this Angel could not be an appearance of the Lord. As He raises His hand toward heaven, the Angel announces that there will be no further delay, which affirms that the time of God's final judgment has now arrived.

10:7 *In the days when the seventh angel is ready to blow his trumpet, the mystery of God will be completed, as he had made this Good News known to his servants, the prophets."*

The stage is set. Six angels have sounded their trumpets (*Revelation 8:6–9:21*), and the sounding of the seventh trumpet is ominously imminent. It is time for the "mystery of God" to be completed. Time has run out, and the final judgment has come due. All that the Lord has made known through the prophets about the events of the final days will be fully revealed and fulfilled. The atrocious events to this point were but a foretaste of the impending calamities to be ushered in with the sounding of the seventh trumpet.

DIG DEEPER: *The Mystery of God*

This mystery is not unknown to the people of God. The mystery had been declared hundreds of years earlier to the prophets. Paul told the church at Colossae, "*²⁶In the past God hid this mystery, but now he has revealed it to his people. ²⁷God wanted his people throughout the world to know the glorious riches of this mystery—which is Christ living in you, giving you the hope of glory*" (*Colossians 1:26–27*). With the sounding of the seventh trumpet, the mystery of God would be revealed to those who do not believe, and they will at last understand their judgment. The tone of God's judgment has been set from the opening words of this book: "*Behold, he cometh with clouds; and every eye shall see him, and they also which pierced him: and all kindred of the earth shall wail because of him*" (*Revelation 1:7*, KJV).

Notes/Applications

Time is captive to God's creation. When the eternal Creator created the heavens and earth, time was born. As the world rushes headlong toward its final days, the Creator Who brought this world into existence will also bring it to its final conclusion. Then, time itself will dissolve into eternity.

In the midst of this creation, the Creator entered His creation for the sole purpose of saving the very people that He had created in His own image. Having paid the penalty for man's transgressions, He returned to His throne in heaven.

Now, however, this same Creator, Jesus Christ, enters His creation a second time, no longer as the suffering Savior, but in His role as the Judge of those who have refused His sacrifice on their behalf. This time, the entry of the righteous Judge is formidable in its scope and fury. Earlier, God's judgments were delivered to the earth by His assigned emissaries. Now, Jesus personally takes charge of the judgment He administers with the pronouncement: "There will be no more delay!"

We can be sure that the time for repentance is past! The time of judgment has now arrived! The mystery of God will be revealed to every tribe and nation and everyone will realize that they have offended their Creator and Redeemer and He will no longer withhold His holy justice.

Scripture admonishes us to redeem time because the present day is our only opportunity to serve the Lord God Almighty. The following poem reminds us to cherish the time God has appointed for us by being wise stewards of the time God has given us:

My Name Is Time

> My name is Time; I am the present moment,
> I am on the move, I measure out life.
> Some men welcome me, some men fear me,
> Some could not care less, but none can stop me.

I have not always been, nor will I always be.
God says I am running out
and He is in control.
When I stop, when I am no longer now,
Eternity keeps on going
and it will be too late for getting right with God,
too late for faith in Christ.
Nothing will be left
but forever and its regrets.
My name is Time. Can you tell me?
If you redeem me, you will find me good.
If you use me, you will find me precious.
My name is Time. I am nearing the end,
and I shall take you with me into eternity.

—Anonymous

Revelation 10:8–11

10:8–9 *[8]The voice which I had heard from heaven spoke to me again. It said, "Take the opened scroll from the hand of the angel who is standing on the sea and on the land." [9]I went to the angel and asked him to give me the small scroll. He said to me, "Take it and eat it. It will be bitter in your stomach, but it will be as sweet as honey in your mouth."*

John is directed to go and take the little book from the Angel's hand. This is an authoritative command, presumably by God Himself, directing John to do something that he likely would not have otherwise done, being intimidated by such a magnificent and powerful Angel.[9] John demonstrated obedience while facing such an overwhelming experience. He approached the Angel and asked for the book, whereupon the Angel gave him the book and instructed John to eat it. It is generally agreed that this was a symbolic gesture whereby John was to absorb the book's contents with complete understanding.[10]

The Angel warned John that the book would be very sweet in his mouth but bitter in his stomach. Many expositors suggest that the book epitomizes the Word of God, which contains the joy of the Gospel message and the path of salvation as well as the certain and inescapable judgment and wrath of God.[11] It seems clear within the context of the entire passage that John was instructed to understand fully the contents of the book, so he could convey them to others at a later time.[12]

10:10 *I took the small scroll from the angel's hand and ate it. It was as sweet as honey in my mouth, but when I had eaten it, it was bitter in my stomach.*

John obeyed what the Lord had told him to do, and the Angel's warning proved to be true. He ate the book, and although it was sweet in his mouth, it soon became bitter in his stomach.

It was surely thrilling for John to "eat" the book and be directly involved in the divulgence of the truth contained within it. However, upon "digesting" its contents, the reality of its truth soon weighed heavily upon him.

10:11 *The seven thunders told me, "Again you must speak what God has revealed in front of many people, nations, languages, and kings."*

The Angel told John that he must prophesy again, though opinions differ regarding whether he would be prophesying "in front of" or *about* these many nations and leaders. The preposition translated as "in front of" in this version is perhaps better expressed as "against," telling John that he would testify both "in front of" and "against" these many people.[13] He recorded everything he had seen and heard in this great vision so that all mankind throughout the ages could likewise be equipped to understand the message and be warned of impending judgment.

Notes/Applications

A lesson can be learned from John's experience in the preceding passage about the impact that the Word of God has on believers' lives. God has gifted us with the Bible as an instruction book concerning His principles and precepts by which we should conduct our lives. The Word is always sweet to us as we read it because it registers a true witness within our spirits. However, when we "digest" the Holy Word, when we seek to apply it to our lives, it becomes bitter as it clashes with our human nature. *"God's word is living and active. It is sharper than any two-edged sword and cuts as deep as the place where soul and spirit meet, the place where joints and marrow meet. God's word judges a person's thoughts and intentions"* (Hebrews 4:12). The Word corrects us as it cuts away the chaff of selfishness and self-centeredness. It implores us to trust and obey that which is godly rather than that which is human.

Praise the Lord that He has given us a glimpse of His script for the end of the world, and He is victorious! We can celebrate the ending yet still mourn the events that creation must endure before this ending will be realized. Surely, this must have been similar to what John experienced when he took and ate the little book the angel presented to him. Such truth is bitter to experience but, oh, so sweet to know:

> *Come, divine Interpreter,*
> *Bring me eyes Thy book to read,*
> *Ears the mystic words to hear,*
> *Words which did from Thee proceed,*
> *Words that endless bliss impart,*
> *Kept in an obedient heart.*
> *All who read, or hear, are blessed,*
> *If Thy plain commands we do;*
> *Of Thy kingdom here possessed,*
> *Thee we shall in glory view*
> *When Thou comest on earth to abide,*
> *Reign triumphant at Thy side.*[14]

REVELATION  11

Revelation 11:1–2

11:1 *Then I was given a stick like a measuring stick. I was told, "Stand up and measure the temple of God and the altar. Count those who worship there.*

Despite the numerous interpretive difficulties found in the Book of Revelation, many consider this passage to be the most challenging to explain.[1] Though this chapter is a continuation of the previous chapter, we are immediately confronted with a shift of events that provokes many questions and stirs vast controversy while inspiring few substantial resolutions. Verses one and two, specifically, appear almost as an isolated incident in which a command is given that reveals no obvious relationship with the events preceding it or with those following it.

As with the little book John had been commanded to take from the Angel's hand and eat, he was again required to play an active role in these prophetic visions. Rather than merely observing and recording the events that he had previously witnessed, John was now instructed to take an active role as the vision unfolded. The Angel introduced in the previous chapter handed John a reed, likely a cane stem similar to those common in the Jordan valley, which grew upward to twenty feet in height.[2] With this reed, John was instructed to measure "the temple of God, the altar, and those who worship there."

What does this "temple of God" refer to? This is a question that has perplexed scholars and commentators for centuries. How one attempts to explain the issue can have inescapable bearing on the interpretation of other scriptural passages from Old and New Testaments alike.

Determining whether this is a literal temple or a symbolic one lies at the core of any interpretation. Most scholars who favor a literal interpretation of these two verses suggest that they refer to a temple that has yet to be rebuilt in the last days for the reinstitution of Jewish offering and sacrifices.[3] In this scenario, then, John was commanded to take a physical measurement of a future temple in Jerusalem. Some also view this as a literal temple, though they see it as the first-century temple before its destruction in A.D. 70 by Titus, the notorious Roman emperor.[4] However, it seems highly improbable that the temple referred to in this passage should be understood as literal or physical.[5] The primary challenge in supporting a literal interpretation lies in the difficulty of proving the biblical substantiation for an end-times temple since the Lord has rendered the temple sacrifices ineffectual with His own sacrifice at Calvary. Furthermore, it seems very unlikely that John would be instructed to measure people—"those who worship"—with a measuring rod, the same tool with which he was to measure the temple and the altar.

It seems more plausible, therefore, that this temple is to be understood in a spiritual sense (1 *Peter* 2:4-5). Even many who might find more reasons than most to view this as a literal temple agree.[6] The strongest and most common interpretation is that the three elements, the temple of God, the altar, and those who worship there, comprise one unit representing the church universal—the body of Christ's redeemed.[7] Like earlier descriptions in John's vision, the Angel shows John another view of those Who have been redeemed (*Revelation* 6:9-10; 7:14-17). This is the church triumphant, safely encircled within the sanctuary of God's protecting temple. God's people are safe in the inner sanctuary, which is then 'measured' to indicate that they are all known to God and therefore safe in his care.[8]

The command to measure, therefore, is not to be accomplished in a physical sense but a judicial one.[9] The Angel instructed John to account for all those included within the body of Christ—those washed in the blood of the Lamb. This explanation does not necessarily answer the question of why John was told to measure the temple. Many commentators argue that this act of measuring in some way implies the protection of God over His people during the tribulation.[10] However, based on the text itself, this or any other explanation is simply speculation.

Moreover, since the beginning of chapter four, John has been in heaven. Everything that he has seen has been seen from his position in heaven. His entire encounter with the Angel, that is Jesus Christ, from the beginning of chapter ten to this moment, has taken place in heaven. This also seems to rule out the possibility that the temple John sees is some literal temple, either the second temple destroyed in A.D. 70 or some future temple built in Jerusalem before the Second Coming of Christ.

11:2 But do not measure the temple courtyard. Leave that out, because it is given to the nations, and they will trample the holy city for 42 months.

The Angel further instructed John not to measure the outer court of the temple. Again, this should be taken as a symbolic gesture, though what exactly is represented is uncertain. Some commentators argue that the outer court refers to those professing to belong to the church but who are not genuinely redeemed, such as those addressed in chapter two for adhering to the doctrines of Balaam (2:14) and Jezebel (2:20).[11] Others insist that both delineations refer to the church but from two different perspectives—the temple of God depicting the spiritual preservation of God's faithfulness in troublesome times and the outer court illustrating the imminent hostility of God's enemies against them.[12] Finally, many believe that the court represents not just imposters within the true church but the entire sum of unbelievers.[13] The Greek word rendered as "Gentiles" in this verse is more accurately translated as "nations," denoting groups of people that are not necessarily segregated by ethnicity.[14] This lends more support to the credibility of the third interpretation. Such an explanation implies that this is not a separation of Jews from non-Jews but of believers from unbelievers.

The reference to forty-two months, as with every other aspect of this passage, has received vastly differing interpretations. Some scholars have allocated these as 1,260 days of years (1,260 years) in an allusion to the rise of the Roman papacy.[15] Others altogether dismiss this as being a specific period of time and instead suggest that these forty-two months symbolize the limitation of evil's free reign over God's faithful.[16] However, this is the first of many times that this specific time period is mentioned in the Book of Revelation, and the duration is depicted in several different ways: forty-two months (11:2, 13:5), 1,260 days (11:3, 12:6), and three-and-a-half years (12:14). It appears that this is done to avoid confusion. Therefore, it seems most likely that this refers to a literal three-and-a-half year period of time during which the antichrist will rise to power and persecute all believers. Again, we have evidence of God's preordained limitation to this persecution.

Many commentators designate "the holy city" as another representation of the true church.[17] However, the Scriptures specifically refer to Jerusalem as the holy city (*Nehemiah 11:1; Isaiah 52:1; Daniel 9:24; Matthew 27:53*). Nevertheless, this could be both a physical and symbolic element of the prophecy. For forty-two months, the nations—that is the unbelievers—will trample with violent aggression the holy city, that is the believers and/or the city of Jerusalem, underfoot, having dominion over them.

Notes/Applications

In the previous chapter, the Angel, the very orchestrator of all history, Jesus Christ, stands upon the land and sea and proclaims with a thundering voice: "There will be no more delay!" Two catastrophes have already destroyed half of the world's population. But Jesus announces that what is about to happen will be far worse! The human mind staggers when exposed to the unstoppable justice that Jesus will visit upon those who are reprobate, rejected by God and destined for damnation.

Nevertheless, this passage opens with an obvious parenthesis, another pause in the unfolding vision that Jesus is showing to John. In between the second and third catastrophes, the sixth and seventh trumpets, Jesus asks John to measure the temple and the people within its courts.

It seems as though this passage does not follow the expected explanation of the preceding narrative. What is John's vision trying to show his readers? What is Jesus, the Author of this revelation, trying to tell His redeemed people?

If we look carefully at these two verses, we understand that Jesus is showing John a vision of the temple in heaven. The vision follows the same architectural pattern that the Lord God revealed to Moses as He outlined the plans for the tabernacle that the Hebrew people built in the wilderness (*Exodus 25–30*). Solomon, David's son, followed the same pattern when he built the temple in Jerusalem. This structure proceeds from the outer wall into the Court of the Gentiles. People from every tribe and nation had permission to enter this courtyard. The inner courtyard was reserved only for the Jews, God's chosen people. Inside the inner courtyard was the Holy of Holies, where the Lord God met with His people and directed their pathway as they journeyed from slavery in Egypt to freedom in the Promised Land.

Following this God-ordained pattern, Jesus shows John the temple in heaven. In this temple, the Lord God continues to dwell in the midst of His people. The people of God fill the inner courtyard, worshiping on bended knee the mighty God and His redeeming Son. In this courtyard, the saints dwell safely, shielded and protected from the violence that occurs outside this sanctuary.

Outside this inner courtyard is the Court of the Gentiles. In this courtyard, the hosts of the nations carry on their rebellious, treasonous acts against the God Who has created them and His Son Who has died on their behalf. John is to stay away from this area. These pagan people will be allowed to trample the Holy City for a period of forty-two months.

What is Jesus telling His beloved saints? He is telling them that even in the midst of the impending disaster that He will visit upon those who have rejected Him, He will still be their God and they will always be His people. They are safe and secure in God's sanctuary, and even though many will lose their lives in faithful testimony to their faithful Lord, He will not fail them or forsake them. Jesus is showing John, and through John all His redeemed people, that in the midst of horrendous judgment they should not lose heart, because the One Who died to save them is alive forevermore and will hold them in the hollow of His hand.

Revelation 11:3–8

11:3 *I will allow my two witnesses who wear sackcloth to speak what God has revealed. They will speak for 1,260 days."*

The One speaking to John is the same Angel that has been speaking to John since the beginning of chapter ten. It should not be presumed that such authority exists in any other created being, and therefore, this verse is further evidence that the speaker is the Lord Jesus Christ.

At that time, Jesus will assign "two witnesses" to prophesy for 1,260 days (three and a half years), the same duration of time that Jerusalem would be trampled underfoot by rebellious, God-hating people (v. 2). One commonly accepted interpretation proposes that these two witnesses would not actually be two individuals but are a symbolic representation of the witnessing church.[18] Many who endorse this position point to biblical principles requiring two witnesses for legal testimony[19] (*Deuteronomy 19:15*). This argument aside, there seems little convincing evidence to nullify the straightforward presentation of this passage. It is apparent that these would be two specific individuals prepared and empowered by God to fulfill a unique purpose during this appointed time.[20]

These two witnesses were dressed in sackcloth, which was a dark, coarse material usually made of goat or camel hair.[21] It was customarily worn as a gesture of mourning (*Genesis 37:34; 2 Samuel 3:31; 1 Kings 21:27; Esther 4:1; Isaiah 15:3*). Though we are not specifically told about their message, we can safely assume that these two witnesses warned people about God's impending judgment and urged them to repent.

11:4 *These witnesses are the two olive trees and the two lamp stands standing in the presence of the Lord of the earth.*

This verse parallels an Old Testament prophecy of Zechariah concerning Joshua and Zerubbabel (*Zechariah 3:1–4:10*).

> [11]*I asked the angel, "What do these two olive trees at the right and the left of the lamp stand mean?" [12]Again I asked him, "What is the meaning of the two branches from the olive trees next to the two golden pipes that are pouring out gold?" [13]He asked me, "Don't you know what these things mean?" "No, sir," I answered. [14]So he said, "These are the two anointed ones who are standing beside the Lord of the whole earth"* (Zechariah 4:11–14).

It is unclear whether this verse is simply a reference to the earlier prophecy or the ultimate fulfillment of it. At the very least, the similarities between these two passages are unmistakable. The entire world would know that these two witnesses were servants of the Lord.

11:5 *If anyone wants to hurt them, fire comes out of the witnesses' mouths and burns up their enemies. If anyone wants to hurt them, he must be killed the same way.*

During the three-and-a-half years that these two witnesses prophesy, no one would be allowed to hurt them. Any who tried would be killed by fire expelled from the witnesses' mouths. If this is to be understood literally, we should not doubt that God is certainly able to defend His prophets with such a remarkable phenomenon. There is Old Testament precedent for such an action: *"Elijah answered the officer, 'If I'm a man of God, fire will come from heaven and burn up you and your 50 men.' Then fire came from heaven and burned up the officer and his 50 men"* (2 Kings 1:10).

However, this expression could also be a figurative representation of the words spoken by these two witnesses, words of judgment delivered with the authority of God's anointed. Whenever they speak, their pronouncement of judgment will be accompanied by equally dramatic fulfillment of their pronouncement. Thus, it seems equally plausible to understand this as a figurative expression similar to that spoken by the prophet Jeremiah.[22]

> *This is what the Lord God of Armies says: Because you've talked like this, I'm going to put my words in your mouth like a fire. These people will be like wood. My words will burn them up.* (Jeremiah 5:14)

11:6 *These witnesses have authority to shut the sky in order to keep rain from falling during the time they speak what God has revealed. They have authority to turn water into blood and to strike the earth with any plague as often as they want.*

The two witnesses will be given the power to stop rain from falling and to summon other types of plagues upon the earth during the 1,260 days that they would be prophesying. To compound the innumerable problems caused by such a great drought, they would be able to turn whatever waters remained into blood. These powers were given to them to be used at their discretion.

Many scholars have devised theories regarding the identity of these two witnesses. Some speculate that the witnesses will be Moses and Elijah, two Old Testament figures who appeared at Jesus' transfiguration, as witnessed by Peter, James, and John *(Matthew 17)*. This conclusion is also drawn because of the similar displays that Moses and Elijah possessed while on the earth[23] *(Exodus 7:17, 8:12; 1 Kings 17:1)*. Other commentators agree that Elijah will be one of the two witnesses based upon the Old Testament prophecy concerning him *(Malachi 4:5)*. However, because Moses died *(Deuteronomy 34:5)*, many conclude that the other witness must be Enoch, since neither he nor Elijah ever experienced a physical, earthly death.[24]

Whereas either of these theories are legitimate possibilities, the fact remains that God has chosen these two witnesses from the beginning of time, and their identity is known only to Him. They could just as easily be Christians that arise from among those living during this period of time. They need not be powerful, influential men, for it is the Lord Who will empower them.

11:7 *When the witnesses finish their testimony, the beast which comes from the bottomless pit will fight them, conquer them, and kill them.*

Once the two witnesses had completed their three-and-a-half-year mission, the beast of the bottomless pit would execute them. Based on previous references in Revelation, one might be inclined to identify this beast as the same "angel of the bottomless pit" named Apollyon. *"The king who ruled them was the angel from the bottomless pit. In Hebrew he is called Abaddon, and in Greek he is called Apollyon" (Revelation 9:11).* However, this is the first of thirty-six references in Revelation to a different beast that plays a major role in the events of the last days and who is commonly identified as the antichrist.[25] In this verse, the allusion to the bottomless pit should be understood in a broader sense as an indicator of this creature's Satanic origin.[26]

For 1,260 days, these two witnesses will be invincible under the power of God's protection. At the appointed time, though, God will withdraw His protection and allow the antichrist to overcome them.

11:8 *Their dead bodies will lie on the street of the important city where their Lord was crucified. The spiritual names of that city are Sodom and Egypt.*

The two witnesses were not given proper burial, but instead, their corpses were laid upon the streets of "the important city" for all to see. The clarification of this city as being the same one "where their Lord was crucified" seems to leave little room for doubt that this could be any place other than Jerusalem.[27] Nevertheless, some expositors insist that this city is Rome or at least represents a revived Roman empire.[28] Others believe that this should not be identified with any particular city but that it is indicative of the paganism existing throughout all civilizations.[29]

However, there is only one city "where their Lord was crucified." This can only be the Holy City, Jerusalem. Yet the spiritual names assigned to what was and is once again the capital of Israel demonstrate that Jerusalem has fallen prey to the godless culture, the same as the rest of the nations of the world. This city was compared spiritually to Sodom and Egypt. In the Old Testament, evil and perversion abounded in Sodom and its sister city Gomorrah *(Genesis 13:13, 18:20–21).* Sodom, then, represents the widespread perversion that will permeate the entire culture not only in Jerusalem, but throughout all the nations. The comparison to Egypt identifies the city as one that likewise serves pagan gods, and relentlessly persecutes and oppresses God's people *(Exodus 3:7–9)*. These are the people who dwell in the outer court of the temple and will rise to trample the Holy City underfoot *(Revelation 11:1)*.

Notes/Applications

Although our human curiosities want to know all the details, it is not necessary to reach an absolute conclusion regarding the identity of these two witnesses. Phenomenal results transpire, not from superior people accomplishing such miracles but from a supernatural Almighty God Who appoints people to perform the wondrous things for which He has ordained them.

We may feel insignificant when we consider the witnesses' mission. We probably consider their assignment to be undesirable. Perhaps we would run away from such spiritually burdensome tasks, tasks assigned by God, Who never asked about our willingness to serve Him in this capacity. Yet Scripture reminds us that God is sovereign and He will do with us as He pleases.

Often we pray in such a way that we tell the Lord how He should use us. We live according to our perception of reasonable commitment. How entangled we become by the limits we place upon the Sovereign God and His power.

But God's plan surpasses human analysis. His righteousness never fails, and His perfection never ends. He will intricately weave together the events of our lives into a significant witness, but such significance begins with ministry founded upon God's appointment to service. Some areas of ministry will be less glamorous, less comfortable, and even less safe. Nevertheless, Christ's followers must live in such a way that the Lord will achieve His purposes through them. When our time is over, when our task is completed, we too will die and, like these witnesses, be welcomed into the arms of our risen, conquering Lord.

Revelation 11:9–19

11:9 *For 3½ days some members of the people, tribes, languages, and nations will look at the witnesses' dead bodies and will not allow anyone to bury them.*

The corpses of the two witnesses would lie in the street for three and a half days, where the whole world could see them. How much these two must have been despised! How offensive their message of judgment must have been that their deaths would be treated with such utter disregard! No one will even remove their bodies from where they lie in the streets. Of course, they are hated not only for the message they proclaimed but also because they kept rain from falling and poured out plagues upon the earth for three-and-a-half years.

11:10 *Those living on earth will gloat over the witnesses' death. They will celebrate and send gifts to each other because these two prophets had tormented those living on earth.*

People all around the world will celebrate the deaths of these witnesses who had tormented them for so long. The two corpses will remain in the street serving as symbols of the antichrist's victory. The elated response of the people evokes the exchange of gifts, celebrating the death of God's hated witnesses.

11:11 *After 3½ days the breath of life from God entered the two witnesses, and they stood on their feet. Great fear fell on those who watched them.*

At the end of three-and-a-half days, God's power will again be displayed and God's breath of life will enter the two witnesses. They will stand on their feet where moments earlier their lifeless bodies had lain in the street. The people's rejoicing will come to an abrupt halt, and those who witnessed the miracle will be gripped with paralyzing fear.

11:12 *The witnesses heard a loud voice from heaven calling to them, "Come up here." They went up to heaven in a cloud, and their enemies watched them.*

A loud voice will summon the two resurrected witnesses to "come up here," inviting them to the gates of heaven. This was also the voice of the Angel, even Jesus Christ, Who has been directing these events each step of the way. The two witnesses will disappear into a cloud and will be taken into heaven. When the world watches these two ascend into the sky, people will be startled by the amazing change that has transpired. One moment these two men were dead, and the next they were disappearing into heaven.

11:13 *At that moment a powerful earthquake struck. One-tenth of the city collapsed, 7,000 people were killed by the earthquake, and the rest were terrified. They gave glory to the God of heaven.*

Within the same hour that the two witnesses were called up into heaven, a devastating earthquake rocked the great city, resulting in the deaths of seven thousand people and in the destruction of one tenth of the city. "The rest," all those who were spared from the annihilation, were paralyzed with fear so intense that they finally recognized the God Whom they had despised. Without repentance, without any remorse for their rebellion, without any significant change of heart, the inhabitants of the world recognized the Lord, not for His mercy and salvation, but for His awesome power and frightening judgment.

11:14 *The second catastrophe is over. The third catastrophe will soon be here.*

The second catastrophe, the judgment of the sixth trumpet, was completed. The third and final catastrophe, the judgment of the seventh trumpet, was imminent.

It is very easy to assume that the events following the sixth trumpet ended in the passage of Revelation 9:16-21. However, we should not try imposing human timing to God's description of these last days. Rather, the events of the sixth trumpet actually transpire from Revelation 9:16 through this verse, where we are clearly told that the second catastrophe is over and the third is about to begin. Thus, the events of the sixth trumpet occur over a period of three and a half years, perhaps even longer.

11:15 *When the seventh angel blew his trumpet, there were loud voices in heaven, saying, "The kingdom of the world has become the kingdom of our Lord and of his Messiah, and he will rule as king forever and ever."*

The seventh angel will blow his trumpet, unleashing God's final judgments upon the earth. The sounding of this last trumpet initiates the pouring out of the seven bowls of God's wrath, as described in chapter sixteen.

However, before the judgments are unleashed, John again finds himself in heaven, witnessing the most glorious moment in all of human history. Loudly, in one accord, many voices in heaven praise the Lord, proclaiming that the kingdoms of earth have now become the Kingdom of the Lord Jesus Christ. There will be tremendous excitement and anticipation that this long-awaited moment has finally arrived.

11:16–17 *¹⁶Then the 24 leaders, who were sitting on their thrones in God's presence, immediately bowed, worshiped God, ¹⁷and said, "We give thanks to you, Lord God Almighty, who is and who was, because you have taken your great power and have begun ruling as king.*

The twenty-four leaders gathered around God's throne fell prostrate before the Lord in worship *(Revelation 4:10–11)*. The leaders praised the Lord with thanksgiving for asserting His rightful position as King of kings. The leaders also rejoiced that the reign of evil upon the earth approached completion and the time for the Lord Jesus Christ to rule the earth was at hand. Paul also looked forward to this time when Jesus would finally take control of all peoples, nations, tribes, and languages. *"At the right time God will make this known. God is the blessed and only ruler. He is the King of kings and Lord of lords"* (1 Timothy 6:15).

11:18 *The nations were angry, but your anger has come. The time has come for the dead to be judged: to reward your servants, the prophets, your holy people, and those who fear your name, no matter if they are important or unimportant, and to destroy those who destroy the earth."*

At this point, mankind has not responded to God's judgments with repentance but with anger. Though the final outpouring of God's wrath has yet to take place, the result is as fixed and certain as though it had already occurred, and the leaders rejoice over the outcome.[30]

Those who endured persecution for Christ, labored for Christ, prophesied for Christ, lived for Christ, and died for Christ would receive their reward—eternal life in heaven. Those who lived in their sin and rejected the salvation of Christ would also receive their just punishment. The saints would triumph over those who had exacted violence and destruction upon God's people while on the earth.

11:19 *God's temple in heaven was opened, and the ark of his promise was seen inside his temple. There was lightning, noise, thunder, an earthquake, and heavy hail.*

Whereas the temple in heaven that John beheld can be understood as a literal temple, it should not necessarily be understood as some colossal, physical structure situated in the clouds. Within this heavenly temple, opened wide for John to see, sat the "ark of His promise." It should not be presumed that this was the tangible, historical ark, which had long since been destroyed, lost, or concealed from the world. Rather, this object seems most likely to serve as some reminder of God's covenant with His people.[31]

The sounding of the seventh trumpet also resulted in an extensive display of great atmospheric upheaval. Thunder, lightning, earthquakes, and hail were also unleashed at the opening of the seventh seal *(Revelation 8:1–5)* and would be observed again at the pouring out of the seventh bowl *(Revelation 16:17–18)*.

DIG DEEPER: *Ark of the Promise*

This imagery finds its roots in Old Testament history. The ark of the promise was housed in the tabernacle and later in the Temple in a place called the Holy of Holies. No one was allowed to enter this place except the high priest on one day of the year, the Day of Atonement, in which he entered with sacrificial blood as the atonement for his own sin and the sin of God's people. In this verse, the ark is fully visible to everyone and is no longer hidden. In the same way, the truth of Jesus Christ will be made known to everyone.

Notes/Applications

Mankind's reaction to the deaths of the two witnesses is almost like that of an international holiday. There is widespread rejoicing and celebration that these two will no longer be able to torment the world's inhabitants with their testimony. The thing so offensive about the two witnesses is that they testify to the truth of the Lord Jesus Christ. The problem for the people of the earth is that this truth is delivered in the context of God's judgment, not His mercy, grace, and salvation. At this time, there is no reprieve. There is no salvation. God's holiness and righteousness will now be dispensed in absolute justice. The world enjoys its sin and does not want to be told or reminded that its actions are sinful. But for three and a half years, these two witnesses have reminded people that they are now under the wrath of God and that there will be no more delay *(Revelation 10:6)*. The plagues and droughts imposed at their word give absolute proof that they are the mouthpiece of God's judgment.

Though opposition to the truth will be epidemic in the end times, it is prevalent even now. Certainly, it is easier for mainstream culture to label Christians as radical, closed-minded, and eccentric simply because believers hold fast to the Savior that has redeemed them with His own blood. The unsaved will never acknowledge that behavior they deem acceptable is, in fact, sin that is abhorrent in the sight of God. In like manner, as the two witnesses in this passage, we must testify to the truth of Christ in a world that does not recognize sin as sin or Christ as the Deliverer.

As Christ's witnesses in this world at this time in history, we have the opportunity to provide a testimony to the grace, mercy, and peace of our Savior. But even in this age, we must also be prepared to tell people of God's inevitable judgment. These two witnesses have a heavy task, one that will end in their death. Even at this time, we must also be prepared to be faithful witnesses to the truth of Jesus Christ, both in His salvation and His judgment.

REVELATION 12

Revelation 12:1-6

12:1 *A spectacular sign appeared in the sky: There was a woman who was dressed in the sun, who had the moon under her feet and a crown of 12 stars on her head.*

John witnessed a vision that was both an integral part of the revelation of the seventh trumpet and also different than that which he had experienced thus far. This chapter describes a vision within a vision, and though the passage might at first seem disconnected, it is intricately interwoven into the events of the chapters surrounding it. The figurative language used in this chapter is typical of prophetic literature (*Daniel 7; Isaiah 27; Hosea 3*) wherein familiar images are often used to depict events of greater significance; therefore, John's emphasis of a "sign" urges readers to look beyond the physical description of the vision to grasp the symbolic meaning.

John saw the figure of a woman clothed in the golden glory of the sun and crowned with twelve stars around her head, and the moon lay under her feet. Speculations about this woman's identity range from Mary, Jesus' mother, to the church universal.[1] The most convincing

arguments seem to be made by those who insist that this woman represents Israel, based on comparable imagery found in other Scriptures
(*Genesis 37:9; 1 Kings 18:31*). This interpretation is better appreciated
by viewing the woman as portrayed throughout the chapter rather
than relying upon this particular verse. Even so, differences persist
concerning whether she embodies the nation of Israel (strictly those
of Jewish heritage) or whether she also includes a "spiritual Israel" as
defined by the apostle Paul[2] (*Romans 2:28–29; Romans 9:6–8*).

12:2 *She was pregnant. She cried out from labor pains and
the agony of giving birth.*

At this point, this sign of a magnificent woman clothed in the vast
array of God's cosmos, dominates John's vision. As he looks at the
woman, he sees that she is pregnant and the child she carries is about
to be born.

This verse offers more evidence of the mother's identity than of
the child's. The imagery of a woman crying out "from labor pains" is
a familiar reference to Israel in Old Testament themes.

> [9]*Now why are you crying so loudly? Don't you have a king?
> Has your counselor died? Pain grips you like a woman in labor.*
> [10a]*Daughter of Zion, writhe in pain and groan like a woman in
> labor.* (Micah 4:9–10)

12:3 *Another sign appeared in the sky: a huge fiery red
serpent with seven heads, ten horns, and seven crowns on its
heads.*

While John watches the sign of a woman struggling in her labor pains,
another *sign* appears in the sky. A frightening creature, a fiery red serpent appears with an outlandish number of heads, horns, and crowns.

The color of the serpent probably holds less significance than the
number of his heads, horns, and crowns, about which much has been
speculated. However, since the text says nothing about the array of the
serpent's heads, it is perhaps wisest to avoid speculation about their

significance altogether. Rather it is best to say that this sign appears in the sky along with the sign of the woman as the Angel continues to unfold the vision to John.

12:4 *Its tail swept away one-third of the stars in the sky and threw them down to earth. The serpent stood in front of the woman who was going to give birth so that it could devour her child when it was born.*

The serpent was a formidable monster. It possessed an enormous power with which it caused "one-third of the stars in the sky" to be cast to the earth. The serpent also desired to destroy the Child of the glorious woman in labor immediately after the Baby was born. The serpent had a plan and the will to use its power to disrupt the future of the Baby. Even though it is not clearly stated, it seems that the serpent knew something about the woman and the Baby that she would soon deliver.

12:5 *She gave birth to a son, a boy, who is to rule all the nations with an iron scepter. Her child was snatched away and taken to God and to his throne.*

The Son Who is born to the woman is the Redeemer Who is born for the salvation of Israel. The scene John witnesses is also the fulfillment of Old Testament prophecy:

> [6]A child will be born for us. A son will be given to us. The government will rest on his shoulders. He will be named: Wonderful Counselor, Mighty God, Everlasting Father, Prince of Peace.
> [7]His government and peace will have unlimited growth. He will establish David's throne and kingdom. He will uphold it with justice and righteousness now and forever. The Lord of Armies is determined to do this! (Isaiah 9:6–7)

The identity of this "male child" as the Lord Jesus Christ is verified by His description as the One Who will "rule all nations with a rod of iron." This imagery was first introduced to the Hebrew people

by the ancient prophets of Israel as they looked for the salvation of
Israel in the birth of God's promised Messiah.

> *[7]I will announce the Lord's decree. He said to me: "You are my
> Son. Today I have become your Father. [8]Ask me, and I will give
> you the nations as your inheritance and the ends of the earth as
> your own possession. [9]You will break them with an iron scepter.
> You will smash them to pieces like pottery." (Psalm 2:7–9)*

John watches the birth of the Child and, almost immediately, the
Child's is snatched away to God and His throne. It is evident that God
is actively involved in the protection of the Child from the serpent
between the time of His birth and the time that God brings the Child
to His throne. While the Gospels recount the biographical history of
Jesus of Nazareth in greater detail, John sees the overall panorama of
the Child's birth and His ascension that returns Him to God. It seems
that the Angel wants John to see the end from the beginning – the
triumph of the Child and the failure of the serpent.

12:6 *Then the woman fled into the wilderness where God had prepared a place for her so that she might be taken care of for 1,260 days.*

The "wilderness" as used in this verse probably is not intended to depict any literal topographical description or geographical location. As
with the other metaphors prevalent throughout this passage, it should
be taken figuratively. The wilderness is simply a symbolic reference to
God's protection of the woman, even though the world seems to be
coming apart at the seams.

Throughout this passage John witnesses signs that are presented
in the context of metaphorical imagery. What John sees represents
God's direction of history over a long span of time. However, the
specific reference to 1,260 days in this verse seems to reduce the time
span to a rather short duration. The use of *then* to open this verse
shows that the action of this verse follows the ascension of the male
Child to the throne of God. The stated time period directs the reader

back to John's vision of the temple in 11:1-2. There, the same time period of forty-two months is defined as the time for God's enemies to trample the Holy City under foot.

Essentially, what John sees is simply another vision of God's protection for His people during a time of extreme dissension among the nations of the world as well as the unleashing of God's punishment on those who are condemned for their unbelief.

Notes/Applications

This passage openly exposes Satan's barefaced and shameless attempt to thwart God's will, purpose, and ultimately His plan to redeem the lost. Again, there seems to be a pause, a temporary period of time before the full revelation of the third catastrophe (11:14). The Angel showed John some very important events that he needed to make a part of his recorded narrative. What John sees is the revelation of three wonders in heaven—the opening of the temple in heaven with all of its magnificence and majesty, a glorious woman attired in heaven's resplendence, and a red serpent furnished with seven heads, seven crowns, and ten horns.

As the woman is in the throes of her labor pains to give birth to her Child, the serpent stands directly in front of her, awaiting the birth of the Child so he can devour the Baby immediately after its birth. The serpent, identified as Satan, knows that the Child being born is the promised Messiah, the Son of God, sent to earth to bring God's salvation to the lost and, to one day ascend His throne to rule the nations with power and authority. Satan was well aware that the Baby's birth was the fulfillment of God's promised redemption. The serpent's vengeful passion to defeat God's plan of redemption is revealed by how viciously he attempts to hurt the child. The intensity of the serpent's hatred for the Child is seen in his desire to crush the Baby's body with its mouth.

This wondrous revelation shown to John represents one of the greatest events in time and eternity. God's plan of redemption fulfilled by the consecrated birth of God's Son is revealed in the presence of massive evil represented by Satan. Even though the woman is at her weakest in her labor pain, even though the Child is most vulnerable at the moment of birth, nothing could thwart God's will, purpose, and plan! Not even Satan with all of his evil monstrosities at his disposal!

The Child was born! The woman was preserved! God's plan of redemption was accomplished! Satan was put to shame! His evil scheme was ineffectual! It was null and void!

Oh, child of God, be of good cheer! The Child is the Victor! Evil is conquered! Nothing or no one can ever obstruct God's perfect plan and sovereign purpose.

Revelation 12:7–12

12:7–8 ⁷*Then a war broke out in heaven. Michael and his angels had to fight a war with the serpent. The serpent and its angels fought. ⁸But it was not strong enough, and there was no longer any place for them in heaven.*

Having lost the battle to hurt the woman and destroy the Child, Satan and his angels engage in a fierce battle against God's angels in heaven. The archangel Michael and the angels of heaven battled Satan, the red serpent, and his legion of fallen angels. Michael is the chief prince of angels and the guardian angel over the children of Israel *(Daniel 10:13; 12:1; Jude 9)*. Satan and his angels were no match for the heavenly host. Satan was not only defeated, but also thrown out of heaven because he had rebelled against his sovereign Creator. Even though Satan knew God, even though he recognized God's authority, Satan was not deterred from his evil schemes. But every one of Satan's plans ended in defeat. He was unable to destroy the Child. He was unable to defeat the archangel, Michael. In the end, Satan's disobedience and rebellion became the cause of his own demise. Surely, even Satan must have realized the futility of his goal, yet his obstinate ambition and atrocious malice would nonetheless drive him to attempt the impossible.[3]

12:9 *The huge serpent was thrown down. That ancient snake, named Devil and Satan, the deceiver of the whole world, was thrown down to earth. Its angels were thrown down with it.*

The huge serpent is also referred to as the ancient snake in reference to a passage from the Book of Genesis. *"Then the Lord God asked the woman, 'What have you done?' 'The snake deceived me, and I ate,' the woman answered"* (Genesis 3:13). He is also called the Devil and Satan so that there can be no confusion that these are all one and the same being. Satan has been cast down to the earth with all of his followers.

12:10–12 *¹⁰Then I heard a loud voice in heaven, saying, "Now the salvation, power, kingdom of our God, and the authority of his Messiah have come. The one accusing our brothers and sisters, the one accusing them day and night in the presence of our God, has been thrown out. ¹¹They won the victory over him because of the blood of the lamb and the word of their testimony. They didn't love their life so much that they refused to give it up. ¹²Be glad for this reason, heavens and those who live in them. How horrible it is for the earth and the sea because the Devil has come down to them with fierce anger, knowing that he has little time left."*

A loud voice bursts forth in exuberant praise with what has become a familiar refrain to the victories attained in the heavenly realms (*Revelation 4:8–10; 7:9–12; 11:15–18*). The identity of the speaker is uncertain but it also has no impact on the full appreciation of the text.

John heard a loud voice proclaiming that the salvation, power, and authority of the Lord's Anointed had come. The Messiah ascends His throne to take full command of all aspects of His creation. Saint and sinner will all acknowledge the supreme authority of Jesus Christ (*Philippians 2:9–11*). Satan is defeated "because of the blood of the Lamb and the word of their testimony," which seems to indicate that there was not much of a physical conflict at all. The victory was determined before the clash began—those on the Lord's side would be triumphant, and those who fought alongside Satan would be conquered and cast out with their evil leader. For too many years, the evil one has accused the saints who have been redeemed by the blood of the Lamb.

Most commentators generally agree that the description of those who did not "love their life so much that they refused to give it up" obviously refers to martyrs, those persons willing to give their lives for the cause of Christ.[4] The war fought in heaven is of a spiritual nature, but it has earthly ramifications. Whatever the hardships endured by believers in the world, the victory is certain and irreversible and is not dependent upon the triumphs over evil in the earthly realm but upon those achieved in the spiritual realm.[5]

There was great joy in heaven because the devil had been defeated. However, there was still great misery in store for those who remained on the earth, for the devil was now among them. The devil's absolute failure in heaven would only incite his anger and wrath against the earth's inhabitants. Further provoking Satan's fury would be his awareness that his time was almost up. God would only allow Satan's unprecedented outpouring of wrath upon the earth for a limited time, and during this period, believers should be encouraged to persevere with great confidence and hope.[6]

Notes/Applications

One of the most difficult concepts for redeemed sinners to understand is the idea that we are at one and the same time both saint and sinner! We know by some feeble recognition of our minds that we are clothed in the righteousness of Jesus Christ, clothed with robes washed in the blood of the Lamb. But our practical everyday experience tells us that we are far from perfect! How can we possibly be absolved of our sin and, at the same time, seen by the eternal God through the lens of His Son's sacrifice as perfectly sinless? Nevertheless, this is the consistently proclaimed truth of the Scriptures. For God and for His Son, Jesus, this is no problem at all. For redeemed sinners, it is a perplexing contradiction of everything we know about ourselves.

One thing is very clear: our perspective is *not* God's perspective. God's Word has made this plain to everyone from the very beginning of the Book. Through His prophet, Isaiah, the Lord tells us: [8]"'My *thoughts are not your thoughts, and my ways are not your ways,' declares the Lord.* [9]*Just as the heavens are higher than the earth, so my ways are higher than your ways, and my thoughts are higher than your thoughts'"* (Isaiah 55:8–9).

In the same way, the human species should not impose their perception of time onto the eternal God. For God, time simply does not exist. As far as God is concerned it may be very possible that the whole span of time from the dawn of history to the dramatic end of this world is nothing more than the blink of an eye.

When we read that Satan *will be* cast out of heaven, we immediately wonder how that is possible? Hasn't Satan already been cast to the earth, perhaps even before the creation of this world? Yet, the Scriptures teach that both time frames are true! Satan *has been* cast out of heaven and he *will be* cast out of heaven. We struggle with great difficulty when we try to get our minds around this concept. Yet, for God it is no problem at all. What God *has already done*, He *will do*! What God *is doing has been completed* before the foundation of the world (*John 17:24; Ephesians 1:4; Revelation 13:8*).

In that sense, for God there is no past, present, or future. There is only the *eternal present*. We should not be confused by those passages that seem to confuse time periods. However, the importance of these passages should teach something about the eternal God, and should, at the same time, help us understand that our confusion about eternal time sequences is insignificant compared with understanding God's purposes in His offer of salvation as well as His righteous judgment.

So, we are simultaneously both saint and sinner. At one and the same time, Satan has already been cast out of heaven and he will be cast out of heaven. The impact of this passage should inform and teach us that God is the victor through the blood of His Son, Jesus Christ, and Satan, though frightful in his furious resentment of the Lord's authority, has already been defeated at the Cross of Calvary even as he will be defeated by Michael and the angels when he dares to oppose his sovereign Creator. Satan is done! God wins! Praise the Lord!

Revelation 12:13–17

12:13 *When the serpent saw that it had been thrown down to earth, it persecuted the woman who had given birth to the boy.*

Drawing on the developing depiction of the woman, we are pushed more strongly toward the interpretation that the woman represents the people of God. Surely, she represents Israel, the covenant people of God who, through their earthly genealogy, gave birth to the male Child, Who is Jesus, the Christ. She also represents the redeemed of the Lord, the saved people of the New Covenant, who will reap the wrath of Satan's fury after he loses the battle with Michael and God's angels. Unable to frustrate the plan of the eternal God, cast down to earth and removed from access to heaven, Satan unleashes his fury upon God's people.

12:14 *The woman was given the two wings of the large eagle in order to fly away from the snake to her place in the wilderness, where she could be taken care of for a time, times, and half a time.*

As discussed in verse six, a place of safety and refuge (the wilderness) was prepared for the woman so that she would not be harmed by the serpent's tactics. The Lord God also provided "two wings of a large eagle" to carry her to that place of sanctuary. This phrasing is similar to imagery used in the Old Testament to depict God's active safekeeping of His faithful. *"You have seen for yourselves what I did to Egypt and how I carried you on eagles' wings and brought you to my mountain" (Exodus 19:4).*

Again, we are told about a specific duration of time that the Lord provides protection to the woman, in this verse referred to as "a time, times, and half a time." Most scholars agree that the time period described in this verse is the same period specified in several other passages of Revelation *(Revelation 12:6).* Although we cannot be absolutely certain, this vision may simply be a parallel to the vision John saw and described at the beginning of this chapter.

12:15–16 *¹⁵The snake's mouth poured out a river of water behind the woman in order to sweep her away. ¹⁶The earth helped the woman by opening its mouth and swallowing the river which had poured out of the serpent's mouth.*

At that time, Satan will attempt to pursue the woman to the place that God had prepared for her safety. He will somehow create some sort of deluge in a vain attempt to cut off the flight of the woman. This flood probably represents an outpouring of the serpent's wrath toward the woman, perhaps an allusion to Old Testament imagery of evils perpetrated against the children of God *(Psalm 124; Isaiah 43:2)*. However, once again, God's hand protects the fleeing woman, preserving her from harm despite Satan's relentless pursuit. Determining the exact meaning of the imagery used in these two verses is unnecessary. The scene simply shows how God's protection of the woman is sufficient to frustrate Satan's attempts to destroy her.

12:17 *The serpent became angry with the woman. So it went away to fight with her other children, the ones who keep God's commands and hold on to the testimony of Jesus.*

Because the serpent was unable to vent his rage against either the Child or the woman, he sought to redirect his rage against "her other children." The woman's seed, the Child of her womb, was her Deliverer and Redeemer, the Lord Jesus Christ. Her other children, therefore, are those people who have been saved by the sacrifice of this Redeemer. Further description identifies them as those "who keep God's commands and hold on to the testimony of Jesus." There can be little doubt, therefore, that these would indeed be Christians.[7]

12:18 *The serpent stood on the sandy shore of the sea.*

Frustrated because his attempts to capture and persecute the woman's children have been foiled by the supreme authority of the sovereign God, the serpent simply stands on the sandy shore of a sea. The specific location of this sea is not given and speculation is not advisable.

Notes/Applications

While many struggle to understand the message of Revelation, trying vainly to interpret all the signs, wonders, and details within its pages, there is merit in taking a few steps back and looking at the overall picture that John presents to his readers at the direction of Jesus Christ. No Christian would question that this New Testament book was authored, not by John the beloved disciple, but by Jesus Christ Himself. Every development of this unfolding revelation is clearly orchestrated by the sovereign God and His conquering Son.

When stepping back from the attempt to understand the details, the overall picture comes into sharp focus. Bible scholars and commentators may vigorously defend one perspective over another, but no one would argue that the revelation of Jesus Christ is a graphic picture of the struggle between good and evil.

From the beginning of time, when Adam and Eve sinned against God's clear instruction in the Garden of Eden, the human race has been embroiled in the divine stress imposed on them by their sin. They know what is right, but fail miserably when they try to do what is right! Every human life is nothing more or less than survival, trying to provide the most basic amenities necessary to sustain life. But imprinted on this most basic need to survive is the more demanding need to make sense of it all.

Why do people have to work so hard just to survive? Is there some malevolent deity that takes perverse pleasure as he watches them scrape and scrounge for food and shelter? Why does he take so much pleasure in their suffering? What do people have to do to appease the appetite of this god, who is both frightening and hateful at the same time?

So people have developed innumerable religious structures in their vain attempt to understand what life is all about. There is little doubt that everyone feels the effects of evil in their lives, and look diligently for the influence of some relieving good to counterbalance the evil. All of these structures fail miserably to explain the stress of life that everyone experiences. There is only one plausible, rational, reasonable answer to life's perplexities—a viable relationship with the

One Who has created this world, Who has provided a solution to life's perplexities, Who offers forgiveness for sin and restoration of fellowship between the Creator and His creation.

When everything is over—when this life ends, when this world comes to its ordained end—then everyone will see the Lord of Creation and understand fully what life is all about! It is the divinely ordained struggle between good and evil, led by the forces of Christ on the one side and the forces of Satan on the other. From birth to death, every human being is personally, intimately involved in this lifelong trial.

In the end, God wins, Satan loses. In the end, God's goodness triumphs over Satan's evil. In the end, God's justice will prevail, and evil will be punished. In the end, those who have been washed in the blood of the Lamb sing the song of victory in praise of the Lamb, and those who have rejected the Lamb's sacrifice will suffer terrible torment. The struggle between good and evil will be over. In the new heaven and new earth only God's goodness, graciousness, and mercy are present. Evil no longer exists, no longer troubles the redeemed saints, no longer permeates the environment. The wonder and praise of the eternal God and His Son, Jesus, forevermore forms on the lips of the people He has saved and gives voice to the eternal song: [10]*"Now the salvation and the power and the kingdom of our God and the authority of his Christ have come, for the accuser of our brothers has been thrown down, who accuses them day and night before our God.* [11]*And they have conquered him by the blood of the Lamb and by the word of their testimony, for they loved not their lives even unto death.* [12]*Therefore, rejoice, O heavens and you who dwell in them!" (Revelation 12:10–12).*

REVELATION 13

Revelation 13:1–6

13:1 *I saw a beast coming out of the sea. It had ten horns, seven heads, and ten crowns on its horns. There were insulting names on its heads.*

Who is standing on the sandy beach next to the sea? Who sees the beast coming out of the sea? There is a discrepancy between the end of chapter twelve and the beginning of chapter thirteen, which is very plain when one reviews different translations. Some have added verse eighteen to chapter twelve. Others have moved this phrase to the beginning of chapter thirteen.[1] The antecedent of the pronoun used for "I/he" is not clear. However, chapters and verses were not added to the biblical text until the sixteenth century. Without these arbitrarily imposed divisions, the text reads more smoothly.

The vision introduces a new figure to the unfolding revelation that Jesus is showing to John. It is John to whom Jesus is revealing the events that occur at the end of this age. It is John, therefore, who looks out at the sea and sees this beast arising from its depths. Like the red serpent in chapter twelve, the beast in chapter thirteen has seven heads and ten horns. Unlike the red serpent however, the beast has ten crowns, one on each horn, and words of blasphemy on its heads. The beast emerges following the failure of the red serpent in its endeavor to hurt the woman and to destroy the Child she delivered. The red serpent is furious and sets out to declare war against the children of the woman—those who keep God's commandments and honor the testimony of Jesus Christ (*Revelation 12:17*).

Whatever the case, the description of the beast so closely resembles that of the serpent itself that we must conclude that the beast is Satan's ploy to create a counterfeit entity frightening in its representation of ungodly power. The beast therefore must be interpreted as more than the spirit of antichrist. The beast must also be viewed as a person who will embody all the characteristics of the serpent. He will be the agent through which Satan will carry out his ultimate plot to make war with the saints (*Revelation 12:17*) and make war with the Lord Himself (*Revelation 19:19*). He will achieve some success in his campaign against God's faithful (*Revelation 13:7*), but his efforts against the Lord will be met with total defeat and ultimately lead to his own eternal destruction (*Revelation 19:20; 20:10*).

13:2 *The beast that I saw was like a leopard. Its feet were like bear's feet. Its mouth was like a lion's mouth. The serpent gave its power, kingdom, and far-reaching authority to the beast.*

Many have attributed significance to similarities between the description of this beast and those described in a vision by the prophet Daniel (*Daniel 7:4–6*). However, with a lack of compelling evidence linking the two visions, it is perhaps most practical to recognize that the physical features of this beast are better compared to those found in the animals described. Metaphorically, the beast may rise to power with the great speed of a leopard, exercise his dominion with the brute strength of a bear, and conquer with the ravenous appetite of a lion.

The beast was given its power and position of great authority by the serpent. The beast could do nothing within its own power and was solely reliant upon Satan for the authority and influence that it possessed.

13:3 *One of the beast's heads looked like it had a fatal wound, but its fatal wound was healed. All the people of the world were amazed and followed the beast.*

John sees that one of the beast's heads is mortally wounded. This "head" could be representative of one of the world leaders that reigns under the hierarchy of the beast and under the power of Satan. It is unclear whether this is indeed some supernatural phenomenon precipitated by the power of the serpent (under the sovereignty of God) or whether John's specific use of words should be taken more literally, indicating that this being *appeared* as if "it had a fatal wound." Regardless of the circumstance, the outward effect would be the same. To the public eye, this beast would display its power and authority when it was healed from some fatal injury. This appears to be another instance of Satan mimicking Christ, specifically in this case, healing some otherwise fatal wound.

In response, the entire world would be amazed at the beast's recovery, and out of respect or fear, or perhaps both, people will begin to worship the beast. People have always been amazed at "miraculous" events, interpreting them as signs that the person has some kind of superior power. This usually leads to some sort of worship of that person with little understanding of the true source of the miracle. When Jesus walked among His disciples, He, too, performed miracles, but, because of the unvarnished truth of His message, relatively few followed Him.

The apostle Paul also caught a glimpse of the complete depravity of the human race and the resultant willingness to follow a false god rather than the living God.

> ⁹*The man of sin will come with the power of Satan. He will use every kind of power, including miraculous and wonderful signs. But they will be lies.* ¹⁰*He will use everything that God disapproves of to deceive those who are dying, those who refused to*

> love the truth that would save them. ¹¹That's why God will send
> them a powerful delusion so that they will believe a lie. ¹²Then
> everyone who did not believe the truth, but was delighted with
> what God disapproves of, will be condemned. (2 Thessalonians
> 2:9–12)

**13:4 *They worshiped the serpent because it had given author-
ity to the beast. They also worshiped the beast and said, "Who
is like the beast? Who can fight a war with it?"***

With the miraculous recovery of the beast, the world will be deceived
and follow the beast. The world's inhabitants would first worship the
serpent who empowered the beast. They knew that this "miracle" was
from a power higher than the beast itself. They then also worshiped
the beast, which they now perceived as being all-powerful. Insomuch
as they accepted him as some incarnate manifestation of deity, they
believed that none could ever oppose him. People thought he was invincible, and that no one would dare contradict his authority. War was
out of the question! People began to hope that peace would now reign.
Their worship mocked that of God's people in the Old Testament.[2]
Early in the sojourn of the Hebrew people after God brought them out
of Egypt and brought them safely across the Red Sea, Moses raised his
voice in thanksgiving to God:

> Who is like you among the gods, O Lord? Who is like you? You
> are glorious because of your holiness and awe-inspiring because
> of your splendor. You perform miracles. (Exodus 15:11)

**13:5 *The beast was allowed to speak arrogant and insulting
things. It was given authority to act for 42 months.***

The beast was "allowed to speak," to communicate with people in an
arrogant and insulting tone. More importantly, this phrase indicates
that the beast was subservient to a higher power. Though the details
of his message are not revealed, the message the beast promoted was
blasphemous. By other biblical accounts, it seems likely that his mes-

sage included the proclamation of himself as a god (*Daniel 11:36; 2 Thessalonians 2:3–4*). Everything the beast said would be a lie, but the people of the world would still willingly follow this beast, unaware of his true identity.

The word *act*, as used in this verse, is translated from the Greek word *poieō*, which means "to make or to do."[3] This simply indicates that the beast would only be allowed to carry out these blasphemous acts for a preordained period of forty-two months (three and a half years), a time span which correlates with that mentioned in other passages of Revelation (*Revelation 11:2–3; 12:6, 14*). This mocking, deriding, blasphemous attitude is very similar to the vision that Daniel witnessed six hundred years earlier: "*He will speak against the Most High God, oppress the holy people of the Most High, and plan to change the appointed times and laws. The holy people will be handed over to him for a time, times, and half of a time*" (*Daniel 7:25*).

13:6 *It opened its mouth to insult God, to insult his name and his tent—those who are living in heaven.*

The detail of the beast's blasphemies is disclosed at last. Satan and his beast leveled their insults not only against God but also against any and all things related to God, including the redeemed of heaven. It is generally agreed that the "tent" mentioned in this verse likely refers to heaven and all those who dwell there.[4]

Notes/Applications

As seen in the above passage, the earth is a place where Satan has been allowed limited power in his quest to frustrate, destroy, and divide the work of God and His people. The evil one is not some animator's creation but the very personification of the Evil One, and his primary tool is deception. Satan mimics the miracles and ways of truth in order to possess the hearts and minds of people and destroy their lives. Paul warned the Corinthians: "*Even Satan disguises himself as an angel of light*" (*2 Corinthians 11:14*).

Why is the serpent allowed the authority that he then extends to the beast? In essence, why would God permit this beast to blaspheme His Holy Name, His tabernacle, and those residing in heaven? The answer to this question is not known. It is held within the councils of the eternal God. Nevertheless, the Scriptures are clear. God does allow His adversary to prowl wickedly according to this hideous being's vile nature. Believers can be thankful that this rebellious beast is only permitted to do this for a specified period of time.

The enemy is a mocker and an imposter. Nevertheless, his time is limited, and praise God, his end is in sight. As we study these disturbing chapters of this world's destiny, we cannot forget the promised conclusion. The adversary and his ways are feeble when compared to the power of the all-powerful living God and His Son, our Lord and Savior Jesus Christ. Satan, too, will one day bow to the Holy Father and His Son!

While we, as believing children of God, live during these times when Satan continues to roam as a lion seeking whom he may devour, let us fall on our knees in worship, and ask our Lord God to protect us and hold us safely in the hollow of His hand, redeeming us with the blood of His Son, the Lord Jesus Christ. *"[7]So place yourselves under God's authority. Resist the devil, and he will run away from you. [8]Come close to God, and he will come close to you"* (James 4:7–8).

Revelation 13:7–12

13:7 *It was allowed to wage war against God's holy people and to conquer them. It was also given authority over every tribe, people, language, and nation.*

As we read in the previous chapter, the serpent will wage war against believers throughout the earth because he will be unable to destroy the woman *(Revelation 12:17)*. We now see that the serpent will continue to wage war with the saints on the earth through the authority given to this beast.

During the end times as throughout history, Satan will only be able to do that which is granted to him by the overriding sovereignty of God. Though we understand that the serpent was ordained to wage war against believers through the beast, the manner in which this war will be conducted remains unclear. It might mean physical conflict with full-blown military battles, though this is unlikely unless all the saints band together to form their own communities or forces of resistance. More likely, the war waged against the saints would come in the form of unrelenting persecution, which will result in the deaths of many believers worldwide without regard to nationality, language, or cultural heritage. No matter where they were located throughout the world, all Christians would feel the impact of the beast's persecution against them.

Also, whatever his method, we are told that the beast would not only be given the power to make war with Christians but also the power to *succeed* in this campaign. It will take full advantage of the opportunity given to him by ruling all nations with stern, unrelenting control.

13:8 *Everyone living on earth will worship it, everyone whose name is not written in the Book of Life. That book belongs to the lamb who was slaughtered before the creation of the world.*

This verse shows the means by which the beast would know those who were redeemed. Every living person upon the earth would be required to worship the beast. The only people who would refuse to worship him would be the faithful believers in Christ Jesus. All unbelievers would worship the beast without exception as emphasized by the phrases "everyone living on earth," which distinguishes them from "everyone whose name is not written in the Book of Life." Only those having received the salvation of God's grace have their names written in the Book of Life, and only these would have the power to resist the deceit of the beast. The believers would have the power within them from the indwelling Holy Spirit to be able to withstand this evil command. Those whose spirits are enlightened by the truth given them by the Holy Spirit would see the beast for what he is—an adversary of the Lord Jesus Christ.

The phrase "the Lamb who was slaughtered before the creation of the world" gives insight that could be overlooked by the impact of the first part of the verse. This is another evidence of Jesus' eternal coexistence with the Father and the Spirit. Jesus did not come to earth in the middle of the world's history as a reactionary decision by God to redeem mankind unto Himself. The Lord God had already determined to send His Son as the sacrifice for mankind's sins before the creation of the world. He had determined to send Himself into the world as the solution (Christ's sacrificial atonement) before the problem (the fall of man into sin) ever developed.

13:9 *If anyone has ears, let him listen:*

Similar to the warnings given to the seven churches in chapters two and three, we are again admonished to listen intently to the message of God's revelation to His saints through the apostle John. The "if" implies that not all people possess the spiritual capacity to hear what God is telling His people. All who read this portion of Revelation have been admonished not to simply read but to study, understand, meditate upon, and assimilate the warnings that are given to John by Jesus Christ Himself.

13:10 *If anyone is taken prisoner, he must go to prison. If anyone is killed with a sword, with a sword he must be killed. In this situation God's holy people need endurance and confidence.*

Herein lies a promise given to believers who stand against the fury of the beast. The saints are assured that their endurance in faith and patience would not be in vain. They should not object to their imprisonment or the sacrifice of their lives at the hands of God's enemies. Truth and righteousness will eventually and ultimately prevail. Their captor would eventually be the captive, and those who had killed as part of this war waged against Christians would likewise be killed.

> *How horrible it will be for you, you destroyer, although you haven't been destroyed. How horrible it will be for you, you traitor, although you haven't been betrayed. When you've finished destroying, you will be destroyed. When you've finished being a traitor, you will be betrayed. (Isaiah 33:1)*

This promise would not lessen the agony of the Christians' persecution, but it would serve as assurance in the midst of great suffering that their endurance would be rewarded, and justice would have its day.[5]

13:11 *I saw another beast come from the earth, and it had two horns like a lamb. It talked like a serpent.*

John witnessed the emergence of a second beast, not arising from the sea like the first but from the earth. This beast had two horns like a lamb. It was again a direct reflection of Satan's response to the things of God. This second beast spoke as the serpent because the serpent was the source for all it said and did. Consequently, this meant that he blasphemed and lied just like the serpent, the father of lies. This verse marks the introduction of the second beast, often referred to as the false prophet (*Revelation 16:13, 19:20; 20:10*).

13:12 *The second beast uses all the authority of the first beast in its presence. The second beast makes the earth and those living on it worship the first beast, whose fatal wound was healed.*

The second beast was given the same power as his predecessor, the first beast. Both received their power from Satan but were ultimately allowed to execute their actions only by the sovereign will of God. The second beast directed all the world's inhabitants to worship the first beast, the global figure miraculously restored to life from a mortal wound. Evidently, the false prophet did not promote the worshiping of himself.

The phrasing of this and related verses suggest that this control will be exercised throughout the earth. The entire world system, including all operations of currency, media, and vital provisions, will submit to the control of the first beast at this point, and it should also be expected that all the world's inhabitants will place their trust and loyalties solely upon this individual. This beast functions primarily as the priest to the false god, the first beast. The entire earth will be permeated with a false religion wherein people worship this false god that opposes Jesus Christ and all His saints.

Notes/Applications

Throughout the last few chapters, a clear hierarchy of evil comes sharply into focus. First, the serpent, that is Satan, attempts to destroy the male Child born to the woman. When that fails, he tries to destroy the woman's other children, that is, the saints who have been redeemed by the blood of the Lamb.

When the serpent fails because the Lord protects His people, John sees a beast arising from the sea. That entity is an arrogant, insulting beast who blasphemes the Name of the Most High. Nevertheless, God allows this beast to have his way for a brief period of time. Now, a second beast arises from the land and receives his power and authority from the serpent. The second beast uses that authority to enforce the worship of the first beast, acting something like a high priest to this counterfeit god.

The hierarchy is now complete! Satan, the ultimate authority in all things evil, gives authority to the first beast who wages war against the saints of God. God even allows the first beast to kill many of those who follow Christ. The second beast enforces the worship of the first beast, thereby creating a fully developed religious structure that powerfully influences everyone living on the earth, except those whose names are written in the Book of Life.

Slowly but surely, like a boa constrictor with its prey, the serpent and his appointed representatives tighten their hold on the people of the earth. They relentlessly pursue those whose names are written in the Book of Life, killing them and wrecking havoc among Christ's redeemed people. As the Christians are wiped out, those remaining unbelievers will turn more and more to their worship of the beast. No one can survive the onslaught of the beast's anger. It is better to worship this false god than to die.

Revelation 13:13-18

13:13 *The second beast performs spectacular signs. It even makes fire come down from heaven to earth in front of people.*

The second beast possessed the ability, as did the first beast, to perform incredible wonders. He causes fire to descend upon the earth from the sky, perhaps in the form of lightning. He does this in front of many witnesses in order to deceive them into believing that he is a god worthy of their worship and adoration.

This fire will be a miracle in the eyes of men but not in the eyes of God. It is a deception of Satan that will be very convincing. This is similar to Old Testament accounts where Pharaoh's magicians reproduced several of the miracles that Moses performed (*Exodus 7*).

13:14 *It deceives those living on earth with the signs that it is allowed to do in front of the first beast. It tells those living on earth to make a statue for the beast who was wounded by a sword and yet lived.*

It is evident that this second beast will fool the great majority of the world's population. The miracles the two beasts performed provided persuasive evidence of their power and authority. The second beast becomes increasingly powerful in his function as the high priest for the first beast. After the world has been deceived into worshipping this false god, the people could more easily be convinced to make an idol of the beast who had been wounded by a sword but was still alive.

Because of the conflict between the beast and Christians described in verses seven and eight, we know that the beast is able to deceive only those who did not belong to Christ. Nonetheless, this second beast now orders the people to erect an image of the beast, which further violates the most fundamental aspect of God's Law. This may very well be a test for the Christians living in that day as it was a test that the Lord God put to the Hebrews as they wandered in the wilderness:

> [1]One of your people, claiming to be a prophet or to have prophetic dreams, may predict a miraculous sign or an amazing thing. [2]What he predicts may even take place. But don't listen to that prophet or dreamer if he says, "Let's worship and serve other gods." (Those gods may be gods you've never heard of.) [3]The Lord your God is testing you to find out if you really love him with all your heart and with all your soul. (Deuteronomy 13:1–3)

13:15 *The second beast was allowed to put breath into the statue of the first beast. Then the statue of the first beast could talk and put to death whoever would not worship it.*

As additional evidence of the "miraculous" powers of these servants of Satan, the second beast will be given the power to breathe life into the otherwise lifeless image of the first beast. In yet another effort to undermine God's might and power, Satan would mimic God's miraculous life-giving creation of Adam by giving life to this statue.[6] This inanimate effigy will come to life, speaking and killing anyone who refused to worship it. The second beast will have the power to give life to the idol that had been built, and the idol consequently would be given power to carry out its own part of Satan's plan.

There is no clear indication that this image would be able to cause the deaths of those who refused to worship it simply by wishing it were so. Rather, it seems more likely that there would be a process of "weeding out" the true believers from those who worship this counterfeit god, the first beast.

13:16–17 *[16]The second beast forces all people—important and unimportant people, rich and poor people, free people and slaves—to be branded on their right hands or on their foreheads. [17]It does this so that no one may buy or sell unless he has the brand, which is the beast's name or the number of its name.*

The second beast and its political structure will make it essential for anyone hoping to carry on life's normal activities to receive a specific mark on his right hand or forehead.[7] This mark will be a prerequisite for transacting both personal and professional business. We know that this "decree" will be required of every individual on the earth because the description specifies all classes of people in just a few, short words—small and great, rich and poor, free people and slaves, reflecting people from all political, financial, and social classes. This description further implies that wealth, status, and power will be of no value. Only those who bear the mark of the beast will be provided with the tools necessary to conduct daily business.

On the contrary, anyone who refuses to receive the mark of the beast either on his forehead or on his right hand will not be allowed to buy or sell anything. For believers who stand firm in their faith and refuse to receive the mark, provisions for health and life will be unobtainable through the world system. They will not be able to buy food, clothing, property, services, medical needs, or anything purchased by means of exchange.

This might be the criterion by which the beast discovers those who refuse to worship it. Once the beast finds out that a citizen refuses to receive the mark, he or she will be executed. God is perfectly aware of these dangers, knowing that an innumerable number of His people will be put to death for their testimony about Jesus.

13:18 *In this situation wisdom is needed. Let the person who has insight figure out the number of the beast, because it is a human number. The beast's number is 666.*

We are advised to pay close attention to what John has recorded in these verses. Though we do not yet know the beast's name and probably will not know until further signs of the end times develop, we are clearly given the number that represents the beast. Herein, John offers wisdom, which is given by God for all to read and understand. Those who follow Christ will be able to identify the beast by its number, which is 666. It is perhaps best to trust that the Holy Spirit will intercede and guide us when such wisdom becomes necessary.

Notes/Applications

As the serpent, the first beast, and the second beast continue to centralize their power, as they continue to tighten their hold on everyone on the earth, political, social, and economic structures are put in place to control every aspect of human activity. Underlying the whole scene is the development of a religious structure, accompanied by amazing miracles, convincing people to worship them. People will be completely fooled by these satanic forces, submitting to the worship of this counterfeit god and its economic and social policies.

This is something that Christians should not fight. Nowhere in this revelation are Christ's redeemed encouraged to resist these ungodly developments. Rather, this is the ordained unfolding of scenes that Jesus shows to John. What God has ordained will come to pass! There is no changing of the future, which God has already designed. Instead, believers are asked to discern the times and realize that the time for their final witness has come. They will be restricted from the normal exchange of goods and services, suffering physically and materially by a world system that is designed specifically to expose the believers' relationship to Jesus Christ.

Once that relationship is discovered by the beast, Christians will be put to death. Believers at this time are to submit to the cruelty of the world that has been ordained by God and to die as faithful martyrs to the testimony of their faithful Lord. In this way, believers become an integral part of God's plan to destroy evil.

This is not what most Christians want to hear! But this vision given to John makes it abundantly clear that this is what God has ordained for them. It is not the power of the beast that destroys them. It is the direct result of God's ordained purpose for them.

Christians are never to agree with or endorse the development of false gods and their evil schemes. Rather, they are to simply accept what God has planned for their lives—and their deaths. He has given them life! He has redeemed them from the pit of hell! He brings them home to Himself as martyrs. In all of these circumstances, Christians should submit to their Lord with the song of praise on their lips.

REVELATION 14

Revelation 14:1–7

14:1 *I looked, and the lamb was standing on Mount Zion. There were 144,000 people with him who had his name and his Father's name written on their foreheads.*

What a glorious scene opens this chapter! It is a sharp contrast to the terrible scenes of persecution and corruption that dominated the previous chapter. John saw the Lamb standing upon Mount Zion with the 144,000 that had the seal of God upon their foreheads. There should be little doubt that these 144,000 comprise the same group described earlier in the book *(Revelation 7:4)* and that this Lamb is the Lord Jesus Christ *(Revelation 5:6)*.

The 144,000 have received the seal of God on their foreheads as John has recorded in Revelation 7:1–8. At that time, the 144,000 were on the earth where 12,000 from each tribe of Israel were given this seal of God. Now, however, John sees the same 144,000 in heaven, standing with the Lamb on Mt. Zion.

John has witnessed the dramatically deteriorating conditions on earth where the serpent, the first beast, and the second beast inexorably weave a pattern of religious deception, controlling all aspects of every person on the planet and putting to death those who refuse to worship this counterfeit god. However, the scene in heaven portrays a calm confidence as he sees the Lamb standing on Mt. Zion.

14:2 *Then I heard a sound from heaven like the noise of raging water and the noise of loud thunder. The sound I heard was like the music played by harpists.*

A sound resounds from heaven like the rushing currents of many waters and like the rumbling boom of great thunder. Music played on many harps is interwoven with the sounds of the raging waters and loud thunder (*Revelation 5:8*).

When John first encountered his risen Lord on Patmos at the beginning of this revelation, he heard the voice of Jesus and described it this way: *"His voice was like the sound of raging waters"* (*Revelation 1:15*). Because of the similarity with other passages of Scripture and the relationship with the Lamb in the first verse, this could be interpreted as a metaphor for the voice of Jesus Christ, Who stands on Mt. Zion.

In other Scriptures, similar imagery is used to describe the voice of God:

> I saw the glory of the God of Israel coming from the east. His voice was like the sound of rushing water, and the earth was shining because of his glory. (*Ezekiel 43:2*)

> His body was like beryl. His face looked like lightning. His eyes were like flaming torches. His arms and legs looked like polished bronze. When he spoke, his voice sounded like the roar of a crowd. (*Daniel 10:6*)

> Do you have power like God's? Can you thunder with a voice like his? (*Job 40:9*)

As John watches the scene and hears the music, it seems that the voice of Jesus Christ is mingled with the praise of those who have been

redeemed. The entire atmosphere is charged with the sound of praise
as the Lamb speaks and His people reply with praise.

14:3 *They were singing a new song in front of the throne, the
four living creatures, and the leaders. Only the 144,000 people
who had been bought on earth could learn the song.*

The assembly of 144,000 was heard singing a song of praise to the
Lord God and unto the Lamb. It was a song that was exclusive to this
group. No one else could understand it or learn it. The song was solely
created for and sung by the 144,000 that had been protected from the
effects of God's judgment visited upon those who had rebelled against
the Lord. They were aptly called the "people who had been bought on
earth," indicating that they were regular men who had lived on earth.
This verse provides additional confirmation of the special relationship
that this group of people have with the Lord and of their distinguished
importance to Him.

14:4 *These 144,000 virgins are pure. They follow the lamb
wherever he goes. They were bought from among humanity as
the first ones offered to God and to the lamb.*

The specific characteristics of these 144,000 are explained more fully.
These people are described as "pure," that is sexually pure. Also the
masculine use of the Greek word *parthenoi* is translated as "*virgin.*"[1]
Most other translations say that these 144,000 had not defiled themselves with women. It is pretty clear from these translations that these
144,000 were men, who were literally virgins who had never had any
carnal relationships with women. It is equally clear that this characteristic was a part of their personal makeup that was given to them by
God, their Creator. Because of their special position they are brought
into a special relationship with Jesus Christ, following Him wherever
He goes.

Again, we are told that these 144,000 were redeemed from among
mankind in the world. Much is made of their being called the "first

194 Revelation: *Tribulation and Triumph*

ones offered to God and to the Lamb." Such a description would seem to indicate that this group of 144,000 cannot comprise the entire sum of the redeemed upon the earth, as some have indicated, for by the word's very definition, the implication is that those included in this group are but the first group gathered at harvest time and presented to the Lord as consecrated or set apart.[2]

14:5 *They've never told a lie. They are blameless.*

In the original language this verse actually goes a step further than to merely say that these people did not lie, though that is certainly true. The meaning here expresses the idea that they do not stretch the truth, cleverly avoid the truth, or even say truthful things that give false impressions. Nothing except truth comes from their mouths. They stood faultless before God, though not suggesting that they are without sin, but as all Christians, they will be justified by the redemptive work of the Lord Jesus Christ on the Cross of Calvary.

14:6–7 *[6]I saw another angel flying overhead with the everlasting Good News to spread to those who live on earth—to every nation, tribe, language, and people. [7]The angel said in a loud voice, "Fear God and give him glory, because the time has come for him to judge. Worship the one who made heaven and earth, the sea and springs."*

This angel will fly over the earth preaching the everlasting Gospel to all people of every nationality and tongue on earth. When Jesus discussed future events with His disciples as they looked across the Kidron Valley at the temple gleaming in the sun, He told them that there would be wars, famines, earthquakes, and pestilence. However, this was not the end. The end would come only after the Gospel was proclaimed to every human being on the earth, regardless of language, national, or cultural barriers (*Matthew 24:14*). This may be the fulfillment of that prophecy. The messenger's purpose was to declare the truth of Jesus Christ to those who were still alive. Previous judgments had already wiped out half the earth's population. Those that were left still refused to repent.

Some commentators have hinted that this moment reveals one last opportunity for repentance and one last offer of salvation to the inhabitants of earth.[3] However, in context of this chapter and in light of the events that follow, it seems more likely that this is a pronouncement of judgment and not one of hope.[4] We have already witnessed how the reprobate of the earth will refuse to repent even when they realize that the horrendous events experienced are a result of the direct judgment of God *(Revelation 9:20–21)*. Even after this angel's task is completed, there is still a noticeable lack of response. There is no record of any people repenting and receiving salvation and redemption. By both the tone of the message and the context in which it was written, it can be assumed that this "everlasting Good News" message that was preached did not accompany an invitation to which the earth's population could respond.

The angel proclaimed two unshakeable statements: first, everyone should fear God, and second, everyone should worship God. In the face of the beast's undeniable dominance of the world's population, this angel directs the attention of this reprobate population to recognize that there is One greater than the beast. Nevertheless, the angel is not offering salvation so much as telling a rebellious people one more time to fear God and worship Him. Whether they agree is unimportant, because when all is over, that is exactly what they will do even as they enter the gates of hell.

Notes/Applications

The Good News is the central message of the entire Bible. From Genesis to Revelation the redeeming work of the eternal God is carefully unfolded and revealed to mankind. It is the theme of Exodus, the recurring story of the Book of Judges, the promise of the prophets. Central to this overarching message of the Scriptures is the atoning sacrifice of Jesus Christ on the Cross of Calvary, affirmed and confirmed by His resurrection. The story of God's redeeming work concludes in

John's vision while exiled on the island of Patmos. Here we read the consummation of what God has done throughout history and what He will do throughout eternity.

Now the Lamb stands on Mt. Zion, surrounded by 144,000 redeemed saints in a scene of unsurpassed beauty. The Lamb speaks and His voice rumbles like thunder across the heavens. The 144,000 respond with a song of quiet, yet uplifting praise to God and the Lamb. In this atmosphere of doxology, an angel appears, flying over the earth pronouncing the Good News to everyone remaining on the earth.

What is the Good News? Many Christians believe that it is the story of Jesus and His atoning sacrifice. That is absolutely true! But it is only half of the message. The Word of God also shows mankind that God is just, righteous, and holy. Therefore, the sacrifice of Jesus for the penalty of our sin is great Good News, and the just punishment of sinners who refuse His sacrifice is equally a part of the Good News.

This passage reveals the presentation of the Good News, not in the light of God's salvation through Jesus Christ, but in the light of the Lamb's judgment on a people who have denied the God Who created them and the Savior Who died to offer them the gift of God's salvation.

Even though these people will never respond to the saving Good News, God will visit them with His judgment. That is what the angel loudly proclaims across the earth: *"Fear God and give Him glory, because the time has come for Him to judge. Worship the One Who made heaven and earth, the sea and springs"* (Revelation 14:7). In this proclamation, there is no invitation to respond to the saving Lord. Rather, it is time for God to judge.

God's judgment is absolutely just without preference or animosity. Everyone will hear the Good News. Some will hear the message with thanksgiving for His salvation. Most will hear the message with the pronouncement of His judgment. God is absolutely good and absolutely right in both aspects of His saving, judging message. Whether a person believes what God has done for them has absolutely no impact on the message or on the inevitability of God's action. At some time in the future, when the angel declares the Good News of God's judgment, everyone, even those who hate God, will bow the knee, fear the Lord, and worship the One Who is greater than the beast, greater than the serpent, greater than evil. *"[10]At the name of Jesus everyone in heaven, on earth, and in the world below will kneel [11]and confess that Jesus Christ is Lord to the glory of God the Father"* (Philippians 2:10–11).

Revelation 14:8–13

14:8 *Another angel, a second one, followed him, and said, "Fallen! Babylon the Great has fallen! She has made all the nations drink the wine of her passionate sexual sins."*

A second angel immediately followed, and like the first angel, his message is presented to every person throughout the earth. Though it is not the Gospel message (like that of the first angel), it is a message of doom for unbelievers: "Babylon is fallen." The godless world system is disintegrating.[5] Despite the misplaced confidence in the beast by the people of the entire world, God is about to bring the whole thing down by His unfailing justice.

This message is a proclamation of judgment against those who participate in the alluring ways of the world and succumb to its temptations. The population of the world will become saturated with sexual sins of all types, boldly defying the perfect design of the Creator. This will be accomplished through idolatry as demonstrated in wholesale worship of the beast.

The imagery that John uses is very similar to the imagery used by Jeremiah, the prophet of Judah, as he watched his nation disintegrate under the onslaught of the Babylonian invasion ordained by God for the sins of Judah.

> [6]*Run away from Babylon! Run for your lives! You shouldn't die because of Babylon's crimes. This is the time for the vengeance of the Lord. He will pay the people of Babylon back for what they have done.* [7]*Babylon was a golden cup in the Lord's hand. It made the whole world drunk. The nations drank its wine. That is why the nations have gone insane.* [8]*Babylon will suddenly fall and be shattered.* (Jeremiah 51:6–8)

14:9–11 [9]*Another angel, a third one, followed them, and said in a loud voice, "Whoever worships the beast or its statue, whoever is branded on his forehead or his hand,* [10]*will drink the wine of God's fury, which has been poured unmixed into* *the cup of God's anger. Then he will be tortured by fiery sulfur in the presence of the holy angels and the lamb. ¹¹The smoke from their torture will go up forever and ever. There will be no rest day or night for those who worship the beast or its statue, or for anyone branded with its name."*

A third angel follows with another proclamation of frightening judgment and inescapable condemnation. Like the two angels before him, this angel also speaks with a loud voice addressing all those who worship the beast and bear its image on their right hands or foreheads. This applies to everyone on the face of the earth except for the redeemed (*Revelation 13:12, 16*).

The angel's message is a promise, though not a very favorable one for those being addressed. Without exception, all who worship the beast and receive its mark would experience the full measure of God's wrath. The description of this wrath being "poured unmixed into the cup of God's anger" shows the intensity at which this judgment will ultimately be delivered. It will not be tempered for any reason, but will be dispensed in full measure at full strength. John's vision of God's unswerving judgment is the fulfillment of prophecy that was written one thousand years before the birth of Christ.

> A cup is in the Lord's hand. (Its foaming wine is thoroughly mixed with spices.) He will empty it, and all the wicked people on earth will have to drink every last drop. (Psalm 75:8)

> He rains down fire and burning sulfur upon wicked people. He makes them drink from a cup filled with scorching wind. (Psalm 11:6)

These people will be tormented with fire and brimstone in the presence of the Lord Jesus Christ and in the presence of His holy angels. God's anger at the depravity of the human race is so intense that He and the host of heaven will watch the torture of the condemned.

The fire and brimstone will never burn out or fade away but will burn forever without being quenched. There will not be even one moment of relief for those who had worshiped the beast and had accepted his mark in their right hands or foreheads. The mark, once accepted, could never be erased. To accept the mark of the beast was to accept eternal damnation.[6]

14:12 *In this situation God's holy people, who obey his commands and keep their faith in Jesus, need endurance.*

Throughout this period of intense persecution, Christians are faced with the loss of purchasing access, material possessions, and the voice to object. Slowly but surely, the beast strips them of every asset necessary to sustain human life. In its intense hatred of the living God and those who belong to God, the beast will attempt to eradicate these people who kindle its anger. There seems to be no way that any sensible believer could remain faithful with such intense hostility.

Nevertheless, John, who witnesses the entire circumstance, encourages believers to remain strong despite their obviously threatening situation. In this environment of openly expressed hostility toward God's saints, John encourages them to remain strong, to persevere, and to endure the hardship as good soldiers of Jesus Christ.

One of the encouragements that helps to sustain believers is the promise that, even though they die, they will live to see the torment of those who have tortured them and put them to death (*vv. 9–11*).

14:13 *I heard a voice from heaven saying, "Write this: From now on those who die believing in the Lord are blessed." "Yes," says the Spirit. "Let them rest from their hard work. What they have done goes with them."*

John hears a voice speaking to him from heaven, and the voice instructs him to record what the voice tells him. John obeys and writes: "From now on those who die believing in the Lord are blessed." The Holy Spirit confirms that these believers will finally have rest in heaven from the rigors of their labors and hard life they had endured. This should not suggest that those who had previously been martyred for the cause of Christ were not equally blessed. We know from earlier chapters that they, too, already possessed their reward in heaven and were simply awaiting the Lord's final judgment upon those who took their lives.

> ⁹When the lamb opened the fifth seal, I saw under the altar the souls of those who had been slaughtered because of God's word and the testimony they had given about him. ¹⁰They cried out in a loud voice, "Holy and true Master, how long before you judge and take revenge on those living on earth who shed our blood?" ¹¹Each of the souls was given a white robe. They were told to rest a little longer until all their coworkers, the other Christians, would be killed as they had been killed. (Revelation 6:9–11)

Notes/Applications

The scene unfolding before John is remarkable in the description of the context in which these events take place. John's vision takes place in the framework of worship—the Lamb stands upon Mt. Zion and the 144,000 sing a hymn that is known only to them.

In that environment, three angels make progressively worsening announcements to all the inhabitants of the earth. The first presents the Good News, not in the context of God's salvation, but in the framework of God's judgment. The second declares the disintegration of the world's religious, political, economic, and social structures. The third angel pronounces inescapable judgment on those who have received the mark of the beast, revealing an intensity of God's wrath so violent that it is difficult to grasp with the human mind. It is hard to imagine that God and the Lamb, along with His holy angels, will watch the torment of those who have received the mark of the beast.

Nevertheless, we should understand that God's anger is kindled, not simply because unbelievers have refused to accept His salvation, but because they willfully and deliberately accepted the beast's deception and worshiped the beast's statue. This is idolatry of such immense proportions that God's righteousness and holiness kindles His intense anger. The Lord has done everything possible for the lost race of mankind, giving His only Son to accept the penalty of people's sin and rebellion. What more could He possibly do?

Inevitably, John's vision eradicates the foolishness of the human race, choosing to live in a world where contradictory perceptions and philosophies exist side by side, as though by human confusion we can make excuses for our failure to believe what God has clearly said. All the gray areas in which mankind chooses to live are erased. In truth, these gray areas have never existed. The absolute, clearly revealed message of the Scriptures shows that there are only two paths by which God directs people's lives—the path of His salvation or the path of His condemnation.

Cast against the backdrop of these dreadful details concerning the spiritual fate of those who will accept the mark of the beast, the Lord offers encouragement to the members of His body who will suffer horribly for His name by refusing to submit to the beast's mark. He will see their sorrow and remember their commitment; they will be blessed for their faithfulness. Their lives will leave His mark, the mark of God and His Lamb—a legacy of His Gospel message, His power, and His authority. In sharp contrast to the condemnation of unbelievers, God's saints are invited to His throne to rest from their labors and enter into the joy of their Lord.

Revelation 14:14–20

14:14 *Then I looked, and there was a white cloud, and on the cloud sat someone who was like the Son of Man. He had a gold crown on his head and a sharp sickle in his hand.*

John watched as three angels made their proclamations to the entire world population. Their messages predicted the consequences of rebellion against the sovereign God—an outpouring of God's wrath of frightening intensity.

Now John's attention was drawn toward a white cloud. Seated on the cloud was the regal figure of someone like the Son of Man. The term Son of Man is the phrase most used by Jesus during His ministry among the twelve men He chose to accompany Him. John certainly knew what the Son of Man looked like and he certainly recognized that he was now looking at Jesus, not as He was when He walked among His disciples, but now clothed in the splendor of a royal king, His head bearing a golden crown. However, rather than a royal scepter carried by earthly kings signifying their authority to rule, Jesus carried a sickle. It seems as though this King does not need a scepter to show His authority, but a sickle, showing that He was ready to initiate some action.

14:15 *Another angel came out of the temple. He cried out in a loud voice to the one who sat on the cloud, "Swing your sickle, and gather the harvest. The time has come to gather it, because the harvest on the earth is overripe."*

An angel appears from within the temple in heaven and calls out to the Lord Jesus, Who is sitting on the cloud with the sickle in His hand. The angel tells the Son of Man that the time has come to reap the harvest that is on the earth. It is not clear who or what is the specific object of this harvest. Nevertheless, the Lord had waited long enough. The time had come and the Lord is equipped to reap the harvest that is already overripe.

204 Revelation: *Tribulation and Triumph*

John's vision follows the normal pattern in which angels both respond to the Lord's commands or announce the events that are about to come to pass. Here the angel makes the announcement to Jesus, Who is seated as King on a white cloud. The angel has the responsibility to make the announcement, but the Lord Himself is the only One authorized to actually reap the harvest. He is the One offended by the rebellion of the unsaved. He alone is the One embraced by the ones He has saved.

14:16 *The one who sat on the cloud swung his sickle over the earth, and the harvesting of the earth was completed.*

John then watches as the Son of Man swings His sickle over the entire earth. Though their identity is not clearly stated, it seems most reasonable to conclude that this first harvest reaped by the Son of Man may consist of believers that remain on the earth.[7] This group, however, does not include the 144,000. They are already in heaven as this chapter states in its opening verse. This group that is harvested, therefore, possibly consists of the remaining believers living in their physical bodies on the earth that will complete heaven's population. This is likely a vision that shows the Lord gathering His own unto Himself before the final judgment.[8] There is a sense in which this is the fulfillment of prophecy spoken by John the Baptizer when he described Jesus, the One Who was to follow him: *"His winnowing shovel is in his hand to clean up his threshing floor. He will gather the wheat into his barn, but he will burn the husks in a fire that can never be put out"* (Luke 3:17).

14:17 *Another angel came out of the temple in heaven. He, too, had a sharp sickle.*

Many commentators suggest that this reflects the harvest of judgment described in verses seventeen through twenty, and that this entire chapter depicts only one event—the judgment of the wicked.[9] However, the specific wording seems to indicate otherwise. The phrase "another angel" expresses a different subject, and the phrase "He, too, had . . ." expresses similarity but not equivalence.

Another angel emerges from within the temple of heaven, and he, too, carries a sharp sickle similar to that used by the Son of Man seated upon the cloud. All of God's angels are at His command to do His will as He requires. In this case, the angel is appointed to help carry out God's judgment upon the wicked.

14:18 *Yet another angel came from the altar with authority over fire. This angel called out in a loud voice to the angel with the sharp sickle, "Swing your sickle, and gather the bunches of grapes from the vine of the earth, because those grapes are ripe."*

Another angel emerges from the altar in heaven. This angel, whom God has given the power over fire, calls from the altar with a loud voice to the angel that had just emerged from the temple with a sharp sickle. He told the angel to swing his sickle across the entire earth in the same manner as the Son of Man had just done. The angel instructs the angel with the sickle to "gather the clusters of the vine of the earth" because the harvest was ripe. As the prophet Joel received his vision of the Day of the Lord, he also witnessed an event that closely resembled what John saw:

> Cut them down like grain. The harvest is ripe. Stomp on them as you would stomp on grapes. The winepress is full. The vats overflow. The nations are very wicked. (Joel 3:13)

The implication in the remaining verses of this chapter is that the Lord had already gathered His redeemed from the earth and that the angel with the sickle is to reap those that remain. Had the Lord already harvested every person from the earth in His righteous judgment, there would be no need for a subsequent harvest. Therefore, by the evidence of what awaits those harvested by the second angel, the conclusion can be drawn that the Lord had already harvested those belonging to Him. All that remains after the first harvest are the unbelievers for whom, as later verses specify, the wrath of God had been prepared. This is the event that Jesus may have alluded to when He spoke to His disciples about the judgment that He would one day dispense upon the earth:

> [30]"*Let both [the weeds and the grain] grow together until the harvest. When the grain is cut, I will tell the workers to gather the weeds first and tie them in bundles to be burned. But I'll have them bring the wheat into my barn....* " [38]*The field is the world. The good seeds are those who belong to the kingdom. The weeds are those who belong to the evil one.* [39]*The enemy who planted them is the devil. The harvest is the end of the world. The workers are angels.* [40]*Just as weeds are gathered and burned, so it will be at the end of time.* [41]*The Son of Man will send his angels. They will gather everything in his kingdom that causes people to sin and everyone who does evil.* [42]*The angels will throw them into a blazing furnace. People will cry and be in extreme pain there.* (Matthew 13:30, 38–42)*

14:19 *The angel swung his sickle on the earth and gathered the grapes from the vine of the earth. He threw them into the winepress of God's anger.*

John watches in amazement as the second angel fulfills that which he had been instructed to do. The angel swings his sickle across the entire earth, gathered up all that remained upon it, and then cast them "into the winepress of God's anger." Evidently, the angel did not kill these people but gathered them together for the purpose of executing the sentence that had already been prepared for them at the direction of the Lord God.

14:20 *The grapes were trampled in the winepress outside the city. Blood flowed out of the winepress as high as a horse's bridle for 1,600 stadia.*

The location where this second harvest is gathered, referred to as the "winepress," is "outside the city," likely the same city that is mentioned frequently throughout Revelation—Jerusalem. This seems to have been done so that the sanctity of the city would not be violated (*Leviticus 24:14; Numbers 5:1–3; Matthew 27:31; Acts 7:58; Hebrews 13:12*). When the souls have been thrown into the winepress of God's anger, there will be so much blood that it will reach the height of horses' bridles for a distance spanning sixteen hundred furlongs or about 180 miles.[10] This vividly illustrates a complete slaughter of the unrighteous in which no trace of hope, peace, or relief could be found. With this, we approach a doorstep in the text where we will cross the threshold to the end of the world as we know it. This, too, seems to be a fulfillment of prophecy as seen through the eyes of Isaiah:

> *3I have trampled alone in the winepress.*
> *No one was with me.*
> *In my anger I trampled on people.*
> *In my wrath I stomped on them.*
> *Their blood splattered my clothes*
> *so all my clothing has been stained*
>
> *4I planned the day of vengeance.*
> *The year for my reclaiming you has come.*
>
> *5I looked, but there was no help.*
> *I was astounded that there was no outside support.*
> *So with my own power I won a victory.*
> *My anger supported me.*
>
> *6In my anger I trampled on people.*
> *In my wrath I made them drunk*
> *and poured their blood on the ground. (Isaiah 63:3–6)*

Notes/Applications

During the earth's final days, the world's population will experience unimaginable pain, suffering, and agony in the great winepress of the Holy God.

But the Lord is the only God. He is the living God and eternal king. The earth trembles when he is angry. The nations can't endure his fury. (Jeremiah 10:10)

The Lord will make his majestic voice heard. He will come down with all his might, with furious anger, with fire storms, windstorms, rainstorms, and hailstones. (Isaiah 30:30)

God's wrath is a righteous reply to man's willful disobedience and refusal to repent and worship Him as the only true and living God. God's wrath is not an act of revenge but an expression of His holiness. God will punish the sinful and will ultimately abolish sin.

Man more readily embraces a God Who loves while rejecting a God Who is holy and just. God's wrath, however, should not be juxtaposed against His love. Both are completely integrated attributes of His eternal being. It is not something that can be measured in any quantitative sense. He has as much love as He has anger; He *is* as much love as He is righteousness. Man's difficulty in surrendering to such a God, the true God, lies in his refusal to admit his sin and need for restoration. The very God Who pours out His wrath against evil is the same God Who poured out His Son as the means to restore His rebellious creation.

If we turn away from looking at God's wrath, we set up an idol—a god with a frail and incomplete nature, and in so doing, we negate what the Cross was all about. We cannot accept a portion of God's character and deny any other aspect of His eternal Being.

Paul, God's appointed apostle to the Gentiles of his day, understood this very well. He explained the fully integrated nature of God, showing both His mercy and His righteousness, both giving reason and validation to His judgment.

³When you judge people for doing these things but then do them yourself, do you think you will escape God's judgment? ⁴Do you have contempt for God, who is very kind to you, puts up with you, and deals patiently with you? Don't you realize that it is God's kindness that is trying to lead you to him and change the

*way you think and act? ⁵Since you are stubborn and don't want
to change the way you think and act, you are adding to the anger
that God will have against you on that day when God vents his
anger. At that time God will reveal that his decisions are fair.
⁶He will pay all people back for what they have done. ⁷He will
give everlasting life to those who search for glory, honor, and im-
mortality by persisting in doing what is good. But he will bring
⁸anger and fury on those who, in selfish pride, refuse to believe
the truth and who follow what is wrong. ⁹There will be suffering and distress for every person who does evil, for Jews first and
Greeks as well. (Romans 2:3–9)*

It is difficult to read the Book of Revelation and not realize the
frightening events targeting believers by the forces of evil. Likewise,
John's vision alerts unbelievers to the wrath of God that is so vividly
described. The Book of Revelation and the intensity of its prophecies
concerning God's destruction of unbelievers is as certain as is death
itself.

This entire revelation given to John by Jesus is not a message
that invites repentance and restoration. Rather, it is a message that
provides knowledge of what will happen when the Lord's patience is
exhausted and the time of His judgment comes. Alternatives do not
exist here. There is no changing the course of events since they have
already been determined within the counsel of the eternal God. It is
what it is! It cannot and will not be changed!

Thus, this revelation is simply the unveiling of the grandeur of
God's dwelling place and, at one and the same time, the horror that
awaits those who live outside the fold of God's redemption. So it is
written! So it will be done!

REVELATION 15

Revelation 15:1–8

15:1 *I saw another sign in heaven. It was spectacular and amazing. There were seven angels with the last seven plagues which are the final expression of God's anger.*

Chapter fifteen introduces the last series of plagues, showing the final wrath of God visited upon those who hate God and defy both His salvation and His righteous judgment. Read in context, it appears that these seven bowls of God's wrath are a detailed account of the "winepress of God's anger" that concluded the previous chapter.

John witnessed another "spectacular and amazing" sign in heaven, making him fully aware of the terrible significance of these visions. "Spectacular and amazing" does not imply that the sign was a good thing but that it was a momentous and critical event. John saw seven angels in heaven, each having one of the last seven plagues to afflict all mankind left on the earth, those prepared for the winepress of God's fury. Each of these plagues is filled up with God's wrath, which had come due because the world's iniquities had reached its full measure.

John's vision confirms other Old Testament prophecies given to God's chosen scribes under the direction of the Holy Spirit:

> ¹⁵*That day will be a day of overflowing fury,*
> *a day of trouble and distress,*
> *a day of devastation and desolation,*
> *a day of darkness and gloom,*
> *a day of clouds and overcast skies,*
>
> ¹⁶*a day of rams' horns and battle cries*
> *against the fortified cities*
> *and against the high corner towers.*
>
> ¹⁷*"I will bring such distress on humans that they will walk like they are blind,*
> *because they have sinned against the Lord."*
> *Their blood will be poured out like dust*
> *and their intestines like manure.*
>
> ¹⁸*Their silver and their gold will not be able to rescue them*
> *on the day of the Lord's overflowing fury.*
> *The whole earth will be consumed by his fiery anger,*
> *because he will put an end, a frightening end,*
> *to those who live on earth.* (Zephaniah 1:15–18)

DIG DEEPER: *The Anger of God*

This term appears only ten times in Scripture, and two of those times occur in this chapter (*vv. 1 and 7*). There is only one occurrence in the Old Testament (*Psalm 78:31*). Throughout the Book of Revelation, however, the theme appears five times, indicating that God's patient lovingkindness does reach a point when He no longer will tolerate the rebellion of the human race. This does not mean that God is at one moment loving and the next moment angry. Both aspects of His eternal Being have been and always will be present. From the opening chapters of Scripture, God offers His love to the human race, and, at the same time, warns of His anger if He is not obeyed. Jesus laid out the terms of His covenant in clear, concise terms: *"Whoever believes in the Son has eternal life, but whoever rejects the Son will not see life. Instead, he will see God's constant anger" (John 3:36).*

15:2 *Then I saw what looked like a sea of glass mixed with fire. Those who had won the victory over the beast, its statue, and the number of its name were standing on the glassy sea. They were holding God's harps*

John saw what he could only describe as a "sea of glass mixed with fire." According to previous accounts in Revelation, this "sea of glass" is around the throne of God in heaven. *"In front of the throne, there was something like a sea of glass as clear as crystal. In the center near the throne and around the throne were four living creatures covered with eyes in front and in back" (Revelation 4:6).* On this crystalline sea stand the redeemed who have refused to worship the beast, or the statue erected in its honor. They also defied the worship of this counterfeit god by refusing to bear its mark or number. John also noted that they are holding God's harps, praising God with the tune arising from their instruments.

15:3–4 *³and singing the song of God's servant Moses and the song of the lamb. They sang, "The things you do are spectacular and amazing, Lord God Almighty. The way you do them is fair and true, King of the Nations. ⁴Lord, who won't fear and praise your name? You are the only holy one, and all the nations will come to worship you because they know about your fair judgments."*

John saw these martyred saints singing as they played their harps. This is a song that is specifically meant for them to sing, much as the 144,000 had their own song to sing. They sing "the song of God's servant Moses." *"Then Moses and the Israelites sang this song to the Lord: 'I will sing to the Lord. He has won a glorious victory. He has thrown horses and their riders into the sea'"* (Exodus 15:1). This song seems to be their response of praise to the Lord for His decisive and overwhelming victory. Even more so, it appears that they magnified the Lord for His mercy and deliverance of His faithful ones from the times of Moses throughout history, even to the consummation of the Lamb's final judgment.[1] Their song proclaims God's ways to be "just and true," and they address Him as the "King of the saints." In declaring at the onset of God's final wrath that His ways are just and true, they acknowledged the perfection of God's justice for the consequences of man's sin.

The praise of God continued in heaven. In a sense, these saints pose a rhetorical question toward both those in heaven and those on earth by asking, "Who won't fear and praise your name?" The word *fear* implies more than mere reverence. It literally expresses dread and horror.[2]

> *Everyone fears you, O King of the Nations. This is what you deserve. No one is like you among all the wise people in the nations or in all their kingdoms.* (Jeremiah 10:7)

Their song also declared that all nations will worship the one and only living God. The use of the verb *will* indicates that this was, even at this moment of rejoicing, a future and ongoing occurrence. The saints also proclaim that God's judgments had been made known to everyone. Every person on earth will finally realize that the suffering he or she experienced was, in truth, the wrath of God and His direct judgment on all people for its impenitent sinfulness.

15:5–6 *[5]After these things I looked, and I saw that the temple of the tent containing the words of God's promise was open in heaven. [6]The seven angels with the seven plagues came out of the temple wearing clean, shining linen with gold belts around their waists.*

John saw that the temple of the Lord in heaven was open. This is the same temple mentioned throughout Revelation and the same one from which the three angels in chapter fourteen emerged. The heavenly temple was first mentioned after the sounding of the seventh trumpet. *"God's temple in heaven was opened, and the ark of his promise was seen inside his temple. There was lightning, noise, thunder, an earthquake, and heavy hail" (Revelation 11:19).*

Seven angels emerge from within the temple, each possessing a plague from God to pour out on earth's rebellious inhabitants. The angels wear pure white linen, and their chests are adorned in gold. There seems to be some similarity to the descriptions of these angels' attire and that of the Old Testament priests *(Exodus 28:22–26; Ezekiel 44:17).*

15:7 *One of the four living creatures gave seven gold bowls full of the anger of God, who lives forever and ever, to the seven angels.*

Each of the seven angels that emerged from the heavenly temple will be given one of seven golden bowls that contain the wrath of God. The bowls will be given to the seven angels by one of the four beasts near God's throne *(Revelation 4:6).* The golden bowls are filled to the brim with different plagues full of God's wrath—the holy and righteousness judgment of God on all those who accepted the mark of the beast.

John acknowledged the eternality of God's Being where he states that God, the one and only living God, is the One "Who lives forever and ever."

15:8 *The temple was filled with smoke from the glory of God and his power. No one could enter the temple until the seven plagues of the seven angels came to an end.*

The temple in heaven will be filled with "smoke from the glory of God and from His power." Biblically, smoke often foreshadows the awesome presence of God, as was the case at Mount Sinai. *"All of Mount Sinai was covered with smoke because the Lord had come down on it in fire. Smoke rose from the mountain like the smoke from a kiln, and the whole mountain shook violently" (Exodus 19:18).* Similarly, Isaiah saw smoke in the temple as God pronounced judgment upon the nation of Israel. *"Their voices shook the foundations of the doorposts, and the temple filled with smoke" (Isaiah 6:4)*. The significance of smoke appears eleven other times in the Book of Revelation. In this instance, the smoke of God's glory and power fill the temple, this time seen in His righteous judgment, so that no other creature could enter until the seven golden bowls of God's wrath had been completely poured out by the seven angels.

Notes/Applications

Chapter fifteen begins to offer a more detailed account of the manner in which the wrath of God will continue to be unleashed on the remaining inhabitants of the earth as foretold at the end of chapter fourteen. It is the introduction to the final phase of God's punishment on those who defy His authority, even though they know that the punishment they receive comes from Him. A grim, sad picture develops quickly as the Lord prepares to dispense the just rewards of His final judgment. As we will see, this dismal prologue to the imminent wrath of God is not to be dismissed lightly. It is the calculated design of the sovereign God to end the rule of sin and evil in the world that He had created.

Many people tend to wonder why a loving God could cause so much destruction and judgment. It would be better to ask why our perfect and holy Creator has not destroyed this sinful, wayward world long before now. God's holiness demands justice, yet every moment that passes without His judgment is an act of incomprehensible, enduring mercy. The apostle Peter interpreted God's patience in his letter to early Christians: *"⁸Dear friends, don't ignore this fact: One day with the Lord is like a thousand years, and a thousand years are like one day. ⁹The Lord isn't slow to do what He promised, as some people think. Rather, He is patient for your sake. He doesn't want to destroy anyone but wants all people to have an opportunity to turn to Him and change the way they think and act"* (2 Peter 3:8–9).

Nevertheless, a day of reckoning approaches, a day of complete victory over the beast, his image, his mark, and his number. The single hope for man to be delivered from God's judgment is an undeserved gift given to those He has chosen to save only on the terms established by God through the means that He has already provided—the Lord Jesus Christ. Praise God for His mercy toward those who are turned from their rebellion and believe in Him!

REVELATION 16

Revelation 16:1–7

16:1 *I heard a loud voice from the temple saying to the seven angels, "Pour the seven bowls of God's anger over the earth."*

A great voice was heard from the temple that orders the seven angels to fulfill their tasks. It can be presumed with relative certainty that this was the voice of God since we know from the last verse of chapter fifteen that no one could enter the temple that was filled with the smoke of God's glory and power. God sent each of the angels to complete His all-encompassing wrath and final judgment upon those who worshiped the beast and allowed its mark to be placed on their foreheads or on their right hands. It was perfect and fitting justice that the world deserved for its sin.

Each developing segment of God's judgment will increase in its intensity as the end of the age approaches until finally, these seven bowls of wrath complete the purpose of God's justice.

16:2 *The first angel poured his bowl over the earth. Horrible, painful sores appeared on the people who had the brand of the beast and worshiped its statue.*

The first angel poured out his first bowl of wrath upon the earth. Immediately, those bearing the mark of the beast were inflicted with "horrible, painful sores." This first bowl of wrath resembles the sixth plague against Pharaoh and Egypt by God through Moses.

> *⁸Then the Lord said to Moses and Aaron, "Take a handful of ashes from a kiln, and have Moses throw them up in the air as Pharaoh watches. ⁹They will become a fine dust throughout Egypt. The dust will cause boils to break into open sores on people and animals throughout Egypt." ¹⁰They took ashes from a kiln and stood in front of Pharaoh. Moses threw the ashes up in the air, and they caused boils to break into open sores on people and animals. ¹¹The magicians couldn't compete with Moses because they had boils like all the other Egyptians. (Exodus 9:8–11)*

16:3 *The second angel poured his bowl over the sea. The sea turned into blood like the blood of a dead man, and every living thing in the sea died.*

The second angel poured out his bowl of wrath into the sea, and all of the world's oceans and seas turned into blood like the blood of a dead man, causing the death of every living thing in those waters.

It is obvious that this plague is far worse than the previous judgment of the second trumpet, in which only a third of the world's seas were turned into blood and only a third of the living creatures within the seas were killed. "*⁸When the second angel blew his trumpet, something like a huge mountain burning with fire was thrown into the sea. One-third of the sea turned into blood, ⁹one-third of the creatures that were living in the sea died, and one-third of the ships were destroyed*" (Revelation 8:8–9).

This plague is far more comprehensive than the previous plague both in the scope of its coverage and in the composition of the blood that strangulates every living thing. The blood of a dead person quickly coagulates and loses it oxygen, because the function of breathing, which keeps the blood a viable river of life no longer exists. This will literally create a river of disease and decay, the effects of which can never be reversed.

16:4 *The third angel poured his bowl over the rivers and the springs. They turned into blood.*

When the third angel pours out his bowl of judgment on all of the earth's freshwater sources, including rivers, streams, brooks, and springs, they also turn into blood. The source of the earth's freshwater supply will be contaminated, including the deepest natural resources. Like the seas afflicted by the second bowl judgment, this bowl will likewise kill every creature within these waters. The plague will also bring an end to the world's freshwater supply needed to sustain life. Slowly, but ever so surely, the Lord God removes the most basic resource necessary for the human race to survive. Without water, the people will quickly die.

The second and third judgments contained in these golden vessels also bear resemblance to the first plague used by Moses against Pharaoh and the Egyptians.

> [20]*Moses and Aaron did as the Lord had commanded. In front of Pharaoh and his officials, Aaron raised his staff and struck the Nile. All the water in the river turned into blood.* [21]*The fish in the Nile died, and it smelled so bad that the Egyptians couldn't drink any water from the river. There was blood everywhere in Egypt.* (Exodus 7:20–21)

16:5 *Then I heard the angel of the water say, "You are fair. You are the one who is and the one who was, the holy one, because you have judged these things.*

Looking at the judgments that God had just poured out on the earth, it is easy to see how people will be horrified at the harshness of its consequences. God has just removed the most basic element from the earth, assuring a quick end to those who are living there at that time. But the angel of the water reminds John and his readers that what God had done was absolutely just. The serpent, the first beast from the sea, and the second beast from the land may have dominated the earth's population for a short period of time. The people of the world may have been amazed at their miracles and eventually bowed down and worshiped the statue of the beast. But the Lord God, Who is the eternal "I AM," is far more powerful than these temporary enemies of God's people. He had created all things and all things were dependent on His goodness for every breath they took. It is also important to note that the angel did not say that God is righteous *and* He has judged according to His righteousness, but rather declares that God is righteous *because* He is holy and righteous in His judgment. This confirms that judgment upon an unholy, unrepentant creation was not only merited but also *necessary* simply by the nature of the perfect, holy, and just Creator. Apart from the quickening of the Holy Spirit, which brings people into a restored relationship with the Creator through Jesus Christ's atoning work at Calvary, there is no possible way for unholy people to stand before or live in the presence of their holy Maker. God's judgment, therefore, is as essential as it is just.

16:6 *You have given them blood to drink because they have poured out the blood of God's people and prophets. This is what they deserve."*

The angel now gives the reason that proves the justness of the Lord's wrath. Because these reprobate followers of the beast had shed the blood of so many "people and prophets" of God, they were aptly given blood to drink. The earth's drinking supply had been turned to blood. Those seeking to quench their thirst had to do so with the unsatisfying blood that flowed from contaminated water sources.

There is a time of reckoning and a time to even the scales. God's vengeance would soon come against all those who had persecuted and killed His faithful ones.[1]

I will make your oppressors eat their own flesh,
and they will become drunk on their own blood
as though it were new wine.
Then all humanity will know that I am the Lord,
who saves you,
the Mighty One of Jacob, who reclaims you. (Isaiah 49:26)

16:7 *Then I heard the altar answer, "Yes, Lord God Almighty,*
your judgments are true and fair."

John then makes a very strange statement. He says he heard the altar
answer. Did the altar really speak? It is likely that John heard a chorus
of saints reply to the angel's declaration of God's justness. God paid
the evil people of the world back for what they had done to the saints.
It is as if God was answering the cry that went up from the altar in Revelation 6:10: *"They cried out in a loud voice, 'Holy and true Master, how*
long before you judge and take revenge on those living on earth who shed our
blood?'" As harsh as these plagues may appear to be, it is the perfectly
just consequence for the sins of those who had shed the blood of God's
saints. Indeed, "true and fair" are God's judgments upon the earth!

Notes/Applications

Consistent with the overall theme of the vision being revealed to him,
John is now introduced to the more severe and frightening aspect of
God's judgment poured out on the earth and its degenerate inhabitants. John also sees God's justice, His righteousness, and His faithfulness in the administration of His judgment. God commands the seven
angels to execute His judgment out of the seven bowls. The first three
angels pour out the contents of the bowls in their hands in succession
discharging God's fury on the children of disobedience.

All who would serve and worship the beast would suffer boils all
over their bodies. All life in the seas and fresh water would be annihi-
lated. Death and destruction along with unbearable pain and anguish
would proceed to consume the earth and its inhabitants. Neither the

serpent nor the beasts serving him would be able to save the world from the wrath of God the Almighty which would rain upon sinful men. The serpent and his beasts would be stripped of their God-given abilities to perform mighty acts or command events in the world. The beasts which once would have had the ability to impress the whole world would now be completely powerless to stop the fury of God's wrath.

Such intensity of divine anger certainly surpasses any human comprehension regardless of one's spiritual condition. The unregenerate are spiritually dead while the redeemed remain confined to the finiteness of their humanness. Nevertheless, the redeemed are called to grow in the knowledge of God their Creator Who also became their Father and Lord by redeeming them with the precious blood of the Lamb—His Son Jesus Christ. But the angels fully know Who God is. They would not be surprised by God's judgment of sin. Nor are the saints who are already worshiping God at the altar in heaven. We read in the present passage that the angels and those at the altar joyfully exchange words of praise and worship because God has righteously judged sin and sinful men. To those who have come to the full knowledge of God's righteous indignation toward sin and His enduring patience and mercy toward those who love and obey Him, God's wrath should appear no less than the righteous and appropriate response to sin and disobedience. God is merciful and loving, but He is also just and holy. To believe in God is also to accept Him in the full expression of Who He is.

Believers, because they are recipients of God's gift of salvation, are comfortable in their loving relationship with the Lord. Consequently, they, too, might find it difficult to grasp God's judgment on sinners. Nevertheless, in accepting the biblical expression that paints a complete picture of God's unchanging character, they should learn to praise God for His judgment as much as they do for their salvation.

Revelation 16:8-14

16:8 *The fourth angel poured his bowl on the sun. The sun was allowed to burn people with fire.*

The fourth angel poured out the bowl of judgment in his hand on the sun, and immediately the intensity of the sun's heat will rise to a level so hot that it will burn people. This does not mean that the heat of the sun will cause those exposed to it to receive severe sunburns. People will actually be charred by the searing heat of the sun, as though brought into direct contact with fire. This could mean that the protective layer of the earth's atmosphere will be removed and no longer able to shield the earth, allowing the scorching heat of the sun to burn everything on the earth's surface.

Whereas the fourth trumpet of judgment also affected the sun, it only does so to the point of lessening its light, as with the moon and stars, by a third *(Revelation 8:12)*. There is no mention of this bowl's effects on the stars or moon, but its ramifications are far more severe than those of the fourth trumpet judgment. Such evidences serve as further proof that the judgments of the trumpets and the bowls were progressive and not concurrent.

16:9 *They were severely burned. They cursed the name of God, who has the authority over these plagues. They would not change the way they think and act and give him glory.*

All of mankind will be affected by the sun's intense heat, but death will not provide any escape. No one will avoid this or any of the final judgments of God's wrath. Nevertheless, rather than repent for their sinfulness, everyone instead will curse the name of the Lord. Like the plague of the scorpions, the pain inflicted is severe, but God, Who both makes alive and kills, will not permit the people to die. It becomes painfully clear that knowledge of God's action, even His judgment, does not always result in repentance and restoration. *"At that time people will look for death and never find it. They will long to die, but death will escape them" (Revelation 9:6).* People will even be stripped of their capacity for suicide, sentenced to experience the full measure of God's judgment.

16:10–11 *¹⁰The fifth angel poured his bowl on the throne of the beast. Its kingdom turned dark. People gnawed on their tongues in anguish ¹¹and cursed the God of heaven for their pains and their sores. However, they would not stop what they were doing.*

The judgment of God at this point directly affects people on a physical level. Nevertheless, physical pain has not induced any repentance on the part of the people. Now the fifth angel pours out his bowl on the throne of the beast, directly attacking the source of people's worship of this false god. Darkness now envelops his kingdom. Whether this is physical darkness or the metaphorical representation of the collapse of the beast's kingdom is uncertain. Nevertheless, it is certain that the beast's kingdom is in the throes of its final days. The religious, political, social, and economic system the beast had developed begins to crumble, and people, who once loved the fact that they could buy and sell on the beast's system, now are challenged to find food and other products. The beast and those who worshiped it are now the recipients of the same sentence that they had imposed on those who followed Christ and refused to have the mark of the beast imprinted on their bodies. With complete acknowledgment of their deplorable spiritual position and despite the severe anguish of the physical pain already inflicted upon them, people are left to gnaw their tongues in response to the agony consuming their bodies.

This is the last verse in the Book of Revelation where it is recorded that the people refused to repent. When the Day of Judgment is present, the opportunity for repentance is past. *"This is what the Lord says: I'm going to bring a disaster on them that they can't escape. Although they will cry out to me, I won't listen to them" (Jeremiah 11:11).*

16:12 *The sixth angel poured his bowl on the great Euphrates River. The water in the river dried up to make a road for the kings from the east.*

The sixth angel will pour out the bowl of wrath upon the Euphrates River, which instantly dries up. The vast banks that once contained one of the world's greatest rivers will become a pathway for an approaching army from the east. Jeremiah also envisioned the destruction of the Lord's enemies, even as he watched the approach of the Babylonian army, making its way toward Judah. The similarities are striking.

> *That day belongs to the Almighty Lord of Armies. It is a day of vengeance when he will take revenge on his enemies. His sword will devour until it has had enough, and it will drink their blood until it's full. The Almighty Lord of Armies will offer them as sacrifices in the north by the Euphrates River.* (Jeremiah 46:10)

16:13 *Then I saw three evil spirits like frogs come out of the mouths of the serpent, the beast, and the false prophet.*

As soon as the Euphrates River dries up, John saw three unclean spirits come out of the mouths of the serpent, the first beast that arose from the sea, and the second beast that arose from the land. Presumably, one unclean spirit comes from the mouth of each of these hosts. To John, these spirits resemble frogs, but they are distinct spirits that possess the supernatural power that has been given to these three evil beings by God, demonstrating the miraculous signs and wonders John had recorded earlier.

16:14 *They are spirits of demons that do miracles. These spirits go to the kings of the whole world and gather them for the war on the frightening day of God Almighty.*

The frog-like spirits that emerged from the mouths of the serpent, the beast, and the false prophet are now defined clearly. They are the spirits of particular demons empowering their host figures to perform miracles and great wonders. These spirits depart from the members of the unholy trilogy and go out to the kings of the entire world. They use their power to summon the leaders of the nations, influencing them to gather for "the war on the frightening day of God Almighty." This will be Satan's final effort to gather a great army in a last desperate attempt to wage war and defeat the Lamb and His saints. These world leaders will be individually and corporately deceived by these spirits to believe that they could do battle with the Lord and possibly defeat the beast's arch enemy. However, the mention of "the frightening day of God Almighty" is a foreshadowing of a great battle that will expose the futility of the serpent's effort.

Notes/Applications

> While men grow bold in wicked ways,
> And yet a God they own,
> My heart within me often says,
> "Their thoughts believe there's none."
>
> Their thoughts and ways at once declare,
> What'er their lips profess,
> God hath no wrath for them to fear,
> Nor will they seek His grace.
>
> What strange self-flatt'ry blinds their eyes!
> But there's a hast'ning hour,
> When they shall see with sore surprise
> The terrors of Thy power.
>
> Thy justice shall maintain its throne,
> Though mountains melt away;
> Thy judgments are a world unknown,
> A deep, unfathom'd sea . . .[2]

Do these words from Isaac Watts, the masterful hymnist, express our attitudes? Believers often find it difficult to understand why the lost will continue along a path of destruction, especially the lost depicted in these verses—those biting their tongues in agony yet still cursing the God of heaven. We easily question God's righteousness or become puzzled by the indifference of the conduct of an unregenerate heart. We forget that the response of such people to their lost situation comes from their unredeemed condition. They will not be saved because they cannot see the truth that is right before their eyes. They will not be saved because the Spirit has not quickened their sin sick hearts. Of all people, those who have been redeemed by Jesus Christ should understand fully the impact of God's Word revealed to them by the regenerating work of the Holy Spirit. Numerous passages throughout the biblical narrative explain the two ways that are open to the human race—the path of righteousness in obedience to God or the path of sin and rebellion in disobedience to God. Yet many believers focus on the love of God so intensely that they forget His judgment, grossly underestimating the power and authority in His judging as it is in His saving.

The truth of God's Word cannot be more clearly expressed than the reading and assimilation of the first of the Ten Commandments:

> "²I am the Lord your God, who brought you out of the land of Egypt, out of the house of slavery. ³You shall have no other gods before me. ⁴You shall not make for yourself a carved image, or any likeness of anything that is in heaven above, or that is in the earth beneath, or that is in the water under the earth. ⁵You shall not bow down to them or serve them, for I the Lord your God am a jealous God, visiting the iniquity of the fathers on the children to the third and the fourth generation of those who hate me, ⁶but showing steadfast love to thousands of those who love me and keep my commandments" (Exodus 20:2–6).

Thus, the redeemed of the Lord should embrace not only God's love for them with intensely grateful hearts, but God's hatred for his avowed enemies.

Revelation 16:15–21

16:15 *"See, I am coming like a thief. Blessed is the one who remains alert and doesn't lose his clothes. He will not have to go naked and let others see his shame."*

John heard the voice of the Lord saying, "See, I am coming like a thief." This language was often used by Jesus to describe His second coming. He would come suddenly when no one was expecting Him and few were ready.

However, in the context of the theme of Jesus' revelation to the apostle John, it seems better to interpret this concept as a matter of proper clothing. As John has witnessed several scenes in Heaven, he has seen saints under the altar and saints before the throne. In both these cases, John has been told that these were those people who had been redeemed and whose clothes had been washed in the blood of the Lamb (*Revelation 7:9, 14*). Obviously, if a person remains alert, but does not have the proper attire, he is still considered naked and not dressed appropriately for the event.

This is much like Jesus' parable about an invitation to a wedding feast. When people gave excuses, the master of the household finally told his servants to go find anyone they could. Many came and were welcomed into the wedding feast, but one person did not have the clothes provided by the host. The master reacted quickly: "*[11]But when the king came in to look at the guests, he saw there a man who had no wedding garment. [12]And he said to him, 'Friend, how did you get in here without a wedding garment?' And he was speechless. [13]Then the king said to the attendants, 'Bind him hand and foot and cast him into the outer darkness. In that place, there will be weeping and gnashing of teeth.'"* (Matthew 22:11–13).

16:16 *The spirits gathered the kings at the place which is called Armageddon in Hebrew.*

As we have read in previous verses of this chapter, the unclean spirits that left the bodies of the serpent, the first beast from the sea, and the second beast from the land sought to deceive the world leaders into coming together to wage war with the beast against God Almighty. In fact, we now know that this would ultimately occur according to God's plan and would have nothing to do with Satan's scheming. The armies of evil would gather at a place called *Armageddon,* which means "hill of slaughter."[3]

This is the only biblical account of this place called Armageddon, and yet, much has been made of this great battle. As the meaning of its name suggests, Armageddon will be a place of great slaughter. As the scene unfolds, the nations of the world are arrayed in battle formation looking for an opportunity to strike at Jesus, the Captain of the opposing army, Whose forces are arranged in battle formation with an innumerable host of His saints. From all appearances, the sheer number of people prepared to do battle makes this look like it will be a battle of monumental proportions. Nothing like it has ever happened previously in human history, and nothing like it will ever happen again.

16:17 *The seventh angel poured his bowl into the air. A loud voice came from the throne in the temple, and said, "It has happened!"*

The seventh angel poured out the bowl of wrath into the air, at which time John heard a great voice coming from the temple in heaven and "from the throne." The voice could only be that of God, Who sat upon the throne and around Whom smoke from His glory and power filled the temple. The Lord announced, "It has happened!" How this must have sent chills down John's spine! God's wrath upon mankind was completed, and the earth would be ready for the return of the Lord Jesus Christ as King of kings.

This phrase, "it is done," is a phrase that is strikingly similar to the outcry of Jesus just before His death on a Roman cross. *"When Jesus had received the sour wine, he said, "It is finished," and he bowed his head and gave up his spirit"* (John 19:30). There, on that Cross, Jesus took the penalty of sin that God placed on His shoulders, and God's work of redemption was finished (*Colossians 1:19–20*). Now, the risen Lord Jesus Christ prepares to do battle with Satan and his minions. Satan had summoned the nations for this one final attempt to defeat his hated Enemy. But Jesus makes the statement: "It is done!" This time, however, Jesus was not talking about His redemption, but about His judgment. Again, both God's salvation and His judgment are presented to the reader as eternal characteristics of God's unchangeable character. In the end, every person ever born will meet Jesus, either as the Savior or the Judge.

16:18 *There was lightning, noise, thunder, and a powerful earthquake. There has never been such a powerful earthquake since humans have been on earth.*

Just after Jesus died on the Cross, there was a powerful earthquake. The curtain in the temple was ripped from the top to the bottom. The earth shook so hard that rocks were split open (*Matthew 27:51*). Now, the Lord announces that His judgment has likewise been completed. Immediately following, a tremendous earthquake again shook the earth. This was accompanied with lightning, noise, and thunder. The only distinction between the two earthquakes is that the one following judgment is much more powerful than any previous earthquake.

16:19 *The important city split into three parts, and the cities of the nations fell. God remembered to give Babylon the Great the cup of wine from his fierce anger.*

The great city, identified in this verse as Babylon, was divided into three parts by the earthquake. Also, the cities of all the nations fell, which either symbolizes or literally describes the destruction of the world-power structures. These cities will join together in their defiance against the holy and righteous God, so God, in turn, will violently and permanently break these cities apart.

The repercussions of the seventh bowl of God's wrath will be poured out on Babylon. For centuries, biblical scholars have debated the interpretation of *Babylon*. Some have argued that Babylon symbolizes the one world-power system that would control the various nations of the world from a united structure of authority.[4] Others maintain that it should be literally interpreted that the city of Babylon would be rebuilt in the last days as the capital city of the world government.[5] Whatever the actual meaning, the intent is clear: Babylon had been disobedient to God, and therefore, "the cup of wine from his fierce anger" will fall heavily upon that city.

DIG DEEPER: *Babylon*

The ancient culture of Babylon, located in Mesopotamia, flourished as early as the sixth century B.C. The city was located along the Euphrates River in what is now Iraq. It was conquered by Sennacharib of the Assyrian dynasty 689 B.C. Later, in the mid-sixth century, the city achieved its greatest glory as the most powerful nation of its time under the rule of Nebuchadnezzar. This mighty king also conquered the southern kingdom of Judah, destroying Jerusalem and taking the vessels of Solomon's temple. Since those days, Babylon has always engendered visions of an evil empire that oppose the people of God.

16:20 *Every island vanished, and the mountains could no longer be seen.*

This verse vividly illustrates the devastating effects that this intense, worldwide earthquake will have upon the earth. The disappearance of islands seems to suggest that all the world's islands will crumble into the sea and be utterly destroyed beyond salvage. Also, the mountains will be leveled, shaken to the ground in massive piles of severed rocks and splintered lumber. As in other passages of this book, which have revealed events of the last days, ancient biblical prophecy also looked forward and saw a very similar scene:

> [4]*Every valley will be raised.*
> *Every mountain and hill will be lowered.*
> *Steep places will be made level.*
> *Rough places will be made smooth.*
>
> [5]*Then the Lord's glory will be revealed*
> *and all people will see it together.*
> *The Lord has spoken.* (Isaiah 40:4–5)

16:21 Large, heavy hailstones fell from the sky on people. The people cursed God because the plague of hail was such a terrible plague.

Another result of the seventh bowl of God's wrath will be a massive hailstorm. Other translations use the original Greek language to describe the actual weight of these hailstones. Enormous balls of ice, approximately one hundred pounds each, will fall from the sky to earth.[6] This phenomenon will certainly result in extensive injury and destruction above and beyond the devastation that had already been caused by the worst earthquake the world had ever known. It is frightening to see how God has preserved those He is punishing so that they could experience the full measure of His wrath. The seventh plague marked the final physical judgment God imposed on mankind, and it would be, by far, the most destructive.

Despite the intensity of the plague—and more accurately *because* of it—people again cursed God for their destruction and torment, even though it was the just consequence of their unrepentant hearts. This verse depicts a final demonstration of man's resistance and hardness to God, even to the very end.

Notes/Applications

Though Armageddon (which loosely translated means "mount of Megiddo" or "hills of Megiddo") appears only in the Book of Revelation, Megiddo is the location of many prominent events in biblical history. Around this area is where Barak conquered Sisera, King Josiah was killed, and many Old Testament battles were fought. Megiddo was once a great city fortified by King Solomon, and it had prospered under the reigns of King Ahab around 900 B.C. and King Jeroboam ben Joash around 800 B.C. It was also of great importance because of its key location along the *Via Maris,* or "the Way of the Sea." Dating back to 3000 B.C., the Via Maris has been an international roadway, connecting Egypt with Damascus and Mesopotamia. Its major crossways intersect in Megiddo, which is located about halfway between the Jordan River and the Mediterranean Sea. This region is also known as the Valley of Jezreel.

Despite the historical rise and fall of this city, it is primarily noted for only one momentous event—the final, decisive moment when the Almighty God will conquer Satan and his evil followers. The foolishness of people who worship the beast will be exposed as God the Lord descends upon the nations with a powerful display of His righteousness dispensed in His unbiased justice, breaking the counterfeit god and his minions in pieces. Even the serpent and the beast display their foolishness by carrying their rebellion to this extreme. Yet, Satan has opposed the Person and work of Jesus Christ since the beginning of time. That opposition has been expressed in so many ways throughout the biblical narrative.

It is astounding that the nations and the serpent they worshiped would actually prepare to battle the One Who had created them in the first place. How do they think that the creature can have any chance of dominating and conquering the source of their very lives? Yet, the depravity of Satan and those who worship him is so deeply ingrained in the human psyche that such people never see the foolishness of their position. With arrogant but futile confidence they march into battle not knowing that they are marching straight into the pit of hell.

REVELATION 17

Revelation 17:1-6

17:1-2 *¹One of the seven angels who held the seven bowls came and said to me, "Come, I will show you the judgment of that notorious prostitute who sits on raging waters. ²The kings of the earth had sex with her, and those living on earth became drunk on the wine of her sexual sins."*

Even though chapter sixteen provides John's readers with the horrible details of God's judgment on a world that has worshiped the statue of the beast, engaging in idolatry of the worst kind, chapter seventeen expands on those details, outlining the deplorable condition of the world's governments. That condition is described within the framework of a woman who seduces the kings with the perversion of her sexual enticement.

After witnessing the outpouring of the seven bowls of God's final wrath, John was approached by one of the seven angels that had been given one of the seven bowls of God's wrath. The angel told John to follow him so that he could reveal the details surrounding the seven bowls that were poured out on the "prostitute who sits on raging waters." "*Sexual sins*" describes metaphorically the association of the earth's inhabitants with rampant wickedness and pagan idolatry throughout the Book of Revelation[1] (*Revelation 14:8, 17:4, 18:3, 19:2*). Pagan worship is considered fornication because it is an abomination and perversion of the truth and a blatant rebellion against the One Who had created them. The intended sentiment seems to be that mankind had committed adultery by turning away from God, its very Creator, to worship a false god of absolute corruption. Therefore, mankind would also share in the wrath and the eternal judgment of its god, Satan. As found in numerous Scripture passages, the relationship between God and His people is very often described as a marriage. Therefore, when people who are connected to God through creation turn away from God, they are often portrayed as an adulterous people.

The "kings of the earth" were also described by their intimate relationship with the prostitute and were, therefore, responsible for leading the multitudes into the same kind of relationship. These kings were the same kings who had allied themselves with the beast and helped enforce its authority (*Daniel 7:24; Revelation 16:13–14; 17:12*), who had joined the beast to make war against God at Armageddon (*Revelation 16:14*), and who would be thoroughly defeated upon the return of the Lord Jesus Christ (*Revelation 19:19–21*).

17:3 *Then the angel carried me by his power into the wilderness. I saw a woman sitting on a bright red beast covered with insulting names. It had seven heads and ten horns.*

The angel carried John away in a similar manner in which the apostle had been carried up into heaven to witness the other visions (*John 4:1*). John was already under the influence and power of the Spirit when the angel came to escort him to "the wilderness." By the Spirit's power, John was simply taken to another setting to witness another vision.

The woman described here—"a woman sitting on a bright red beast" and the woman described in the opening verses—"a notorious prostitute who sits on raging waters" are likely a portrayal of the same entity, which becomes apparent in subsequent verses.

The blood-colored beast upon which she sat had names of blasphemy written on it, and it had seven heads and ten horns. This beast is strikingly similar to the beast that has been described earlier in John's vision.[2] *"I saw a beast coming out of the sea. It had ten horns, seven heads, and ten crowns on its horns. There were insulting names on its heads"* (Revelation 13:1). The beast depicted in chapter twelve personified the characteristics of the red serpent, identified as Satan. *"Another sign appeared in the sky: a huge fiery red serpent with seven heads, ten horns, and seven crowns on its heads"* (Revelation 12:3). The only dissimilar details in this description are the color of the beast and the ten crowns on the ten heads. Though the serpent and the beast in chapters twelve and thirteen appear strikingly similar to this beast, it is impossible to be absolutely certain whether they are one and the same or different entities.

17:4 *The woman wore purple clothes, bright red clothes, gold jewelry, gems, and pearls. In her hand she was holding a gold cup filled with detestable and evil things from her sexual sins.*

The woman was adorned in the finest jewelry made of the most precious gems and pearls, and she was dressed in purple and scarlet garments, the colors of royalty. This woman possessed great wealth, power, and influence. The description of her glamorous attire signifies that 1) she appeared, at least to the unbeliever, to offer all the luxuries that the world could provide, and that 2) she was dressed as a figure of royalty, depicting her relationship with the authorities of the world. She will hold a golden goblet, another emblem of her glamorous outward appearance, but the contents of the cup will reveal her true ambition. To those who succumb to the allure of a prostitute, everything about the woman is intoxicating. However, like a prostitute, she appeared beautiful and enticing on the outside, but her true character is revealed by the cup she holds, filled to the brim "with detestable and evil things from her sexual sins." All that she had to offer were temporary pleasures that lured her consorts far from the eternal joy found in Christ Jesus.

17:5 *A name was written on her forehead. The name was Mystery: Babylon the Great, the Mother of Prostitutes and Detestable Things of the Earth.*

Some Bible translations and commentators prefer to separate *mystery* as a description of the woman's title rather than as a part of it.[3] The Greek word for *mystery* is *musterion*, which connotes an unknown thing. The apostle Paul often speaks about the mystery of faith that was hidden for ages, but was revealed when Christ died for the sin that so strongly holds people in its power. *"[26]In the past God hid this mystery, but now he has revealed it to his people. [27]God wanted his people throughout the world to know the glorious riches of this mystery—which is Christ living in you, giving you the hope of glory" (Colossians 1:26–27).* In the same way, this woman's name is shrouded in mystery. However, the angel now shows John what her name really means. Just as the Lord has revealed the mystery of faith to those He has redeemed, so now the Lord reveals the mystery of this adulterous woman. Thus, the description of her name reflects "a spirit of disobedience to God"[4] *(2 Thessalonians 2:7).* She is Babylon the Great, the Mother of Prostitutes and Detestable Things of the Earth. Now John reveals the truth about the deplorable character of this woman. Those who belong to Christ should understand the mystery of this woman as clearly as they understand the mystery of their revealed faith in Jesus Christ.

17:6 *I saw that the woman was drunk with the blood of God's holy people and of those who testify about Jesus. I was very surprised when I saw her.*

The woman is obsessed with her hostility against the followers of the one true God. Her ambition was predicated on her all-consuming hatred of God and His people *(Revelation 13:15).* She is described as being "drunk with the blood of God's holy people and of those who testify about Jesus." The emphasis on her drunken state illustrates her ravenous and insatiable appetite for the blood of those who followed

Christ. This is not a picture of passive resistance to God's will but a violently furious assault on all things of the Lord.

John was not merely awed by the sight of this woman. On the contrary, he simply could not believe the spectacle before his eyes. He was "very surprised." In a sense, John watched with dumbfounded horror. He observed with revulsion the beautifully decorated woman who so voraciously craved the blood of Christ's faithful.

Notes/Applications

The Holy Spirit continues to show the apostle John those things, which will come to pass (Revelation 1:1). In the unfolding of Christ's revelation, the angel shows John a woman who appears to be extremely powerful, luring the kings of the earth to indulge in her adulterous worship of the beast. Even though her sins are described in graphically sexual terms, it is apparent that her hatred of God has motivated her to worship something other than the eternal God. That fact is the exposure of her adulterous heart. Not satisfied with her own debauchery, she drags the kings of the earth into the crucible of her idolatry, thus misleading and deceiving the great mass of the earth's population.

The woman's worship of a counterfeit god is no accident. She not only rejects and defies God, she deliberately turns away from God and worships the beast, not because she was somehow misled by others, but because she knew God and hated Him for what He represents—a Savior and a Judge. That knowledge was not a saving knowledge, but a knowledge that induced a hatred for God so intense that she tries to draw the kings of the earth into a battle with God. Obviously, her hatred for God also incites a violent hatred for God's people. In the course of events, she persecutes those who belong to God, killing them and drinking their blood in such quantities that she is now drunk.

We read the epitaphs of men, women, and children with common names and stations in life who all died for one cause—serving their Lord and master Jesus Christ. We hear the truth of the Scriptures reminding us: "We must suffer a lot to enter the kingdom of God" (Acts 14:22).

Throughout history, Christian saints have been persecuted and will continue to be persecuted for carrying the banner of Christ. Jesus warned His followers of impending trial and torture for His name. *"You will be thrown out of synagogues. Certainly, the time is coming when people who murder you will think that they are serving God"* (John 16:2). Before Christ's return, such persecution will intensify to the point that the prostitute of Babylon will become drunk with the blood of the saints.

Thomas Benet, a martyr burned in Exeter in 1531 proclaimed: "I will rather die, than Worship such a Beast, the very Whore of Babylon, and a false Usurper, as manifestly doth appear by his doings ... I thank Christ, and with all my heart will allow all things done and used in the Church to the Glory of God, and edifying of my Soul."[5]

We may feel overwhelmed by the task before us because our human frame rebels against such violence to Christ's followers. Yet this is the unfolding plan of God's salvation on those He has redeemed as well as His judgment on those who rebel against Him. The saint follows his Lord wherever that leads, even if the pathway leads through death to eternal life. This revelation is no longer some warm tranquilizer given to God's saints to remove them from the pain of torture and death. Rather, it is the plain teaching of Jesus Christ through the visions that John witnessed on the Isle of Patmos.

Revelation 17:7–11

17:7 *The angel asked me, "Why are you surprised? I will tell you the mystery of the woman and the beast with the seven heads and the ten horns that carries her.*

John was shocked by the vision of the woman drunk with the blood of Christian martyrs, but the angel tells the apostle that he should not be surprised by it. The angel first asked John about his bewilderment and then assured him that the full importance of the woman and the beast would be explained.

17:8 *"You saw the beast which once was, is no longer, and will come from the bottomless pit and go to its destruction. Those living on earth, whose names were not written in the Book of Life when the world was created, will be surprised when they see the beast because it was, is no longer, and will come again.*

The angel started to explain the beast to John. As people attempt to understand what is going on throughout this book, they immediately encounter a phrase which does not seem to help. It seems that this beast had existed at some previous time. However, the beast no longer exists at the particular time in the sequence of events that John had been witnessing. Whether that means that the beast has died or is somehow confined, we cannot be sure. However, the beast no longer exerts his influence on the nations of the world. Stranger still, the beast will once again appear, coming out of the bottomless pit only to be condemned, permanently confined to the place reserved for him under the sovereign authority of God.

Whenever the beast is removed from the scene, the unregenerate people of the world will be astounded. They had given themselves to the beast because of the signs and wonders that it had performed under the agency of the demons that lived in it. They thought their religious devotion was directed toward a god that could not be vanquished. They had watched him persecute and kill the saints of God. They had seen the establishment of a religious system that worked out practically in a political, economic, and social structure that allowed them to buy and sell, but prevented the same privileges to those who remained steadfast in their testimony for Jesus Christ. Now that beast was gone! Everything they had hoped for, all the prosperity and safety that their false god offered was dashed to pieces. Now they knew that the god they had worshiped, although very persuasive and powerful, was a fraud.

17:9 *"In this situation a wise mind is needed. The seven heads are seven mountains on which the woman is sitting.*

The angel urged both John and his readers to understand the significance of the vision. True understanding in matters pertaining to the almighty, transcendent God does not arise from human intelligence, but requires spiritual insight, given and nourished by the Holy Spirit. This is similar to the urgings of Jesus as He addressed the seven churches of Asia Minor in chapters two and three, "He who has an ear, let him hear what the Spirit says to the churches." The Lord was not speaking of physical ears but of spiritual understanding, and the angel appears to be doing the same at this moment. Those with wisdom should understand the explanation.

This verse has long served as the foundation for understanding the intended significance of this beast as Rome, which has been called "the city of the seven hills."[6] However, most contemporary scholars now dismiss this once popular explanation.[7] Rome, while the epitome of hatred and violence towards Christians in the first and second centuries, now seems hardly a fitting solution for what is said about the "important city" in this chapter and the next. Essentially, the angel is simply telling John that the seven heads represent seven mountains, which make up the seat on which the woman sits. It is impossible to say whether these are seven mountains in one city or mountains found on seven different continents. It may simply depict the woman as the powerful, seducing force that will lead the kings of the earth into battle against the Lord and His saints.

17:10 *They are also seven kings. Five of them have fallen, one is ruling now, and the other has not yet come. When he comes, he must remain for a little while.*

The angel, despite promising to reveal "the mystery of the woman and the beast," seems to speak in riddles. The beast's seven heads just depicted as seven mountains are now further explained as seven kings. Though there are many interpretations regarding the identity of these leaders, within the context of this passage it seems that we are to understand this as a succession of kings and not necessarily as kings ruling concurrently as a part of the beast. Another difficulty is these kings could be interpreted as individual rulers or as kingdoms.

Of these seven kings, we are told that five have fallen, which means that they are no longer in power during the time period represented in this passage. The problem is exacerbated by the angel's description that fails to specifically define the time line relating to these kings. However, following the context of the recent chapters, it is best to interpret the time frame as existing at some future time in relation to the period following the seventh bowl of God's wrath after the beast's authority has been stripped from him, and his political structure lies in ruins. Any attempt to identify these leaders specifically is full of dangerous pit falls. While several interpretations have been offered to count these rulers and determine the identity of the seventh king, each interpretation is admittedly problematic and cannot be argued convincingly.[8]

17:11 *The beast that was and is no longer is the eighth king. It belongs with the seven kings and goes to its destruction.*

The beast on which the woman rides, the woman whose name is Babylon the Great, the Mother of Prostitutes and Detestable Things of the Earth, has been described as an entity that has seven heads and ten horns. Now these seven heads, the seven mountains, that are also the seven kings or kingdoms, emerge as an eighth kingdom, which succeeds the previous seven. This is a succession of kings or empires that eventually develop into one large kingdom. The beast, consisting of all seven previous kings along with the eighth king, is described together by the angel as the object of God's destruction.

Notes/Applications

Despite the best resources available—knowledge, technology, and science—the world continues to rush headlong in its disobedient course to its ultimate destruction. Blinded by its depravity and satiated with its inordinate lust for power, money, and glamour, it never sees the culmination of its perverse perspective. They are completely focused on filling their belly with the immediate gratifications of their perversion. The people of the world never see that they are rebelling against the God Who has created them and the Christ Who has suffered the penalty for their sin. Eventually and inevitably God's righteousness will bring forth God's justice, resulting in the condemnation of those who have turned away from the living God to worship a false god.

The woman, who is the mystery of Babylon the Great, entices the kings of the world, drawing them into the perversion of her adultery. As she reaches toward the culmination of her ambition, she arrives at the climax of her power, glamour, and authority, bringing the leaders of the nations along with her to the pinnacle of their rejection of God's authority. The closer she gets to her own godless ambitions, drinking the blood of the saints of God, the more she becomes drunk with her success. As the kings of the earth engage in their illicit relationship with her, they, in turn, drag an innumerable host of people with them to the brink of God's unfailing justice.

By the same token, when God's redeemed children are enticed by the allurements of the material world—its money, power, glamour, and ambition—they too suffer a breach in their relationship to Jesus Christ. The pitfalls of living in the world are many! As members of the human race, we are subject to the temptations that surround us on all sides.

While God's children are tempted to submit to the allurements of the world's passion and rebellion, while some of the redeemed succumb to the world's seductions, they are still kept by God until that day when their salvation will be consummated at His triumphal return to judge the earth. God's children are preserved by the intercession of the Holy Spirit until that day when they see their Savior face to face even as those who are the children of perdition are preserved by God until that day when they receive His judgment and perish for their sin.

Revelation 17:12–18

17:12 *"¹²The ten horns that you saw are ten kings who have not yet started to rule. They will receive authority to rule as kings with the beast for one hour. ¹³They have one purpose—to give their power and authority to the beast.*

The angel continued to explain that the ten horns represent ten kings who had "not yet started to rule." This clearly refers to a future occasion from the time of John's writing. Nevertheless, this future event occurs while the eighth king, which is the beast described in the previous passage, consolidates his power. These kings will be actual persons to whom a territory will be assigned and to whom authority will be given. Their ascension to power will occur during the time that the eighth king dominates the world scene. Again, God in His sovereignty will only allow these evil rulers to reign with the beast for a short time, depicted in this verse as "one hour."

These ten kings will join forces with only "one purpose." They will rule their corresponding kingdoms under the dominion of the beast, that is, the eighth king that the beast represents. Because of the hatred of the beast for the living God, this consortium of kings will be single-mindedly hostile toward God and His people, merging their forces to rise up against the Lord God on a global basis.

17:14 *They will go to war against the lamb. The lamb will conquer them because he is Lord of lords and King of kings. Those who are called, chosen, and faithful are with him."*

The purpose of the kings unified mission is clear—to make war with the Lamb, the Lord Jesus Christ. In response to the attack on the Kingdom of God, Jesus Christ will engage the battle and defeat the world's kings and kingdoms. Jesus is, in the final analysis, the Lord of lords and the King of kings. He has created all things and orchestrated the events by which He dispenses His judgment on those who have rejected the salvation offered to them by His Own blood. When Jesus engages the forces of the evil world kingdoms, He does so with those who have been called, chosen, and redeemed by Him.

The overarching purpose of these kings is similar to the scenes John has already witnessed. John saw the serpent pursue the saints of God when he could not destroy the Child born to the woman as described in the twelfth chapter: "The serpent became angry with the woman. So it went away to fight with her other children, the ones who keep God's commands and hold on to the testimony of Jesus" (*Revelation 12:17*). John had watched the gathering of forces intent on attacking the stronghold of the Lord's Kingdom: "They are spirits of demons that do miracles. These spirits go to the kings of the whole world and gather them for the war on the frightening day of God Almighty" (*Revelation 16:14*). Now he watches the same scene, not from the perspective of those in Heaven, but from the perspective of those on the earth as the ten kings under the authority of the eighth king, the beast, join forces to go to war against the Lord.

17:15 *The angel also said to me, "The waters you saw, on which the prostitute is sitting, are people, crowds, nations, and languages.*

The angel continued to explain the meaning of the scene he had witnessed. When one reads the opening verse of this chapter, the image that appears seems riddled with puzzles. At that time, John saw a "notorious prostitute" sitting "on raging waters." Now, the angel interprets the scene for John.

John saw this woman seated on a beast. But the image represented the forces of the world united under one authority whose sole purpose was to engage in battle with the forces of Jesus Christ and His redeemed saints. Now the angel tells John that the waters represent the host of the earth's inhabitants—people, crowds, nations, and languages.

17:16 *The ten horns and the beast you saw will hate the prostitute. They will leave her abandoned and naked. They will eat her flesh and burn her up in a fire.*

When John saw the woman, the angel explained that she seduced the kings of the earth. The political leaders became drunk with "the wine of her fornication." This illicit indulgence on the part of these leaders in turn permeated the entire population of the world. Even though this relationship is described in graphically sexual terms, it seems best to interpret this as the adulterous indulgence of the world, fleeing their legitimate relationship with their Creator, and committing their allegiance to the counterfeit god who was presented to the people by the serpent, that is, Satan.

Now, however, the beast and the ten kings, represented by the ten horns of the beast, will turn on the woman who has seduced them. The description of their actions is shocking if not somewhat confusing since these entities were fully engaged with this woman, which is really *"Babylon the Great"* (v. 5). The violent reversal of their roles shows how the Lord will confuse His enemies so that they will eventually devour each other, resulting in a systematic destruction of the city that had once served the kings so well. This destruction will be both thorough and irreversible. These kings completely annihilate the woman so that she can never be revived.

17:17 *God has made them do what he wants them to do. So they will give their kingdom to the beast until God's words are carried out.*

What a paradox! These ten kings fully believed that they were in charge of their own destinies, submitting their authority to their leader, the beast. They will align themselves with God's enemy. However, the beast and his servants will eventually turn on the woman and, like cannibals, completely devour her. Now the angel tells John that this unholy alliance was orchestrated by God Himself. By submitting to the beast, they will unwittingly fulfill the sovereign design of Almighty

God. While seeking to *"give their kingdom to the beast,"* they unknow-ingly fulfilled the purpose of the very God that they hated. Paul, God's chosen apostle, clearly described the authority of God that overrides even the most evil schemes of His most powerful enemies: "[11]That's why God will send them a powerful delusion so that they will believe a lie. [12]Then everyone who did not believe the truth, but was delighted with what God disapproves of, will be condemned" *(2 Thessalonians 2:11–12).*

17:18 *The woman you saw is the important city which domi-nates the kings of the earth."*

The woman that John saw represents the great city called Babylon, the capital of idolatry and apostasy *(Revelation 17:5).* The specific identity of this city cannot be easily defined, but its identity will one day be revealed. During that time, while the archenemy of Christ, the beast, consolidates his position among the nations of the world, this city will dominate the world scene, offering all the material enticements the world extends to those destined for destruction. She will seduce the world's inhabitants with her beauty, wealth, and opportunities, but her destiny is destruction by those she has seduced. This center of the anti-Christian empire will be utterly ruined when the seventh bowl of God's wrath is poured out *(Revelation 16:19–21).* All of these events are the outcome of God's decree, not the futile design of God's enemies.

Notes/Applications

The nations, leaders, and the people of this world march onward and upward in the development of their political, social, and economic structures that provide the security needed to survive the troubles and adversities that plague the human experience. At least that is what the world thinks! Deeply embedded in the mindset of the human race are the dangerous, illusive ideas that people can do anything they want, controlling their environment and defining their futures. The capac-ity to improve the conditions of their human experience lies solely within their own capabilities to create the best world they possibly can. They do so believing that they are the originators and sustainers of all wisdom and authority. But this passage shows the foolishness of such self-indulgent audacity.

As the angel continues to explain the vision that John witnesses, believers are surprised to discover that the world will one day turn against its own. In the violence of that betrayal, the city, which has dominated the world scene, will be completely destroyed. At the height of its importance, this city will direct the political and economic strategies of the entire world. Everyone, both great and small, will look to this city as the shining example of wealth and prosperity. However, such external enticements hide a much deeper cancer that eventually destroys the city from the inside out. Those who once looked on her with undisguised desire and lust will turn against her, exposing her shallow beauty and destroying her influence on the nations of the world.

As Christians look at the world around them they do not find it difficult to see the pitfalls of today's world. Stores are full of merchandise which people don't really need, but which they desperately want. Many of those stores capture the eye of the potential buyer with sexually explicit language and graphics. The leaders of countries are drunk with the power of their positions, overriding the needs of the people they govern in their lust for more wealth and power. Then, the leaders of the nations gather together in great convocations to discuss the distribution of wealth among the nations, environmental concerns, and profitable political alliances. They believe with unswerving stupidity that they are equipped to solve all the world's problems. According to John's record of events that Jesus has shown him, all of this will come crashing down when the nations of the world turn on each other, directing their anger toward the city that has dominated their prosperity over a long period of time.

However, the most important aspect of this passage that believers should grasp is the part that God plays in the unfolding of these events. While people look on from the perspective of an unregenerate heart, they simply see a world that they expect to provide security and wealth simply dissolve before their eyes into a mass of unparalleled chaos. Many believers who do not fully understand the truth of God's Word will be duped into a false sense of security, trusting vainly in the provisions of this world's economic system. However, a close look at this chapter in the Book of Revelation will wipe out any misguided delusions. It is God and God alone Who has arranged, orchestrated, and decreed the end of this world's headlong pursuit of false gods. He speaks and the world trembles! He raises His right hand and the kings of the earth rise up and destroy the city that has provided their prosperity. The Lord tramples upon the rebellious of the earth in His righteous judgment! And everything that people have planted their hopes and dreams on comes to a bitter, frightening end. And all God's people say, "Amen!"

REVELATION 18

Revelation 18:1–8

18:1 *After these things I saw another angel come from heaven. He had tremendous power, and his glory lit up the earth.*

After the angel helped John understand the seven bowls of God's wrath and its relation to the woman and the beast with seven heads and ten horns *(chapter seventeen)*, another angel came down from heaven having two distinguishing characteristics—great power and glory, which lit up the earth. During God's judgment on the unregenerate inhabitants of the earth, the brightness of the sun had been dimmed by the impact of God's pronouncement of condemnation *(Revelation 8:12; 9:2)*. Now, following the final outpouring of God's wrath, the earth is brightened, not by a restoration of the sun's rays, but by the presence of an unusually powerful angel.

18:2 *He cried out in a powerful voice, "Fallen! Babylon the Great has fallen! She has become a home for demons. She is* *a prison for every evil spirit, every unclean bird, and every unclean and hated beast.*

This angel's voice was powerful, proclaiming loudly, *"Babylon has fallen! It has fallen! All the idols they worship lie shattered on the ground"* (*Isaiah 21:9b*). The center of religious devotion to the beast lay in ruins. The economic, political, and social structures headquartered in the capital of the anti-Christian empire had suffered the penalty of God's judgment. The angel showed how the city had become a habitation for devils and evil spirits. The great city that at one time ruled the world will be inhabited by unclean birds—detestable, aggressive animals that survived on the dead flesh lying in its streets.

18:3 *All the nations fell because of the wine of her sexual sins. The kings of the earth had sex with her. Her luxurious wealth has made the merchants of the earth rich."*

Before her fall, the city had enjoyed the adulation of her paramours. She had reveled in the attention that the leaders of the nations had showered upon her. Many merchants had achieved great wealth as they traded within her economic structures. Other translations, using a more literal approach, show how her current condition is the result of wrath, the just consequence of her adulterous behavior. Kenneth Wuest's translation puts it this way: "because as a result of the wine of the wrath [that fell upon her], because of her fornication all the nations have fallen."[1] This powerful city falls apart as the just consequence of her excessive appetites, dragging all the nations down with her as they collapse in economic chaos.

18:4 *I heard another voice from heaven saying, "Come out of Babylon, my people, so that you do not participate in her sins and suffer from any of her plagues.*

John heard another voice from heaven, urging God's people to come out of this profoundly corrupt city. Since this city influences all of the political, economic, and social structures of the entire population of the world, how do God's redeemed people come out of her? It seems that God's people are urged to withdraw from the influences of this world system. Earlier the beast had placed its mark on people's foreheads or right hands (13:17–18). The only people who did not receive this mark were those who remained faithful to the testimony of Jesus (12:17; 20:4). The redeemed of the Lord remain within the world, but are to refrain from submitting to the influences of a material world that draws them away from their calling in Jesus Christ. In a sense, this angel called God's people to live in perfect harmony with the prayer of Jesus, their Savior, which He expressed to His Father the night before He died for the sins of the world: *"I'm not asking you to take them out of the world but to protect them from the evil one"* (John 17:15). Jeremiah, the Lord's prophet during the siege of Jerusalem by Babylon made a similar plea to the inhabitants of the besieged city:

> *Run away from Babylon! Run for your lives!*
> *You shouldn't die because of Babylon's crimes.*
> *This is the time for the vengeance of the Lord.*
> *He will pay the people of Babylon back for what they have*
> *done. (Jeremiah 51:6)*

18:5 *Her sins are piled as high as heaven, and God has remembered her crimes.*

In a clear description of the immensity of Babylon's wickedness, John was told that the accumulation of the city's sins piled high enough to reach heaven. The expression of her crimes reveals that God had not turned a blind eye to Babylon's extensive wickedness but was simply reserving judgment that He had determined by His own counsel. *"God remembered to give Babylon the Great the cup of wine from his fierce anger"* (Revelation 16:19).

18:6 *Do to her what she has done. Give her twice as much as she gave. Serve her a drink in her own cup twice as large as the drink she served others.*

God will repay this corrupt city with the same cruelty that she had meted out against God's redeemed people. In fact, God will repay Babylon twice the cruelty with which she pursued and persecuted the people of God. The cup of her punishment will be twice as large as the drink she served others.

Earlier, John saw that this woman, this completely debauched city, was drunk on the blood of God's saints *(Revelation 17:6)*. Now she would be served a portion of blood twice the amount that she and her consorts had shared. The blood that she would now be forced to consume came not from God's people, but from those who had shared her hatred of the living God. Perhaps this is another expression of that moment when the kings of the earth would turn against this city, completely destroying her *(17:16)*.

18:7 *She gave herself glory and luxury. Now give her just as much torture and misery. She says to herself, 'I'm a queen on a throne, not a widow. I'll never be miserable.'*

From the perspective of the woman, there was no place she would rather be. She was on top of the world, consorting with the leaders of the nations, enjoying the wealth heaped on her, and persecuting God's saints. She reveled in her luxury, looking at herself as a queen on a powerful throne. She thought it would never end. She would never be a widow. She would never be alone. She would always have her lovers. She would never experience the misery of loneliness and poverty. She had convinced herself that she had risen above God's description of her as a notorious prostitute, failing to acknowledge the truth of her debauchery and rebellion.

In response to this self-serving, self-indulgent attitude, the Lord repays her with as much torture and misery as she had received in glory and luxury. When this happened, she would receive the just reward for her failure to worship God rather than her own tenuous position of power and authority.

18:8 *For this reason her plagues of death, misery, and starvation will come in a single day. She will be burned up in a fire, because the Lord God, who judges her, is powerful.*

The woman's conceit blinded her to the dangerous precipice on which she was seated. Her conceit was so deceptive that she could not understand God's evaluation of the immensity of her idolatry. In her opinion, her ego trumps God's truth. Because of this blind conceit, the Lord will repay her swiftly for her sins, which had consumed every moment of her life. Now the Lord would trample the conceit of that notorious prostitute, completely obliterating her existence in death, misery, and starvation. That will certainly be a painful death. But the Lord is not done with her. He will further destroy her completely with fire.

There is no doubt that this woman, this corrupt city, was supremely important in terms of the world's perspective. She was truly wealthy, prosperous, and powerful. She was the center of the world's attention and dominated the nations with her strategically powerful position. However, she failed to recognize that she was not the most powerful force in the world. She forgot the Lord! She forgot the Lord God, Who was far more powerful than she was. When the Lord God raises His voice in her judgment, nothing can save her. Her destruction is sure! She had dominated the world scene for years, but her fall will be as swift as it will be complete.

Notes/Applications

It has been stated that "Babylon is a counterfeit church," whose mission is to "attack with seduction . . . to destroy the purity of the saints."[2] In fact, some scholars consider the prostitute, Babylon, to be a direct antithesis to the Bride of Christ, the Church.[3]

The prostitute, Babylon, will live in a lewd, perverted relationship with the devil, whom she worships. She will seek to seduce the world, turning people from God's eternal truth. Corruption will characterize the heart of her home as seen in the waywardness of her children. She will "buy" her followers with economic benefits and worldly opulence. She will arrogantly exalt herself, believing herself to be a queen, when in fact she will be a slave to sin, serving the master of spiritual bondage, Christ's archenemy, Satan.

The Bride of Christ, the Church, is characterized by her purity, which is the righteousness of Christ that clothes her. She continuously lives in blessed assurance according to the faithful covenant made by Jesus Christ, her Bridegroom. She worships the only true God, and she possesses eternal wealth incomparable to the prostitute's temporary enticements. This heavenly treasure can only be found in a sacred union sealed by the Spirit of the living God. Her Bridegroom has given His life for her and purchased her with His own blood. Nothing will sever this bond of love, sealed for eternity by the Holy Spirit.

During such troubling times, the rewards for following the prostitute will tempt people in the form of material promises, whereas the cost of obedience to God will be persecution and possibly death. Although the prostitute will seek to lure the Church from the Bridegroom, her evil attempts will fail completely. Believers may want the comforts enjoyed by those they see partaking of the prostitute's prosperity, but the price of such temporal gratification is too great. The truth of God's Word imprinted on believers' hearts by the Holy Spirit keeps those washed in the blood of the Lamb safely in the fold of God's redemption. God's truth will help them see the dangers that surround such a worldly perspective. They will recognize the wrath that will befall the prostitute and her followers for their attachment to the world's temporary treasures.

Let us rejoice in the secure union that we have in our Lord Jesus Christ, the true Bridegroom, Who has bought us with His own blood and Who will return to gather us unto Himself.

Revelation 18:9–19

18:9–10 *⁹"The kings of the earth who had sex with her and lived in luxury with her will cry and mourn over her when they see the smoke rise from her raging fire. ¹⁰Frightened by her torture, they will stand far away and say, 'How horrible, how horrible it is for that important city, the powerful city Babylon! In one moment judgment has come to it!'*

At the very heart of the world system, directed and controlled by the serpent and the beast that attracted the worship of the world's unregenerate inhabitants, lay a religious devotion, an emotionally charged worship of the counterfeit god. Using that religious foundation, the beast developed a political, economic, and social structure that controlled and managed the world's commerce. The city of Babylon, although not specifically identified geographically, became the financial and political center for the transactions conducted by the leaders of the world. Together, the woman, Babylon, and her consorts, the kings of the nations, managed to control the entire population of the world.

However, at some point and for some unknown reason, the leaders of the nations turned against the city and viciously attacked and destroyed her (17:16). These leaders now stand at a safe distance and witness the consequences of their actions. As the city lay in ruins and flames continued to reduce her once great buildings to rubble, the leaders react with shock and dismay, bewailing the demise of this once great city that had been the center of their political and economic lives.

There is a sense in which these kings actually wondered what caused them to destroy the city. Surely, they had argued the merits of their policies and, at times, probably wanted to destroy others associated with them. But their relationship in the pursuit of wealth and luxury was so intertwined that the destruction of one would affect those that remained. What these kings failed to realize was that the Lord God Himself had implemented the whole catastrophe, directing His divine judgment through the hands of the world leaders who once worshiped this great city (17:17). It is not difficult to understand that they would now look at the ruins and wonder what had gotten into them. The only conceivable answer, even from the perspective of these depraved leaders, was that they now were looking at the results of God's judgment, which had changed the great city into a smoldering ruin in just a very short time.

18:11–13 [11]*"The merchants of the earth cry and mourn over her, because no one buys their cargo anymore.* [12]*No one buys their cargo of gold, silver, gems, pearls, fine linen, purple cloth, silk, bright red cloth, all kinds of citron wood, articles made of ivory and very costly wood, bronze, iron, marble,* [13]*cinnamon, spices, incense, perfume, frankincense, wine, olive oil, flour, wheat, cattle, sheep, horses, wagons, slaves (that is, humans).*

Like the world's leaders, the world's merchants will also grieve the loss of the city. These merchants had become tremendously wealthy through their alliance to this great city and the anti-Christian authorities that governed it (18:3). But now the economic system operating within her global structure had collapsed. The merchants' had now lost their wealth along with the destruction of the world's financial center. Like the kings, the merchants mourned the loss of the city. It seems, however, they grieved not so much for the loss of the city as for the loss of their own prosperity. Nobody would be able to buy or sell anything, including food, clothing, medical supplies, or any other vital provisions. The merchants mourned the ruin of their financial security as well as the threat to their physical well-being.

Another of the ancient Hebrew prophets, under the influence and instruction of the Holy Spirit, made this proclamation to the people of Judah:

> [18]*Their silver and their gold will not be able to rescue them on the day of the Lord's overflowing fury. The whole earth will be consumed by his fiery anger, because he will put an end, a frightening end, to those who live on earth. (Zephaniah 1:18)*

John then goes on to list some of the products and services that provided the financial stability of this great city. The list is impressive by its size as well as by its diversity. The high quality of craftsmanship also adds to the value of these products. Because of Babylon's destruction at the hands of the nation's leaders, all of these products will now be in short supply. With the collapse of the global economy, there would be no one to buy anything under the best of circumstances. No one will have the money!

In the holy justice of the eternal God and His Son, Jesus Christ, the merchants and the earth's inhabitants were stripped of their power to buy and sell, imposing on them the same sentence that these leaders had imposed on those who followed the testimony of Jesus Christ. Surely, God had meted out His justice in greater proportion to that which Babylon, the wicked prostitute, had imposed on the saints of God (18:5–6).

18:14 *'The fruit you craved is gone. All your luxuries and your splendor have disappeared. No one will ever find them again.'*

Food and the nourishment it provides are fundamental to sustaining human life. Now, with the destruction of Babylon, even this most basic need is gone. The luxury and glamour of the products once offered will disappear from the stores. The food and products, which had once stocked the shelves in abundant quantities, will no longer be available. Money no longer will have any meaning. Whether a person was rich or poor, the lack of available products and services will force everyone to subsist on the same level of poverty and destitution. She, who was once the glowing center of the world's adoration and ungodly worship, will now be deprived of the products that made her rich, stripping her of her pride as well as her power.

18:15–16 *[15]"Frightened by her torture, the merchants who had become rich by selling these things will stand far away. They will cry and mourn, [16]saying, 'How horrible, how horrible* *for that important city which was wearing fine linen, purple clothes, bright red clothes, gold jewelry, gems, and pearls.*

Like the world leaders, the merchants who had become wealthy because of their association with Babylon's success will stand at a distance and express their grief, remembering the wonderful merchandise they had previously bought and sold within her borders. The memory of her riches will be as painful to the merchants as the reality that the city was now gone. Broken by their grief for their loss, they will be more gripped by their fear of what they are watching. The sight of the city, burning from one border to the other, will induce fear into the souls of the strongest, most loyal subjects. That fear will keep them far away from the scene of conflagration, torture, and destruction.

18:17–18 *¹⁷In one moment all this wealth has been destroyed!' Every ship's captain, everyone who traveled by ship, sailors, and everyone who made their living from the sea stood far away. ¹⁸When they saw the smoke rise from her raging fire, they repeatedly cried out, 'Was there ever a city as important as this?'*

The merchants could only lament the quickness with which this tremendous calamity had struck the great city. Not only will they grieve the actual loss of this center of commerce, but they will also be shocked at the swiftness that so dramatically reversed their financial fortunes.

Apparently the city of Babylon was also a significant seaport, rising to prominence even as the city grew in importance as the financial center of the world's markets. Those who engaged in commerce by shipping products to and from Babylon joined others in the expression of their shock at the rapid collapse of the world's markets. Like everyone else, leader, merchant, or common man, the seafarer will also be financially impacted by the collapse of the global economy. On the horizon, they see the smoke of her fire rising toward the sky and with that smoke they see the end of their financial schemes and fortunes.

18:19 *Then they threw dust on their heads and shouted while crying and mourning, 'How horrible, how horrible for that important city. Everyone who had a ship at sea grew rich because of that city's high prices. In one moment it has been destroyed!'*

In a gesture common among Middle Eastern cultures, the shipmasters cast dust on their heads as a public display of their grief and anguish. In the midst of their weeping and grief, they called out much like the kings and the merchants before them. In a moment's time, the great system in which they had prospered and to which they had devoted their allegiance was wiped out.

Notes/Applications

God's judgment descends swiftly and decisively on the city of Babylon. The great city glowed in the light of its wealth and prosperity, dispensing essential services to national leaders, merchants, and tradesmen from the four corners of the earth. In the next moment, a raging fire was consuming the city, and the horrific sight frightened those who once dwelt within her borders.

From a purely human perspective, the destruction of the city could be interpreted simply as the outcome of the jealous tensions that will exist among the world's leaders. However, the angel shows John a dramatically different picture. Recording what he sees, John provides believers with evidence of God's involvement in the cataclysmic events that bring the world's political, financial, and social structures to its knees. That evidence should provide believers with a calm and peaceful outlook on a world that will one day come apart at the seams. God's peace should rule in the hearts of His people even in the midst of paralyzing calamity. The revelation of Jesus Christ as shown to the apostle John makes it very clear that the city of Babylon is destroyed at the direct decree of God. That is why everyone was frightened by what they saw. The leaders of the nations had just destroyed the city with their own hands. They were as frightened by the conflagration they had started as they were by their own involvement in its destruction. However, John tells believers that God had caused these consorts of the woman to turn on her and destroy her *(Revelation 17:17)*.

From the beginning of this book to this very passage, one thing should be perfectly clear. No matter what is happening on the earth or in heaven, God is the One Who has orchestrated every event, executing His justice on unbelievers even as He protects and saves those He has redeemed. The details may at times become confusing, but above it all, God reigns supreme in His heaven and the Lamb, Jesus Christ, judges the world for its sin even as He has died for the sins of the world.

Revelation 18:20–24

18:20 *"Gloat over it, heaven, God's people, apostles, and prophets. God has condemned it for you."*

Earlier, a voice urged God's people to flee Babylon, avoiding the sins that ravaged the great city and, consequently, the judgment God had decreed as punishment for their unyielding stubbornness and intransigence (*vv. 4–5*). The owner of this voice continued to show John the way Babylon would fall apart, destroyed by those who had once done business within her borders (*17:16*). After describing the horrible scene of Babylon's destruction, the voice now changes his audience, continuing to speak to John, but also addressing the host of heaven, the saints for whom Jesus died.

The tone of this address seems to contradict everything that Christians believe is good conduct and basic courtesy, even when dealing with one's enemies. This is not a lament for the loss of life, for those souls who, in the judgment of God, are cast into hell. Rather, this is a celebration for the blood of God's people is finally avenged.

18:21 *Then a powerful angel picked up a stone that was like a large millstone. He threw it into the sea and said, "The important city Babylon will be thrown down with the same force. It will never be found again.*

John saw a powerful angel heave what looked like an enormous boulder into the depths of the sea. The mighty angel then spoke, comparing what he had done with the destruction of the city, saying that Babylon would be "thrown down" in the same manner, meaning that it would have a tremendous, far-reaching impact and it would occur instantaneously. *"Say, 'Babylon will sink like this scroll. It will never rise again because of the disasters that I will bring on it.' The words of Jeremiah end here"* (*Jeremiah 51:64*). Like a huge stone thrown into the ocean, Babylon would be gone, never again to be found on the face of the earth, and the effects of her destruction would ripple out and reach every corner of the world. Babylon—the great city, the globally influential core of paganism, idolatry, and sinfulness—will be violently and utterly destroyed by the wrath of God, and no person on the face of the earth will remain unaffected.

18:22 *The sound of harpists, musicians, flutists, and trumpeters will never be heard in it again. Skilled craftsman will never be found in it again. The sound of a millstone will never be heard in it again.*

The mighty angel introduced in the previous verse continued speaking, further describing the utter destruction of Babylon. There would be no more music played or heard within her borders. Craftsmen will disappear from her streets. The sound of the millstone or any other type of tool used for producing the basic foods necessary to sustain life would be distinctly absent. The mention of these trades demonstrates the far-reaching impact of Babylon's destruction, even on those who would seemingly have little if anything to do with her prosperity. Unpretentious things that bring simple joy will never again grace Babylon's streets. The wealth and prosperity, which bathed the city in materialism and leisure, were distinctly absent from the streets of this once prosperous city.

18:23 *Light from lamps will never shine in it again. Voices of brides and grooms will never be heard in it again. Its merchants were the important people of the world, because all the nations were deceived by its witchcraft.*

Not even the light of a candle or a lamp will be present after God's wrath falls on this city, for Babylon will lie in utter ruin. No light of any kind will survive the devastation to illuminate the once exalted city.

Again, the extent of the destruction is illustrated with a specific example. The merriment and festivity of such things as weddings will be gone forever. The normal routines of life will not be just disrupted, but entirely extinguished.

The powerful merchants of the world dominated the life of the city. They had created policies and procedures to which they had enslaved the entire population of the world. But the entire commercial structure was built, not on sound business and financial principle, but on the deception of a false religion, the worship of the beast. The whole structure of the city's existence was predicated on the illusion of witchcraft, sorcery, and the false glamour of greatness.

18:24 *"The blood of prophets, God's people, and everyone who had been murdered on earth was found in it."*

Externally, Babylon will be a very prosperous, glamorous city. Life will be exciting with all the allurements she offers. The political, economic, and social structures will appear to be an impregnable fortress, providing health, wealth, and security to those who fall under her authority. Underlying its external appeal is the religious framework which directs and determines the course of her world dominance. That religious framework, exalts the beast, who serves Satan, the archenemy of the Lord God and His Son, Jesus Christ. People who participate in the life of this city do so because they have first given their allegiance and worship to the beast, the counterfeit god.

Therefore, it is perfectly reasonable to conclude that anyone who fails to worship the beast, but embraces the only living God and the salvation given them through the sacrifice of Jesus Christ will be considered the enemy of the state. The religious devotion to the beast will demand the blood of God's people in its vain attempt to wipe out those who remind them of their sins. On the outside, the city is bright and cheerful, bustling with commercial activity, but inside they are covered in blood. There is a sense in which the guilt for all those who have been murdered, whether redeemed or not, lies at the door of this great city.

Notes/Applications

When some Bible scholars and commentators foolishly debate the identity of this city, the overriding theme sometimes gets lost in the confusion of the arguments. Forgetting this unprofitable endeavor, it is far better to see specifically what God is saying as He explains to John through different angels and voices exactly what He is doing.

In essence, this city's actual location and identity are not nearly as important as her fate. Babylon represents everything that contradicts and rebels against God's sovereign authority, and dripping from her hands will be the blood of God's saints. The city's actual identity is unimportant when seen in the absolutely certain light of God's perspective: Babylon will be judged by our holy and righteous God, Who will completely destroy her in His wrath according to His predetermined measure *(Revelation 18:4–6).*

Some may wonder how a loving God could unleash such fury upon His creation. Where is the long-suffering, loving God with Whom the multitudes more easily identify? It is far easier to look at God in the aspect of His love and forgiveness than to look at Him in the aspect of His righteousness and holiness, because this latter aspect of God's unchanging character ends in His judgment, punishing both sin and sinner in the violence of His just wrath.

Our sinful nature has confused the issue and, therefore, perverted our perception of the full revelation of God's attributes. The long-suffering God, Who has been ruling the universe from all eternity, is also the righteous Warrior of truth, and righteousness requires an accounting for evil. *"The Lord ... patient, forever loving ... He forgives wrongdoing and disobedience ... He never lets the guilty go unpunished, punishing children ... for their parents' sins to the third and fourth generation"* *(Numbers 14:18).* Therefore, the same God Who lovingly sacrificed His Son on Calvary's cross and raised Him from the dead as the penalty for our transgressions will, in His righteousness, rightfully avenge the torture of His faithful saints by completely decimating the great city, seen as the prostitute who rides proudly on the beast.

REVELATION 19

Revelation 19:1–10

19:1–3 *¹After these things I heard what sounded like the loud noise from a large crowd in heaven, saying, "Hallelujah! Salvation, glory, and power belong to our God. ²His judgments are true and fair. He has condemned the notorious prostitute who corrupted the world with her sexual sins. He has taken revenge on her for the blood of his servants."³A second time they said, "Hallelujah! The smoke goes up from her forever and ever."*

After the voice shows John the destruction of Babylon, the tone of the message of Revelation begins to change into one of praise (*18:20*). One last affirmation again confirms the thoroughness with which God had punished the city, removing all remnants of human civilization within her borders. There will be no more music, marriages, or commerce (*18:21–24*).

Now John returns to witness the courts of heaven. What he sees there is a startling contrast to the devastation he had just witnessed. In heaven there is no sound of grief, no wailing, no mourning the loss of a city that was patently corrupt. In heaven there is only the sound of an enormous crowd praising the Lord, acclaiming the salvation, glory, and power that belongs to God alone.

Such an outpouring of praise was motivated by the scene that the saints of heaven had just witnessed—the judgment of God. The saints first acclaim that what God does in the violence and horror of His judgment on the notorious prostitute is absolutely above question. God is absolutely just in the punishment that He has meted out. He is absolutely righteous, dispensing His judgment within the context of His eternal Truth. He has done nothing that He had not already told the human race He was going to do! The inhabitants deserved the full measure of His wrath, because they turned away from the living God to serve an evil god, and, in so doing, removed themselves from the goodness of His grace.

Interestingly, this is the only passage in the New Testament where the word *Hallelujah* appears, and it seems quite appropriate that such distinctive praise and adoration should come on the heels of God's total destruction of that city which was thoroughly permeated with the greatest concentration of evil the world will ever know.

19:4 *The 24 leaders and the 4 living creatures bowed and worshiped God, who was sitting on the throne. They said, "Amen! Hallelujah!"*

John then saw the twenty-four leaders and four creatures that were seated around God's throne fall prostrate in adoration and worship. These unique beings along with the elders join the massive throng of redeemed people in praise to God, again repeating, "Amen! Hallelujah!" These twenty-four leaders and four creatures exist solely for the purpose of praising and worshiping God on the throne *(Revelation 4:8–11)*. Now, these specially assigned servants of God join with the host of God's saints in a resounding chorus of praise.

19:5 *A voice came from the throne. It said, "Praise our God, all who serve and fear him, no matter who you are."*

A voice emerged from the throne in heaven inviting all God's servants to praise the Lord. The believers were characterized as those that fear him. Those who have feared the Lord and served Him during their earthly sojourn, now praise the Lord in the courts of heaven. Even though the host of heaven has been praising the Lord, the voice coming out of the throne continues to encourage God's people to raise their voices in an ongoing song that will continue to exalt the salvation, glory, and power belonging to God.

It is difficult to determine the identity of the voice of the one speaking from the very throne of God. It seems that the only Person with that kind of authority in that location would be God Himself, or His Son, Jesus. However, the use of pronouns, as in "Praise *our* God" and "all who...fear *Him*" suggest that this was more likely the voice of one of the twenty-four leaders or of the four creatures near the throne. Again, the source of the voice is not as important as the message—a call to worship the One Who sits on the throne as He dispenses His judgment.

19:6 *I heard what sounded like the noise from a large crowd, like the noise of raging waters, like the noise of loud thunder, saying, "Hallelujah! The Lord our God, the Almighty, has become king.*

In response to the invitation by the voice coming from the throne, the host of heaven raises their voices even more passionately as they continue to praise the Lord Who has judged Babylon for its sin and has redeemed these saints from the same destruction by the power of His glorious salvation. That sound coming from such an enormous gathering reminded John of the sound of a large crowd, a cacophony of glorious noise like raging waters and loud, pealing thunder. Again, for the fourth time, a resounding Hallelujah spills joyously from God's people, seeing now that He has become King, not just in the hearts of those who follow Him, but in the fullness of His Kingdom as decreed before the foundation of the world.

19:7 *Let us rejoice, be happy, and give him glory because it's time for the marriage of the lamb. His bride has made herself ready.*

The scene continues the outpouring of praise that began in the first verse of this chapter. The hosts of heaven celebrate the victory of Christ over His enemies. The reason for rejoicing and celebration is revealed. It was time for the marriage of the Lamb, and the bride is finally prepared to meet her Groom. The bride is the gathering of God's elect from the dawn of creation to the end of time. This redeemed assembly is gathered before the throne of God and the Lamb that was sacrificed for their salvation. While on earth, this assembly is sometimes described as the Church, and other times as the Body of Christ (*Ephesians 5:25–32*). The word *marriage* describes the relationship between Christ and His Church to demonstrate an eternal union that is intimate, loving, and faithful (*2 Corinthians 11:2*).

19:8 *She has been given the privilege of wearing dazzling, pure linen." This fine linen represents the things that God's holy people do that have his approval.*

Christ's bride is dressed in the finest, purest, whitest linen. This ends John's record of the praise offered to God by the great assembly of His redeemed people. Then John interprets what this clothing represents. As described in this translation, this clothing represents "the things that God's holy people do that have His approval." But this should not be understood as the means by which these saints are brought into the halls of heaven. Earlier, an angel had told John what these white robes meant: "These are the people who are coming out of the terrible suffering. They have washed their robes and made them white in the blood of the Lamb (*Revelation 7:14*). The saints that comprise the bride have had the sins of their human lives washed away and forgiven forever by

God at Calvary when Christ's substitutionary sacrifice accepted the penalty for man's sin *(2 Corinthians 5:21)*. They are a pure, sinless assembly of God's redeemed people, who stand before the perfect holiness of the righteous Lamb of God, clothed in the righteousness of Christ that had been given to them.

19:9 *Then the angel said to me, "Write this: 'Blessed are those who are invited to the lamb's wedding banquet.'" He also told me, "These are the true words of God."*

The angel told John to write down what he was going to tell him. This emphasis demonstrates the importance of the message that Jesus wants to get across to His people. The angel told John: "Blessed are those who are invited to the Lamb's wedding banquet." It is important that God's people recognize that God has given them an invitation to a magnificent feast hosted by Christ Himself. Then, adding further significance to this invitation, the angel tells John that the eternal God, Who always does what He promises, gives this invitation. The words of God and of His Son, Jesus, are the expression of the eternal Creator, revealing His message to the lost race of mankind.

The prayer of Jesus in the Garden of Gethsemane also expressed the truth with which God has spoken throughout the troubled history of the human race. *"Use the truth to make them holy. Your words are truth"* (John 17:17).

19:10 *I bowed at his feet to worship him. But he told me, "Don't do that! I am your coworker and a coworker of the Christians who hold on to the testimony of Jesus. Worship God, because the testimony of Jesus is the spirit of prophecy!"*

Overwhelmed by the invitation Christ offers to His bride, John fell prostrate at the feet of the angel who gave him this wonderful message. But the angel immediately rejected this gesture of John's worship. Urging John to get up, the angel reminded John that he was not to be worshiped. Such worship was reserved for the Lamb Who sits on the throne. Instead, the angel made it clear that he was simply a "coworker." Although he was an angel, his position was no greater than that of John or of other "Christians who hold on to the testimony of Jesus." They were both servants of God. Neither was greater than the other and each was a servant only of the Lord, to Whom the angel redirected John's worship. Then, he further explained that this testimony of Jesus was "the spirit of prophecy." In saying this, the angel redirected John's focus on Jesus Christ, from Whom these visions were given and to Whom all authentic prophecy pertains.[1]

Notes/Applications

After a lengthy description explaining the thorough annihilation of Babylon, the notorious prostitute that has deceived the nations, the revelation of Jesus Christ continues with a dramatic change in tone and substance. In contrast to the horror of God's judgment, dispensed within the framework of His justice and truth, John's readers are escorted into the courts of heaven. There we see a scene that is as amazing in its beauty as it is overwhelming in the sound of praise.

In the city of Babylon, the inhabitants continued to worship the beast that served Satan. Despite the magnitude of the cosmological events that plagued the entire world, the people of the world raised their fists in the face of God and cursed Him for their troubles. They defied God and cursed Him to the bitter end, until that moment when the great city went up in flames.

In contrast to that God-hating scene, God's saints praise the Lord for His judgment, even as the smoke from Babylon's ruins rises into the sky. In heaven, we hear shouts of "Hallelujah," and songs of praise so loud and so powerful in its expression that the hearts of God's saints on earth today cannot wait to join that happy, redeemed throng.

In both scenes, that of Babylon's destruction and that of heaven, one theme is absolutely consistent—the judgment of God. Yes! The judgment of God evokes the cursing of God in Babylon and the praising of God in heaven.

Should God's people rejoice in the destruction of the wicked? Is it right that Christians should rejoice in the death and damnation of those who curse God?

The answer is simple and straightforward—absolutely! This is not a matter of vengeance on the part of the saints, but it is a matter of agreeing fully with the judgment that God dispenses on those who have rejected Him. This is a matter of seeing clearly the absolute truth unveiled in God's Word, showing the eternal God Who is as great in His judgment as He is in His salvation. God's people, who have suffered greatly at the hands of God's enemies, look at the destruction of Babylon and praise the Lord for avenging the blood of the saints that the world has spilled from the earliest moment of human history.

Like David, the great king of Israel, the one who penned so many of the Psalms, God's people today and in every age sense the injustice of the unregenerate people of the world. They seem to prosper as God's people suffer. With David and with the saints in heaven following the destruction of Babylon, believers cry out: *"Shouldn't I hate those who hate you, O Lord? Shouldn't I be disgusted with those who attack you?" (Psalm 139:21).* Now at the end of time, God's people are invited to the wedding feast of the Lamb. In that glorious moment, they see the fulfillment of His salvation *and* His judgment. With the saints of the ages they join their voices and say: *"Hallelujah! Salvation, glory, and power belong to our God" (Revelation 19:1).*

Revelation 19:11–16

19:11 *I saw heaven standing open. There was a white horse, and its rider is named Faithful and True. With integrity he judges and wages war.*

John now sees one of the most awe-inspiring scenes ever witnessed by a human being—the majestic arrival of Jesus Christ as the King of kings, the Victor over sin and death, and the triumphant, majestic Ruler of the world! The gates of heaven stand open and John sees a radiant figure riding on a white horse. He sees the Lord Jesus Christ, called "Faithful and True" not as adjectives but as a title depicting His authority and unassailable righteousness.

The Rider of this horse "judges and wages war." His judgment is executed in perfect righteousness and He rightly goes to war against His enemies. Following the graphic description of the judgment with which God punished the inhabitants of the earth, this portrayal of Jesus as a mighty warrior removes any doubt about the purity and rightness of His justice. He was angry with the sin of those who turned away from His salvation, and He was perfectly righteous and just when He visited them with frightening devastation.

19:12 *His eyes are flames of fire. On his head are many crowns. He has a name written on him, but only he knows what it is.*

After describing the appearance of Jesus as a righteous judge and a mighty warrior, John offers a physical description of the glorious Rider seated on the white horse. His eyes are like flames, seeming to emphasize the Judge's inescapable and penetrating gaze[2] (*Revelation 1:14*). The many crowns atop His head draw attention to an immediate contrast far superior to the beast's ten crowns (*Revelation 13:1*). This has been commonly accepted as referring to Christ's endless dominion and unlimited sovereignty.[3]

John also notes that the triumphant Messiah has a name written that cannot be understood by anyone other than Himself. Though many people wonder what that name is, it is best to let God have His place and agree to accept the unknown name of God's Messiah. At the very least, the fact that God does not reveal the name to John seems to exhibit Christ's transcendence. Even though Jesus came to earth and was clothed in human flesh, God's people need to remember that He was also conceived by the Holy Spirit. Therefore, Jesus is the very human form of the invisible God. He resides both within His redeemed people and in the heavens at the right hand of the throne of God. He is immanent and transcendent, immeasurably closer than the breath that sustains human life and infinitely greater than anything the human mind can conceive.

19:13 *He wears clothes dipped in blood, and his name is the Word of God.*

John sees that the King is wearing clothes dipped in blood. As a mighty warrior, it is not hard to imagine that Jesus' clothes would be bloody. It is difficult to go into combat and not get stained by the consequences of war. However, the bloody clothes of this Rider could be a representation of His own blood, which was shed for the remission of sin for those He redeems—the redeeming blood by which the victory over sin and death was accomplished for God's faithful.[4] It is also possible that the blood on the robe belonged to the Lord's enemies, both those whose judgment had already taken place and those whose judgment was now imminent. In context to the recent judgment poured out on the rebellious citizens of the world and in agreement with Old Testament prophecy, this might be the better perspective:

> I have trampled alone in the winepress.
> No one was with me.
> In my anger I trampled on people.
> In my wrath I stomped on them.
> Their blood splattered my clothes
> so all my clothing has been stained. (Isaiah 63:3)

The name of the Rider on the white horse is the Word of God. This is the One and same Jesus Christ Who formed the earth and later entered His own creation to purchase redemption for those He came to save *(John 1:1–3, 14)*. He now reappears at the conclusion of earth's history as the conquering King to avenge the blood of His servants *(Revelation 19:2)*, to abolish forever sin and His enemy *(Revelation 20:10)*, to judge the reprobate for their unfaithfulness *(Revelation 20:12–15)*, and to establish His eternal Kingdom *(Revelation 21:1–3)*.

19:14 *The armies of heaven, wearing pure, white linen, follow him on white horses.*

The armies of heaven will follow the Lord as He prepares for battle. They, too, will ride white horses. Like the saints described earlier (v. 8), these armies are dressed in fine linen, which represents the righteousness they received from their Leader *(v. 8)*. This multitude assembled to accompany the great warrior, Jesus Christ, as He prepared to return to the earth, not because the Lord required their assistance to secure His victory, but so that they could participate in the celebration of His victory with Him.

It seems consistent with other Scriptures to say that, at the very least, this group will consist of those whose redemption was purchased by the Messiah's sacrifice at Calvary. *"They will go to war against the lamb. The lamb will conquer them because he is Lord of lords and King of kings. Those who are called, chosen, and faithful are with him"* *(Revelation 17:14)*.

19:15 *A sharp sword comes out of his mouth to defeat the nations. He will rule them with an iron scepter and tread the winepress of the fierce anger of God Almighty.*

This verse employs imagery familiar from the Old Testament that portrays the Lord's judgment. The Lord, Who returns to earth with the armies of heaven, will defeat the nations with the sharp sword, which emerges from His mouth. It is certain that a physical sword does not come out of Jesus' mouth, but the imagery defines the deadly accuracy of Christ's penetrating evaluation of the sins of mankind. It is with His truth and unswerving rightness that their deceptions will be exposed and their sins will be judged. The words of truth spoken by the Lord Jesus Christ will be the only weapon necessary to judge and condemn all who oppose Him. As Isaiah prophesied: *"He will strike the earth with a rod from his mouth. He will kill the wicked with the breath from his lips"* *(Isaiah 11:4b).*

When Christ returns to earth, He will rule the nations with an iron scepter, which displays the firm, unbending characteristic of His authority.[5] The reign of Christ will be black and white. There will be no room for leniency or tolerance of wickedness. *"You will break them with an iron scepter. You will smash them to pieces like pottery"* *(Psalm 2:9).* *"Those people will rule the nations with iron scepters and shatter them like pottery"* *(Revelation 2:27).*

Finally, the Lord Jesus Christ treads "the winepress of fierce anger." The glorious Messiah riding a white horse will dispense the intense fury of God's wrath on mankind as the consequences of its sinfulness and disobedience.

19:16 *On his clothes and his thigh he has a name written: King of kings and Lord of lords.*

John records another of Jesus' royal titles written on His robe and on His thigh: King of kings and Lord of lords. Nobody could ever underestimate the absolute sovereignty of this majestic Champion. Though many did not believe that Jesus was the promised Messiah when He came to earth as an unassuming teacher, there would never again be any mistaking His identity when this imposing Warrior returns to the earth the second time. This revelation of the last days was given to the apostle John, but Paul, God's messenger to Gentiles, also gave testimony to the glory of the Messiah he served: *"God is the blessed and only ruler. He is the King of kings and Lord of lords"* *(1 Timothy 6:15).*

Notes/Applications

The Lord and Savior Jesus, the Christ, the Son of the Living God, will one day return to earth in all of His glory to judge the earth for its sin and stubborn disbelief. He, as the Word, the Truth, the Amen, and the Faithful Witness, will descend from His place at the Father's right hand to judge His archenemy and rule the earth according to His holy banner of truth and righteousness.

Furthermore, when Christ returns to battle Satan and his minions, He will not ride a lowly colt as He chose to do when He entered Jerusalem during the Passover. Instead, He will triumphantly return upon a white stallion, and we, as His Bride, will follow on white horses, because He has redeemed us with His precious blood.

The scene John records challenges the wildest imagination of the human spirit, yet Scripture confirms that this will happen as surely as the names that adorn the Son of God. If believers remember the gift of God's promises wrapped in these prophetic words, it will help them endure present tribulation with prayerful and hopeful anticipation.

> *Faithful and True, O Living Word, we anticipate your triumphant return, for then our eyes shall behold as You wage war against the serpent of old. By the sword of Your mouth, You will bring the archenemy to shame, crushing his evil empire and casting him into the brimstone's flame. Lord of lords, King of kings, faithful witness of the Father, we await the day when every tongue will proclaim that Jesus Christ is the name above all names.*

Revelation 19:17–21

19:17–18 *¹⁷I saw an angel standing in the sun. He cried out in a loud voice to all the birds flying overhead, "Come! Gather for the great banquet of God. ¹⁸Eat the flesh of kings, generals, warriors, horses and their riders, and all free people and slaves, both important or insignificant people."*

John then saw an angel standing in the brightness of the sun. He called out with a thunderous, commanding voice to all of the birds that flew in the heavens—a call that could be heard throughout the earth. The angel invited the birds to come and to perform a specific task—to gather for a huge feast he referred to as "the great banquet of God." These birds were invited to feast upon the flesh of the enemies of God who would be slain at the great battle that was about to take place.

> *¹⁷Son of man, this is what the Almighty Lord says: Tell every kind of bird and every wild animal, "Assemble, and come together from all around for the sacrifice that I'm preparing for you. It will be a huge feast on the mountains of Israel. You can eat meat and drink blood there. ¹⁸You can eat the meat of warriors and drink the blood of the princes of the earth. All of them will be killed like rams, lambs, goats, bulls and all the best animals of Bashan." (Ezekiel 39:17–18)*

These verses indicate that none who followed the beast into battle and opposed God would be spared, whether the greatest of leaders (kings, captains, and mighty men) or the most common of men (free and slave, small and great). It was much more than a great battle that would take place. It would be unrestrained carnage.

19:19 *I saw the beast, the kings of the earth, and their armies gathered to wage war against the rider on the horse and his army.*

This scene is an elaboration on the earlier scene, which John had witnessed. In that scene, the leaders of the nations are gathered together to engage Jesus and His saints in battle, attempting a futile effort to remove Jesus from His rightful place at the right hand of the Father: "¹⁴They are spirits of demons that do miracles. These spirits go to the kings of the whole world and gather them for the war on the frightening day of God Almighty... ¹⁶The spirits gathered the kings at the place which is called Armageddon in Hebrew" *(Revelation 16:14, 16)*

In this scene, John saw the beast—the figure through which Satan would mount His campaign—and all of his armies led by the world leaders, the kings of the earth. In a battle where size and strength might have been a decisive factor, the armies of the beast would seem to have the advantage. However, this war will be won without the clash of swords other than the sword of truth and judgment that proceeds from the Lord's mouth. This great multitude had been deceived and was now gathered to make war against Jesus Christ and His heavenly army, still unaware of their imminent and certain destruction when they engaged Jesus Christ in battle. God had determined the actions of the beast to mislead the multitudes only for His preordained purposes of judgment and only for the preordained period of time, both of which are now fulfilled.

19:20 *The beast and the false prophet who had done miracles for the beast were captured. By these miracles the false prophet had deceived those who had the brand of the beast and worshiped its statue. Both of them were thrown alive into the fiery lake of burning sulfur.*

The battle will be over before it ever begins. The beast and his cohort will be immediately subdued. There is no mention of an actual, physical conflict because it was entirely unnecessary for the Lord to engage the enemy in order to secure the victory. In His perfect sovereignty, God is able to bring anything and everything to pass by the simple force of His will.

These two will be the most powerful and influential beings that the world will ever know, yet their destruction will come in a moment. They will not be killed but will be thrown alive into the "fiery lake of burning sulfur." The beast, which rose from the sea and the second beast, which rose from the land, known also as the false prophet, had conspired to draw the earth's inhabitants into the web of their deceit. The false prophet had erected a statue of the first beast and demanded that everyone bow down and worship the statue. This was accomplished by the sole determination of the Lord God for the purpose of reserving His enemies for the full measure of His righteous judgment.

> **DIG DEEPER:** *Lake of Fire*
>
> This is the first of four times this term appears in Revelation. As the theme develops in the following chapter, we find that the devil, the beast, and his prophet (20:10) and all those who are not found in the Book of Life (20:15) are cast into this place of everlasting torment. Throughout the gospel narratives, Jesus also uses the imagery of a fiery judgment for those who do not believe in Him (*Matthew 5:22; 7:19; 13:40-42, 50; 18:8-9; 25:41; Mark 9:43, 48-49; Luke 16:24; John 15:6*).

19:21 *The rider on the horse killed the rest with the sword that came out of his mouth. All the birds gorged themselves on the flesh of those who had been killed.*

After the beast and the false prophet are thrown into "the fiery lake of burning sulfur," the Lord will then kill the rest of those who gather to make war against Him. Their destruction will be as complete as it will be instantaneous. The countless number of people assembled to make war against the Lamb of God will be slain immediately. They will not be thrown into the lake of fire with the beast and his false prophet. Instead, at this time, the sword that comes out of His mouth will physically kill them. Again, this does not mean an actual, physical conflict but, rather, the sovereign act of God's wrath that will result in the immediate deaths of all who had aligned themselves with Christ's enemy,

providing the birds with the flesh they consume as they celebrate the
"*great banquet of God*" (*v. 17*).

Notes/Applications

Following John's observation of a host of people gathered before the
throne to praise the Lord God and His Lamb, John hears the voice
of an angel inviting birds to a feast prepared by God. Consistent with
the pattern that John has witnessed throughout this revelation given
to him by Jesus Christ, moments of heart-inspiring praise are followed
by moments of such frightful destruction that his mind suffers mental
and emotional overload.

Without preamble, John witnesses a battle of immense size, but
little actual conflict. The world leaders gather an enormous army to
engage the Lord in battle. With the sword of His mouth, the unassailable rightness of Christ's justice and resulting judgment, Jesus
remands the beast and his false prophet to the fiery lake of burning
sulphur. Then in one swift action, Jesus kills the massive army arrayed
against Him. The banquet prepared by God will feed a huge gathering
of birds who will eat until they are gorged with human flesh.

No matter which scene John's readers witness through the care-
ful record he has written, the saints of God should see the hand of
God moving through history both in the salvation of those who are
assembled at the throne of God and the judgment of those who gather
to oppose the Lord. In both situations, the Lord has determined the
unfolding history of His creation, determining the ending from the
beginning. He determines the salvation of those He intends to save
as well as the judgment of those that inhabit the earth excluded from
the boundaries of His saving grace. The Lord does nothing by some
capricious reaction to human offenses. Rather, everything He does is
accomplished within the sanctity of His own counsel, executing His
dominion over His creation with absolute rightness and infallible
justice.

The beast's temporary reign over the leaders of the nations and
thereby the whole world's population results not from God's inability

to act, but precisely because of His divine decree. He sends His enemies a delusion so that they will believe the lie of the beast, reserving them for His judgment. And then, with perfect righteousness, He destroys the entire army that has been assembled by the beast.

As God's people make the difficult journey through the maze of their human experience, it is very easy to succumb to the notion that everything happens by the chance confluence of actions and reactions. It is very difficult to see the hand of God that has brought them within the fold of His saving grace. But this paradox is not the result of God's inaction, but the dimness of our sin-laden souls. Even though redeemed, believers still discover that the influences imposed on them by the cares of this world dominate their thinking and often lead them to question God.

Nevertheless, the irrefutable witness of the Scriptures and particularly of this passage in Revelation reminds God's people that God is always on His throne and He is always directing their pathway throughout the entire journey of their lives until that moment when they all stand together before His throne, singing His praise with the countless host of the redeemed.

And all God's people say, "Amen!" Holy and just is our God! May His name be praised forever!

REVELATION 20

SPECIAL NOTE

One of the most debated passages concerning the last days is found in this chapter—the Millennium. There are essentially three positions regarding this period of time: 1) premillennial, which generally views these as one thousand literal years during which time the Lord Jesus Christ will reign following His second coming; 2) postmillennial, which views these one thousand years as depicting the consummation of the church's history during which time the saints will ultimately accomplish their gospel mission of evangelizing the world through those agents provided them, namely, the Holy Spirit and the Word of God, after which time the Lord will return to the earth, as described in chapter nineteen; and 3) amillennial, which generally considers this period as referring to the span between the Messiah's first and second advent but views these thousand years as referring only to themes of spiritual significance.[1]

Each position poses certain inherent complexities whose examinations are better reserved for other academic or theological endeavors. However, certain matters deserve mention for the sake of determining a perspective from which to approach this commentary. First, those who view 19:19-21 as depicting the same event as that presented in 20:9-10 encounter an obstacle in the description of Satan being thrown into the lake of fire "where the beast and the false prophet were also thrown," which appears to refer to different entities experiencing the same fate at different points in time. Furthermore, the events depicted in each chapter noticeably portray different events with different characters and different outcomes.

With these things in mind, the presentation of this commentary interprets this chapter as subsequent events depicted in the previous chapter, whereby the thousand years portrayed follows the triumphant return of the Lord Jesus Christ. Although some question whether this period is definitively ascertained as a span of one thousand literal years, the identical designation of this period occurring six times in the first seven verses seems to support a literal reading in the text. Despite the differences in interpretation, it is most important to note that these disputes should never undermine the magnitude of the last four chapters (*Revelation 19–22*), which tell God's people about the marvelous return of the Lord Jesus Christ; His final wrath, judgment, and punishment of all sin and evil; the vindication of all who have placed their faith in the one true God; and the establishment of God's glorious, eternal Kingdom where all His faithful will dwell forevermore in His presence.[2]

While these differences are an integral part of the fabric of the Christian Church, they should never be the cause of discord among those who are called by His Name. The text of Revelation as well as other passages of Scripture may provide difficulties of interpretation relating to portions of the biblical record on the last days, but inabilities to properly and uniformly interpret the Scriptures on a particular issue should have no significant impact on the Church's understanding of the work of Jesus on the Cross of Calvary. People who have been born again by the work of the Holy Spirit Who shows them Christ's sacrifice for their sin may disagree on some aspects of prophecy concerning the last days, but they may also have warm, invigorating fellowship with each other. On the work of Christ, His life, death, burial, resurrection, and ascension there can be no debate. For this reason, any disunity among the Body of Christ should be dispelled in the light of God's salvation through His Son, Jesus Christ, reducing debate about the end of days to a position of lesser significance. It is important, because it is a part of God's Word. But, because of the complexities involved in interpretation, it should never be used as a reason to break fellowship with believers who hold a different view.

Revelation 20:1–6

20:1 *I saw an angel coming down from heaven, holding the key to the bottomless pit and a large chain in his hand.*

After witnessing the warrior Messiah overcome the beast, false prophet, and all those who gathered to join them in battle, John saw another angel descend from heaven. The angel held in his hands a large chain and the keys to the bottomless pit. This may have been the same angel who had earlier released some demons for judgment *(Revelation 9:1)*.

Whether this bottomless pit depicts a literal or symbolic place is uncertain, but within the context of this verse and similar verses in chapters nine and eleven, it can be assumed that it was a place designated by the Lord to exile certain spiritual beings *(Revelation 9:1–11; 11:7)*.

20:2–3 *²He overpowered the serpent, that ancient snake, named Devil and Satan. The angel chained up the serpent for 1,000 years. ³He threw it into the bottomless pit. The angel shut and sealed the pit over the serpent to keep it from deceiving the nations anymore until the 1,000 years were over. After that it must be set free for a little while.*

God dispatched this angel to bind Satan and cast him into the bottomless pit for one thousand years. There can be little doubt regarding the identity of the one being overcome since he is referred to by every name that he is called in the Book of Revelation—the Devil and Satan *(12:9)*, the serpent *(12:3)*, and the "huge serpent" *(12:9)*.

As with the overthrow of the beast and the false prophet in the previous chapter, there is no description of a struggle. The angel was in no danger of being harmed by Satan because he was carrying out Almighty God's will.

The bottomless pit has been portrayed as the place where evil resides. Earlier in this book, a horde of locusts was released from the bottomless pit to wreak havoc upon the earth for a predetermined time of judgment (*Revelation 9:2–3*). In Revelation 11:7, John tells his readers that the beast who makes war with God's two witnesses came from the bottomless pit. This time, the Lord binds Satan and sends him into the bottomless pit *"to keep it from deceiving the nations anymore."* For one thousand years, escape will be impossible. After this time, as this verse forecasts and later verses explain in more detail, Satan will again be loosed upon the earth for a short period.

Some commentators have suggested that Satan was bound as a result of Christ's sacrifice at Calvary. There is a sense in which this is true. Those who have been saved from the foundation of the world have also been sealed by the Holy Spirit for redemption. In this perspective, Satan is prevented from snatching the redeemed from the hand of their Redeemer.[3] However, in this developing passage, Satan is imprisoned in such a way that he can no longer directly influence the nations with his ongoing deceit. Other biblical references clearly portray the devil as actively and aggressively pursuing the destruction of believers in our present age (*Acts 5:3; 2 Corinthians 4:3–4; Ephesians 2:2; 2 Timothy 2:26; 1 Peter 5:8*). There are several Old Testament passages, which seem to refer to a future period absent of Satan's influence[4] (*Isaiah 11:6–9*).

20:4 *I saw thrones, and those who sat on them were allowed to judge. Then I saw the souls of those whose heads had been cut off because of their testimony about Jesus and because of the word of God. They had not worshiped the beast or its statue and were not branded on their foreheads or hands. They lived and ruled with Christ for 1,000 years.*

John saw thrones, a symbol of authority. That authority is exercised in the framework of judgment. Nothing more is said. No information is given about the number of people assigned this task. At this point, John does not even identify the people who are to be judged. John also does not specify the location of the thrones.

At the same time, John saw the souls of those who were killed for their unwavering faith in Christ Jesus and for refusing to bear the

mark of the beast. It seems that John's identification of the saints who
live and rule with Christ is a little more narrowly defined. He specifically states that these saints are martyrs, saints who were executed for
remaining faithful to the testimony of Jesus Christ. These saints are
then given the honor of living and ruling with Christ for one thousand years.

20:5 *The rest of the dead did not live until the 1,000 years
ended. This is the first time that people come back to life.*

Now John observes that the saints that he sees have all been brought
back to life during the first resurrection. This statement is more inclu-
sive than his observation that the saints who live and rule with Christ
are the martyrs. Here it seems that John includes all those saints who
were arrayed for battle and followed their King as He engaged and
destroyed His enemies *(Revelation 19:14)*.

This first resurrection serves as a contrast to those who participate in the second resurrection, which does not occur until the end
of these thousand years. The implication shows that inclusion in the
first resurrection is something to be desired. Inclusion in the second
resurrection is to be avoided at whatever cost.

It is clear in light of the entirety of Scripture that this event will
include all of God's redeemed. However, it should also be noted that
the verses in this chapter do not necessarily describe this resurrection so much as make reference to it. Though it is very difficult to
delineate chronologically the scope of events described in the Book of
Revelation, it is generally agreed that the Bible depicts this resurrection as occurring in conjunction with the second coming of the Lord
Jesus Christ.

Because scriptural evidence confirms that the resurrection of the
redeemed will coincide with Christ's return, the event would appear
to have already occurred by this point *(Revelation 14:14–16; 19:11–13)*.
Sometime earlier, the redeemed of the Lord are returned to their resurrection bodies, join the Lord as He goes into battle, and then share

in this extended period of relative peace and calm as Jesus rules the earth with a rod of iron and Satan is bound in the bottomless pit.

20:6 *Blessed and holy are those who are included the first time that people come back to life. The second death has no power over them. They will continue to be priests of God and Christ. They will rule with him for 1,000 years.*

Those to whom this first resurrection pertains are considered "blessed and holy." It can hardly be thought that such a description should ever be made of an unbeliever. While these verses do not clearly identify those seated on the thrones of judgment, this is the verse by which many contend that the honor of judgment is bestowed upon all of God's faithful. The case is made by the evident link within the statement that whoever has part in the first resurrection will reign with Christ a thousand years. They would also have no part in "the second death," which will be described later in verse fourteen. Again, John stated that this resurrected group will reign for one thousand years as "priests of God and Christ," indicating their unhindered access to the Lord God and His Lamb. Peter, Christ's apostle, wrote a letter to early Christians, telling them: "You are chosen people, a royal priesthood, a holy nation, people who belong to God. You were chosen to tell about the excellent qualities of God, who called you out of darkness into his marvelous light" *(1 Peter 2:9)*. As priests, all believers not only have direct access to the throne of God, but they are also chosen to enter the ministry of reconciliation, telling the nations about God's salvation in and through Jesus Christ.

Notes/Applications

As chapter nineteen draws to a close, John tells his readers that the hosts of heaven followed the One called "The Word of God." This mighty warrior, Jesus Christ, then engages His enemies in a battle that is won simply by the sword that proceeds from the mouth of the Son of God. In one swift blow, Jesus captures the beast and his false prophet and throws them into the fiery lake of burning sulphur. Those who followed the beast into this futile battle were then slain by the same sword, resulting in a great banquet for the birds of the air.

Even though the beast and his cohort had been condemned to their fiery destination, the serpent, that is, Satan, was still attempting to deceive the nations with his treachery. So the Lord God dispatches an angel to imprison Satan in the bottomless pit for one thousand years. Now with Satan removed from the scene, the beast and the false prophet thrown into the fiery lake of burning sulphur, there is relative peace on earth. In the providence of God, Christ has defeated His enemies, engaged His saints in the administration of His Kingdom, and established a physical Kingdom on the earth.

Although not clearly depicted, the first resurrection of the redeemed in Christ had taken place some time during this period coinciding with the victory of the mighty warrior, the Lord Jesus Christ. The saints that have joined their Lord in battle have the honor to live and rule with Christ during this thousand-year rule of peace under the exclusive authority of Jesus Christ. In all the years of human history, this period of time will be as close to heaven that the world will ever get.

Whatever interpretations people give to these verses, it is clear that Jesus is King, not just in the hearts of His people, but throughout the whole world. Even though Christ's position as sovereign ruler of His entire creation is incontestable, He has now vanquished His enemies and ascended His throne on earth, governing the inhabitants of the earth under His authority. Under His divine Kingdom, His people will finally live with their Lord, not in the struggle their earthly pilgrimage has required of them, but in the simple glory of His presence and the security of His rule.

Revelation 20:7–15

20:7–8 *⁷When 1,000 years are over, Satan will be freed from his prison. ⁸He will go out to deceive Gog and Magog, the nations in the four corners of the earth, and gather them for war. They will be as numerous as the grains of sand on the seashore.*

At the close of chapter nineteen, Jesus condemns the beast and his false prophet to the fiery lake of burning sulphur. Then, with one swift blow, Jesus destroys the army that the beast assembled to make war against Him—its kings, generals, and foot soldiers, both small and great (*Revelation 19:19–21*). After that momentous battle, the remaining inhabitants of the earth were subjected to the rule of Christ and His redeemed people, who had come back to life in the first resurrection. It can be safely assumed that the earth's population grew and again replenished the earth.

Now at the end of one thousand years God releases Satan from his prison, the bottomless pit in which he had been confined for one thousand years (*v. 2*). The purpose for his release is explained clearly— to deceive Gog and Magog, that is, the nations from the four corners of the earth. Satan, the archenemy of Jesus Christ, had witnessed the devastation poured out on his beast and the false prophet. He had witnessed the massive carnage of the army that had been assembled in a futile attempt to destroy the Lord and His armies. However, Satan was not influenced at all by this disastrous outcome. Since Satan is not motivated by logic, but only by his hatred for his Creator, he assembles a host of the world's inhabitants to again attempt to defeat Christ. This army will be much larger than the one assembled by the beast and his false prophet.

For reasons not revealed to John and his readers, the Lord will release Satan for the sole purpose of deceiving the nations and gathering a massive army to again engage in a battle with the Lord and His saints. Even after one thousand years of relative peace under Christ's authority, it appears that much of the world's population, though directly and personally governed by Christ, will not willingly submit to His rule. The presence of Jesus ruling over the affairs of the nations will not automatically win the hearts of those He rules. Thus, the resources for Satan's new army will be immense.

20:9 *I saw that they spread over the broad expanse of the earth and surrounded the camp of God's holy people and the beloved city. Fire came from heaven and burned them up.*

The nations joined Satan in his doomed effort to defeat Christ and those who reigned with Him. People came from throughout the earth and surrounded "the beloved city," where the "camp of God's holy people" was located. This city is often identified as Jerusalem, reestablished as the world's capital city under Christ just as Babylon served as the capital under the beast and his false prophet.[5] Isaiah, the prophet of Israel, wrote nearly 750 years earlier: "In the last days the mountain of the Lord's house will be established as the highest of the mountains and raised above the hills. All the nations will stream to it" *(Isaiah 2:2)*. However, the "camp of God's holy people" and "the beloved city" may also represent the saints scattered throughout the world, confronted by God's enemies wherever they lived across "the broad expanse of the earth."[6] In contrast to the battlefield, Armageddon, this battlefield would know no boundaries.

Despite Satan's long-awaited and well-attended scheme to overcome Christ and His faithful people, his greatest efforts will meet immediate destruction. In the same way that the Lord dealt with those gathered for battle at Armageddon, those who follow Satan will be destroyed without any physical confrontation. Rather, the Lord's unconditional victory will be secured in a mere moment when the Lord sends an all-consuming fire down from heaven, instantly and utterly consuming Satan's vast armies.

20:10 *The devil, who deceived them, was thrown into the fiery lake of sulfur, where the beast and the false prophet were* *also thrown. They will be tortured day and night forever and ever.*

This will be God's final act of judgment against Satan, the final elimination of sin and evil. The devil will be thrown into the fiery lake of sulfur, joining the beast and false prophet, who had been permanently consigned there by the Lord at His second coming *(Revelation 19:20).* Now, the instigator of all evil, the devil himself, would at last join the two chief agents of his deceit.

These three—Satan, the beast, and the false prophet, which formed the unholy trilogy—will be tortured in this lake of fire forever. People often entertain mental images of Satan as the ruler of hell, the place where those who die in unbelief descend to its depths and become slaves or servants of this cruel and commanding taskmaster who has horns and wields a spear. This verse should wipe out such false notions about hell and the lake of fire. This lake of fire has been created and controlled by God for the sole purpose of eternal condemnation. It is not a place where Satan will govern as ringleader but the location where he will receive God's just sentence of eternal punishment. This verse clearly unveils a place of eternal conscious torment prepared for Satan as just condemnation for his persistent, ruthless campaign against the Lord God and His elect.[7]

20:11 *I saw a large, white throne and the one who was sitting on it. The earth and the sky fled from his presence, but no place was found for them.*

John observed a great white throne upon which sat One before Whom not even the earth and the sky could remain. Because of the magnificence of His transcendent glory, the earth and the sky will attempt to flee from His presence. Even though other Revelation passages place God the Father on the throne *(Revelation 4:2-11; 7:9-10; 12:5),* this and other scriptural references suggest that this would be a throne of judgment appointed for and occupied by the Lord Jesus Christ *(John 5:19; 5:28-30; 8:16).*

Heaven and earth and the whole universe around them were terrified by the majesty of Jesus Christ seated upon His throne of final and ultimate judgment. The whole of God's cosmic creation was not just trembling, but had no place to hide. The universe could not get away fast enough and far enough. There is nothing or no one who could shield God's creation from the glory and the power of Jesus Christ's blinding brilliance and terrifying authority in His absolute sovereignty to condemn and to save. This is the time when heaven and earth see Jesus Christ revealed in His ultimate glory like never before.

> *Look at the sky. Look at the earth below. The sky will vanish like smoke. The earth will wear out like clothing, and those who live there will die like flies. But my salvation will last forever, and my righteousness will never fail.* (Isaiah 51:6)

20:12 *I saw the dead, both important and unimportant people, standing in front of the throne. Books were opened, including the Book of Life. The dead were judged on the basis of what they had done, as recorded in the books.*

John saw "important and unimportant people" standing before God, indicating the inclusion of all people regardless of earthly significance. Some commentators see this as the whole of mankind, both believers and unbelievers, standing before this throne of judgment[8] (*Matthew 25:31-33; John 5:28-29; Romans 14:10; 1 Peter 4:5*). Others view this as a resurrection only of unbelievers to receive their condemnation[9] (*John 3:18; 5:24*). Nevertheless, John's emphasis recorded the fate of those who died in unbelief.

The dead were judged according to books that were opened before the Lord, including the Book of Life. Specifically, they were judged "on the basis of what they had done." Unbelievers can be judged *only* according to their works because they have never received Christ's sacrifice on their behalf. Therefore, they will be judged by the unwavering truth of the Law, the Word of God. The redeemed, too, are guilty of transgressing the Law of God, but their sins have been washed away by the sacrifice of Christ's blood. Therefore, they will not be judged according to their works, which would otherwise condemn them also, but by the righteousness of Christ, Who willingly accepted the penalty for their sin.

20:13 *The sea gave up its dead. Death and hell gave up their dead. People were judged based on what they had done.*

To further emphasize that this judgment included the entire host of the dead, John tells his readers that even "the sea gave up its dead," and "death and hell gave up their dead."[10] Despite many errant ideas that hell is the eternal destination of those who die in unbelief, this verse clearly establishes the lake of fire as the ultimate destination for hell and all those who await God's final judgment.[11] Again, it is stated that all will be raised from the dead to face the judgment of God according to their works, which can only testify against them. It makes little difference how long the physical body has laid in the grave, no matter the violence or location of death, by the power of God's command, all bodies will return to life to face God's judgment.

20:14 *Death and hell were thrown into the fiery lake. (The fiery lake is the second death.)*

Death and hell, which contains the souls of all of those who died apart from faith in the Lord Jesus Christ, were cast into the lake of fire with Satan, the beast, and the false prophet. John specifically called this "the second death." All unbelievers throughout history will receive this sentence and experience this condemnation of eternal torment.

Hell holds the souls of God's unrepentant creation, and now this domain, including all its occupants, will be thrown into the eternal lake of fire. Death, too, will finally be eradicated. Their purposes no longer will exist, but God's unassailable truth and righteousness still requires the continued and eternal punishment of unbelievers. In Paul's great chapter on the resurrection, he, too, saw God's final action that concludes His work among His creation, both in salvation and judgment: *"The last enemy he will destroy is death"* (1 Corinthians 15:26).

20:15 *Those whose names were not found in the Book of Life were thrown into the fiery lake.*

This verse plainly states that those whose names were not written in the Book of Life were "thrown into the fiery lake" for eternal condemnation with Satan and his demons. They would exist in eternal, indestructible bodies that would forever suffer the consequences of their sins.[12] Conversely, believers in the Lord Jesus Christ and His finished work at Calvary have their names written in the Book of Life and will live eternally in the presence of God and His Lamb. With all evil finally relegated to the fiery lake of burning sulphur, only the establishment of God's eternal Kingdom remains unsettled, and this blessed event, serving as the pinnacle of this extraordinary book, is revealed in the final chapters.

Notes/Applications

When Satan is bound for the thousand years that the Lord Jesus Christ rules the earth, the devil will no longer be an influence for rebellion and treason against the Most High God. The overall environment of Christ's reign will be couched in peace and justice. Israel's beloved prophet, Isaiah, seems to capture the broad sweep of redemptive history when he penned these words:

> [6]For unto us a child is born, unto us a son is given: and the government shall be upon his shoulder: and his name shall be called Wonderful, Counselor, The mighty God, The everlasting Father, The Prince of Peace. [7]Of the increase of his government and peace there shall be no end, upon the throne of David, and upon his kingdom, to order it, and to establish it with judgment and with justice from henceforth even for ever. The zeal of the Lord of hosts will perform this. (Isaiah 9:6–7, KJV).

Thus, the apostle John and the prophet Isaiah, separated in time by more than seven hundred years, are forever linked together in that moment when they see the reign of Jesus Christ consummated in this time when Jesus rules the earth in peace with justice.

Nevertheless, there is an underlying current of rebellion among those who still refuse to submit to the King that rules the earth with such unswerving truth and righteousness. At the end of this one thousand year period, the Lord sets Satan free for a short time to deceive the nations and attempt once again to wage war with God's Lamb. From the vast resources of unrepentant people still inhabiting the earth, Satan is able to amass an army of immense proportions.

However, the fate of this army is the same as the army of the beast and his false prophet. In one moment, the Lord throws Satan, hell, and death into the fiery lake of burning sulphur. Jesus destroys the rest of the army of unrepentant humanity with fire that descends from heaven and consumes them. Then, Jesus ascends the throne as king and judge, and proceeds to hand out the verdict on every unbeliever who has ever lived from the dawn of human history to the end of time.

Those whom God has redeemed through the blood of the Lamb will rejoice in this moment for the gift of their salvation will be consummated. They will at long last become God's redeemed saints in the sinless environment of God's presence, no longer working out their salvation with fear and trembling. When the Spirit opened their eyes and showed them the truth of their sin and the hope of their salvation in Christ, the Lord clothed His people with His righteousness. But that righteousness was born in fragile vessels of the flesh. Now at last, they stand before the throne of Christ, not in the decay of their mortal flesh, but in the brightness of their immortal bodies, confident, not in themselves, but in the Lord Who has saved and preserved them. Now the words of Paul in his letter to the Corinthians will be fulfilled:

> [51]*I'm telling you a mystery. Not all of us will die, but we will all be changed.* [52]*It will happen in an instant, in a split second at the sound of the last trumpet. Indeed, that trumpet will sound, and then the dead will come back to life. They will be changed so that they can live forever.* [53]*This body that decays must be*

changed into a body that cannot decay. This mortal body must be changed into a body that will live forever. [54]When this body that decays is changed into a body that cannot decay, and this mortal body is changed into a body that will live forever, then the teaching of Scripture will come true: "Death is turned into victory! [55]Death, where is your victory? Death, where is your sting?" [56]Sin gives death its sting, and God's standards give sin its power. [57]Thank God that he gives us the victory through our Lord Jesus Christ. (1 Corinthians 15:51–57)

Those who have continued to rebel and reject the salvation Christ died to bring to the world will at this moment realize with new understanding that they have pursued their own goals at the cost of their own souls. Now there remains no more hope of salvation. Now before them yawns the gateway to the fiery furnace where they will suffer torment, not for a short time, but for all eternity. They will be for all eternity what they have always been during their earthly lives—the spawn of Satan and children of the devil. With him, they will endure untold torture, knowing now that Jesus is everything He said He is.

And so, in this passage, we arrive at the final outcome of life—life eternal with Christ or life eternal with Satan. At long last, by the predetermined counsel of God, the earth's inhabitants receive the consequences of the choice they have made in life. Jesus Christ, both Savior and Judge, mitigates the eternal destinations of those who have loved and served Him as well as those who have hated and rejected Him.

The words of Moses gain significant force when looking at this frightening scene that plays out for all to see. "[19]*I call on heaven and earth as witnesses today that I have offered you life or death, blessings or curses. Choose life so that you and your descendants will live. [20]Love the Lord your God, obey him, and be loyal to him. This will be your way of life, and it will mean a long life for you" (Deuteronomy 30:19–20).*

REVELATION 21

SPECIAL NOTE

So much of Revelation seems to raise more questions than offer answers. Which things are to be taken literally and which are to be taken metaphorically? What does this city refer to, and what does that character depict? When will this event take place, and who will be affected? Readers of all ages find themselves raising these kinds of questions as they read this book.

One pattern that becomes evident in the description of the new heaven and new earth in this chapter is the recurring use of numbers with multiples of twelve. Much has been made of the symbolic relevance of this number, primarily that it represents completeness.[1] The number twelve plays a big part in God's Word throughout both the Old and New Testaments. When God formed the nation of Israel in the wilderness of the Sinai Peninsula, He divided the nation into twelve tribes as derived from the twelve sons of Jacob. When the time came for Jesus to select His apostles, He chose twelve men. Around the throne of God are twenty-four elders, two two sets of twelve, which some say represent the twelve tribes and the twelve apostles. Whether there is some symbolic significance to this number in John's record of Christ's revelation is difficult to determine.

One thing, however, is certain. Though debates still arise concerning certain details of these last two chapters, the relevance of these disparities is relatively insignificant when compared to the glorious majesty and splendor contained within these passages. While people disagree about the details of these chapters, everyone agrees that chapters twenty-one and twenty-two assure believers that they will one day enjoy an eternal inheritance in the glorious presence of God the Father and the Lamb of God, His Son.

Revelation 21:1–8

21:1 *I saw a new heaven and a new earth, because the first heaven and earth had disappeared, and the sea was gone.*

As chapter twenty draws to a close, the thousand year reign of Christ ends, Satan is released from the bottomless pit to once again deceive the nations, and the Lord completely vanquishes the armies amassed against Him, throwing Satan, death, and hell into the fiery lake of burning sulphur.

Now John sees a new heaven and a new earth. Exactly when the old heaven and earth had been destroyed is uncertain. It is possible that this is what John witnessed when he saw the earth and the sky "flee away" from the presence of the Almighty God *(Revelation 20:11)*. However, John states specifically that the old order of the universe no longer existed. In this newly created world order, there is no more sea. Fulfilling the prophecy of Isaiah, God has created a new universe: *"I will create a new heaven and a new earth. Past things will not be remembered. They will not come to mind" (Isaiah 65:17).*

21:2 *Then I saw the holy city, New Jerusalem, coming down from God out of heaven, dressed like a bride ready for her husband.*

The new Jerusalem descends from this new heaven to be placed on the new earth. Some commentators interpret this symbolically because of the description of the new city as a bride that has made herself ready, much like the saints were earlier portrayed[2] *(Revelation 19:7)*. God will provide this new city, a holy city set apart for His redeemed people. John found it difficult to describe the magnificence of the vision he saw. For this reason, he did his best to describe the city in a way that human language could understand, portraying the city as a bride arrayed in radiance on her wedding day.

21:3 *I heard a loud voice from the throne say, "God lives with humans! God will make his home with them, and they will be his people. God himself will be with them and be their God.*

John heard a loud voice coming from the throne, presumably the throne of God, unveiling an incredible revelation about this new heaven and new earth. The saints of God redeemed by the sacrifice of Jesus on Calvary will no longer be separated from God. Now in their immortal bodies, clothed in the righteousness that Christ has given to them, it is possible for the Creator to live with His people without the requirement for a mediator. Instead, the throne of God announces that God will dwell with His people, making His home with them. Now the saints would experience the reality of the salvation that God had given to them, not in a spiritual or theological sense, but in the concrete real-world environment of God's new creation.

John, the writer of this revelation, is the same man who wrote an account of Jesus' earthly ministry. In the opening verses of that Gospel, John tells people that the eternal Word became a flesh and blood human being, coming to earth to dwell among His sinful people. The language of that description literally says that God, in the Person of Jesus Christ, pitched His tent among men. Because of sin, God had to initiate the action that would redeem and restore those He had determined to save. Now, this same John sees the New Jerusalem descend from heaven, and hears God tell His people that He will dwell with them, not in the environment of their sin-permeated lives that dominated their existence prior to the consummation of their salvation, but in the glory of a new, sin-free environment. In both cases, God is the One Who orchestrates the events that bring about salvation for His people and, at the end of days, provides in His new world a place for those He has preserved for this day.

21:4 *He will wipe every tear from their eyes. There won't be any more death. There won't be any grief, crying, or pain, because the first things have disappeared."*

In this new environment John now begins to see the full significance of these new circumstances. No longer will the pain, distress, and grief that accompanied their earthly lives impact them in this new and perfect world created by God for His redeemed people. Never again will God's people be subject to the influences of sin and its God-ordained consequences. In the presence of the eternal God, His people are ushered into their eternal home where death, sorrow, and pain will never again haunt them.

21:5 *The one sitting on the throne said, "I am making everything new." He said, "Write this: 'These words are faithful and true.'"*

The reason for this dramatically altered life is unveiled to John, not by some angel or messenger of God, but by God Himself. The Lord God, seated majestically on His throne, declared, "I am making everything new." Those things that were corrupted by the sin of man's existence in the old earth no longer mattered. The new earth bore no resemblance to what had existed before.

To further emphasize the reliability of God's promise, the Lord instructed John to record: "These words are faithful and true." As hard as it is for people to comprehend the difference between this present world and the world described in these verses, God wants His people to know that what He has decreed cannot be changed. His promise is absolutely reliable. God is asking His people to trust Him, to trust the revelation that He has given to John. This new world is barely imaginable in the dreams of God's people, but it is the sure promise of God. This is the world that God has prepared for His people to inhabit when He gives them a new city where they will live in His presence.

21:6–7 *⁶He said to me, "It has happened! I am the A and the Z, the beginning and the end. I will give a drink from the fountain filled with the water of life to anyone who is thirsty. It won't cost anything. ⁷Everyone who wins the victory will inherit these things. I will be their God, and they will be my children.*

On the sheer authority of His own Name, God tells John, "It has happened!" In words reminiscent of Jesus' words on the Cross, "It is finished," God is telling His people that He has accomplished what He has determined from the dawn of history. At the Cross, God provided salvation for the people of the world by giving His Son as the perfect sacrifice for sin. Now, God tells His people that He has brought His plan to its intended end. He has brought His people safely into the fold of His eternal Kingdom. Now, the ultimate consummation of Christ's redemption is complete.

Then the Lord reminded John of the glory of His eternal Being! He tells John that He is the beginning and the end. The Lord repeats the same phrase that He used when He first commissioned John to write this revelation: "'I am the A and the Z,' says the Lord God, 'the One who is, the One who was, and the One who is coming, the Almighty'" (*Revelation 1:8*). As with all people bound in their sinfulness, John needs to be reminded of the One Who is speaking with Him. This is the promise of the eternal God. What He says, He will do! It is evident throughout the Scriptures and in this revelation that God is the One Who orchestrates the events that bring His plan to its intended conclusion.

The beauty of this new world that God promises His people is seen in the way that God's care for His people is so evident. He gives His people water from the fountain of life. It is not an additional item, which will cost God's saints. Rather, it is an integral blessing that comes with the whole gift that God gives to His redeemed people, and the best gift of all is that God promises that He will be their God and those He has redeemed will be His children. All these things will be given to those whom God has redeemed and brought safely through fiery trials to this moment of eternal happiness.

21:8 *But cowardly, unfaithful, and detestable people, murderers, sexual sinners, sorcerers, idolaters, and all liars will find themselves in the fiery lake of burning sulfur. This is the second death."*

In stark contrast to the rewards the Lord gives to His redeemed people, the Lord tells John of the end of those who experience the second death, the judgment and condemnation of those who had died in their sin apart from the saving grace of the Lord Jesus Christ (*Revelation 20:13-14*). The Lord provides a list that describes a sample cross section of those who will be consigned to the eternal lake of fire. "Detestable people, murderers, sexual sinners, sorcerers, idolaters, and all liars" will be condemned to this place of eternal torment. This was not simply a list of specific sins that condemned a soul to hell but, rather, was indicative of the nature of those controlled by their selfish desires and the evil influences of the world and not by the Spirit of the living God.

All people have sinned, including every believer. But those whose sins are not covered by the blood of Christ's sacrifice will be judged by their actions alone because they had not received the faith and saving grace of Jesus Christ. These sinners could only be judged by their sinful, unbelieving hearts and will be condemned to the lake of fire. This list of offenses committed against their forgiving, but righteous Creator is not comprehensive, but the characterization of such people as cowardly and unfaithful makes it clear that these people do not believe in the One Whom God had sent to the earth to pay the penalty for their sin. A person's position in Jesus Christ will be the only criterion by which God will make His determination from His great white throne and sentence people to their eternal condemnation in the lake of fire. John the Apostle wrote these words in his narrative of the life and ministry of Jesus: "Those who believe in him won't be condemned. But those who don't believe are already condemned because they don't believe in God's only Son" *(John 3:18).*

Notes/Applications

As Scripture says: "No eye has seen, no ear has heard, and no mind has imagined the things that God has prepared for those who love him" *(1 Corinthians 2:9).* Paul wrote this reminder to the church in Corinth, encouraging the redeemed to think about that time when God Himself would dwell in the midst of His people. While that may appear to be a means of escaping the harsh realities of this earthly struggle, it is, in truth, a vision that strengthens the believer's resolve to live for Christ and His Kingdom at this present time. Such a vision should never be used as a rosy picture of some future time that somehow helps God's people to avoid their present responsibilities as citizens of heaven. Instead, it should make Christians uncomfortable for not doing more to witness faithfully to the salvation that is offered by the Cross of Christ.

Nevertheless, it is difficult to read this passage, knowing that God is speaking directly to John and through John to those who read these pages, and not long for that day when the struggles of this earthly life are past. Who would not want to live in a place where evil no longer influences the people? Who would not want to live in a place where there was no more sorrow, grief, or pain—where physical, emotional, and mental anguish is banished forever? More important than any of these, who would not want to live in the presence of the One Who has created them and bask in the glory of the One Who has redeemed them?

Yet, still living on earth, surrounded by all the influences of a profoundly chaotic world, the human mind has difficulty in believing or even imagining "the things that God has prepared for those who love Him." Nevertheless, God has placed great emphasis on the reliability of His promise. He reminds His children that He is the eternal God, the One Who is, the One Who was, and the One Who is to come. Then, with an oath sworn on the integrity of His Own Holy Name, God tells His people that these words are "faithful and true."

So believers of all ages have taken Jesus at His word. They have believed that what He has promised is far superior to anything else this world has to offer. Equipped with the promises of their Lord, believers have faithfully testified to the saving work of Jesus Christ, and shunning the fear of pain and death, many have died at the hands of Christ's enemies. Even as their physical lives go to the grave, they die with the praise of God on their lips, rejoicing in His salvation and His reliable promise of eternal life.

So may all the saints of God be equipped to tell of the Lord's greatness without fear or hesitation, even as they look to that day when God will dwell with them in the new city that He has prepared for them.

Revelation 21:9–14

21:9 *One of the seven angels who had the seven bowls full of the last seven plagues came to me and said, "Come! I will show you the Bride, the wife of the Lamb."*

John was then approached by one of the seven angels responsible for carrying out a portion of the seven bowl judgments of God's wrath. It is not specified which of these seven angels came and spoke with John, but that has no bearing on the angel's message. However, it is interesting to see how this angel was once an agent of God's wrath and was now the agent used to show John the vision of Christ's Bride.

The angel told John to follow him so that he could show John "the Bride, the wife of the Lamb." This Bride of the Lamb will be dramatically different from the unbelievers described previously. As explained in chapter nineteen, the Bride includes all believers, those who had received righteousness through God's grace and atonement for their sins by the blood of Jesus Christ at Calvary.

21:10–11 *¹⁰He carried me by his power away to a large, high mountain. He showed me the holy city, Jerusalem, coming down from God out of heaven. ¹¹It had the glory of God. Its light was like a valuable gem, like gray quartz, as clear as crystal.*

It was important that John could see and record this vision of the Bride of Christ. So the angel swept John away and took him to a high mountain. From this vantage point he could see the whole scenario that was to be laid out before him.

From this "large, high mountain," John witnessed the holy city, specifically named Jerusalem, coming down from heaven. God was the source and the architect of this city. The scene is a further expansion on John's earlier description of the city that he saw coming down from heaven (*Revelation 21:2*). The Lord had told John that this city was to become the eternal dwelling place of God and His Bride, those who had been made righteous in Christ.

The New Jerusalem shone brightly with God's glory. John said the light resembled a precious gem, specifically "like gray quartz, as clear as crystal." This does not necessarily mean that the city was constructed entirely of precious stones. More likely, this was the best description John could give of the beautiful city that he saw. He could only compare the magnificence of the city to the finest things in the world that he had seen. John attempted to describe a city that was otherwise indescribable and unimaginable in its brilliance, grandeur, and beauty.

21:12–13 *¹²It had a large, high wall with 12 gates. Twelve angels were at the gates. The names of the 12 tribes of Israel were written on the gates. ¹³There were three gates on the east, three gates on the north, three gates on the south, and three gates on the west.*

An enormous wall surrounded the city. John obviously saw all four sides of the city. He described the wall as though it was one long wall, only to show later that the wall had four sides, each with three gates. Here the number twelve comes into play. There are twelve gates guarded by twelve angels. Each of the gates was named for one of the twelve tribes of Israel. Each tribe will be represented on the gates of this magnificent city. John records what he saw without comment.

When God organized the children of Israel into a national entity, He instructed Moses on the construction of the tabernacle. This tent represented the dwelling place of God, encamped in their midst. Then He commanded Moses to organize the social structure of the nation around the tabernacle, placing three tribes on each of four sides arranged on the north, south, east, and west *(Numbers 2)*. Now the New Jerusalem comes down from heaven, having the names of the twelve tribes on twelve gates facing north, south, east, and west. In this new city, God actually dwells in the midst of His people, not merely in the symbolism of cloud and fire, but in the glory of His eternal presence.

21:14 *The wall of the city had 12 foundations. The 12 names of the 12 apostles of the Lamb were written on them.*

The massive walls surrounding the New Jerusalem were supported on twelve foundations. There is a sense in which this vision became the fulfillment of Abraham's dream: "Abraham was waiting for the city that God had designed and built, the city with permanent foundations" *(Hebrews 11:10)*. The twelve foundations will bear the names of the twelve "apostles of the Lamb." These names undoubtedly refer to the Twelve who had walked with the Messiah, witnessed His miracles, learned from Him, taught others about Him, and witnessed His resurrection and ascension. It is the doctrine of the apostles upon which Christ built His church. Paul affirmed this fundamental source of Christian doctrine in his letter to the Ephesians: "You are built on the foundation of the apostles and prophets. Christ Jesus himself is the cornerstone" *(Ephesians 2:20)*. Just as the doctrine of these twelve apostles provided the theological basis upon which the church of Jesus Christ was built on earth, so too will their names grace the foundations of this eternal dwelling for God's chosen people.

Notes/Applications

The whole of Scripture is nothing more and nothing less than God's message to all people, showing them His lovingkindness in salvation and His wrath in judgment. Essentially, there are two ways to live: with the Lord or without the Lord. Because it is impossible for people to live the way God created them to live, the situation appears to be hopeless. Everyone, even the best among us, fails to live uprightly in the light of God's standard of righteousness. Only God can remedy this situation and He does so in the Person of Jesus Christ. The beloved Son of the Holy God was born to bear the punishment for the offenses of sinful, rebellious people. That is the only means by which people can be reconciled to their Creator and restored to fellowship with their Redeemer.

Along with the clear call of God to live in harmony with Him through the sacrifice of Jesus, His Son, God gives people images of what He has planned for those who love Him. The tabernacle is one of those images. There in the wilderness God creates an environment that reflects the greatness of His heart. The tabernacle was to be constructed precisely as God told Moses. Sacrifice was necessary so that people could come into the presence of God. Otherwise, people who attempted to approach God died. So with sacrifice and worship, people looked to the tabernacle as the place where God lived. The image is absolutely clear: God lived in the midst of His people.

When Israel became a nation, Solomon built a temple, constructed in the same architectural layout as the tabernacle. God no longer dwelt in a tent, but in a house of stone. Still, sacrifice was necessary to approach their Holy God. Because of the people's sin, God brought the Babylonian armies against Judah and the unthinkable became a harsh reality—the temple was looted and then destroyed. But the image is still clear: God lived in the midst of His people.

A second temple was built and became the most beautiful structure in the Jerusalem of Jesus' day. The image of God dwelling among His people still remained. But Jesus warned His disciples that this temple, too, would be completely destroyed. In its place, Jesus told His disciples that He would send the Holy Spirit to dwell in the hearts of those God redeemed because of the sacrifice of His Son. Thereby God still demonstrates that He dwells in the hearts of His people, who become His living temple.

Now at last with Satan, hell, and death thrown into the lake of fire, God shows His people a city that He has prepared for them. Now the image of things to come vanishes in the mists of worlds long forgotten as God actually gives His people a place to live, not with some shadowy image that represents God's presence, but with the concrete reality of His living, glorious presence in their midst. The dawn of God's new creation breaks forth in shining beauty and holiness as He gives His people the New Jerusalem, promising them that this will be their dwelling place for all eternity. Within its sacred walls, He promises that He will be their God and they will be His children.

Revelation 21:15–27

21:15 *The angel who was talking to me had a gold measuring stick to measure the city, its gates, and its wall.*

The angel that guided John's tour of the New Jerusalem possessed a golden measuring stick. This angel continued to describe the city that God had prepared for His people by providing John with specific dimensions about its size. The measuring stick provided a specific standard, which John understood from his human perspective.

This vision is very similar to a vision that God gave to Ezekiel. In that vision, God uses a measuring stick to show the dimensions of the temple that would one day be rebuilt in Jerusalem. The purpose of this temple was the same as John's vision of the New Jerusalem. God told Ezekiel: *"The voice said to me, 'Son of man, this is the place where my throne is and the place where my feet rest. This is where I will live among the Israelites forever'"* (*Ezekiel 43:7*).

21:16 *The city was square. It was as wide as it was long. He measured the city with the stick. It was 12,000 stadia long. Its length, width, and height were the same.*

The results of the angel's measurements reveal a city of astonishing scale. The New Jerusalem was a perfect cube, having equal length, width, and height. Each side of the city measured twelve thousand stadia. One stadium equals approximately 607 feet (185 meters). The city was approximately 1,380 miles cubed (2,220 kilometers cubed), covering nearly two million square miles (3.2 million square kilometers).

When Solomon built the temple during his reign, the dimensions are clearly described in 1 Kings 6. In that passage, the dimensions of the Holy of Holies is described. *"The inner room was 30 feet long, 30 feet wide, and 30 feet high. Solomon covered it and the cedar altar with pure gold"* (*1 Kings 6:20*). This was the place where God symbolically lived among His people. Like the temple, the city that God has designed and built for His people is also a perfect cube. Again and again through the Scriptures, God shows His people that His intention is to live in the midst of the people He has redeemed.

21:17 *He measured its wall. According to human measurement, which the angel was using, it was 144 cubits.*

John watched the angel measure the wall of the city, which measured 144 cubits. A cubit equals approximately eighteen inches.[3] Since the height, width, and length of the city are given in the previous verse, it is probably best to interpret this measurement as the thickness of the wall. The phrase, "according to human measurement," appears to emphasize that the measurements given were being calculated in human terms for the sake of John's understanding and ultimately for the understanding of his readers.[4]

21:18 *Its wall was made of gray quartz. The city was made of pure gold, as clear as glass.*

John's description of gray quartz may either be a literal description of the wall's physical composition or a figurative description of some heavenly element whose beauty John could only describe in the best way that human language allowed. A figurative interpretation is further recommended since John also described the city being made of pure gold, yet at the same time like clear glass. Nevertheless, it is easy to understand that John had a difficult time describing a city of such immense size and structural beauty. Surely, if God was the architect and builder of the New Jerusalem, it is also easy to understand that He may use materials that no human eye has ever seen. There is no restriction on the resources that God can draw from when He builds this city for His people. The limitations are distinctly human.

21:19–20 [19]*The foundations of the city wall were beautifully decorated with all kinds of gems: The first foundation was gray quartz, the second sapphire, the third agate, the fourth emerald,* [20]*the fifth onyx, the sixth red quartz, the seventh yellow* *quartz, the eighth beryl, the ninth topaz, the tenth green quartz, the eleventh jacinth, and the twelfth amethyst.*

The foundations of the wall, each of which contained one of the names of the twelve chosen apostles, are garnished with a variety of precious stones. This does not imply that the foundations will be made of these stones, but that they were decorated with gems of incredible beauty. Their use is not for structural purposes, but for decorative reasons, designed to exhibit God's glory throughout every aspect of His new creation.

21:21 *The 12 gates were 12 pearls. Each gate was made of one pearl. The street of the city was made of pure gold, as clear as glass.*

John explained that the twelve gates were made of twelve pearls. Then, as if to accentuate what he had just recorded, he described each gate as being constructed of one solid pearl shining with iridescent splendor. Like all elements of God's new creation, these gates would be beautiful beyond human imagination. John then described the streets of the city, constructed from the same material as the city itself. The streets were made of "pure gold, as clear as glass."

21:22 *I did not see any temple in it, because the Lord God Almighty and the Lamb are its temple.*

No temple existed within the city called the New Jerusalem. There was no structure where God's faithful could gather to worship because the Lord God and the Lamb will live in the midst of God's people forever. From His throne, God Himself tells John and his readers: *"I heard a loud voice from the throne say, 'God lives with humans! God will make his home with them, and they will be his people. God himself will be with them and be their God'"* (*Revelation 21:3*). There will never again be a need for temples, tabernacles, churches, or any other organized places of worship since worship would take place daily and continually in the very presence of God. Unity would finally be restored between God and His people.

21:23 *The city doesn't need any sun or moon to give it light because the glory of God gave it light. The Lamb was its lamp.*

Throughout eternity in the new heaven and new earth, there would never be the need for the sun or the moon. God created the sun and the moon for our benefit and for His glory. These celestial bodies will have served their purposes throughout the temporal duration of the earth for its inhabitants, but they will no longer be necessary in the New Jerusalem. In their place, the radiant glory of God Almighty and the Lamb will illuminate the new earth and new heaven.

> *The sun will no longer be your light during the day,*
> *nor will the brightness of the moon give you light,*
> *But the Lord will be your everlasting light.*
> *Your God will be your glory. (Isaiah 60:19)*

21:24 *The nations will walk in its light, and the kings of the earth will bring their glory into it.*

All of those who were saved by the redemptive work of Christ Jesus will walk in the light of His glory. John further illustrated the vast number of the redeemed by describing them as *nations*.[5] The use of the word *nations* in this verse should not be understood in the sense of political structures with geographical boundaries. Rather, John uses this word to emphasize the enormity of the multitudes who have been saved and come from every ethnic and cultural background. There is a sense in which John is describing the way in which the Gospel had broken down all political, social, and cultural barriers, which at one time separated and divided the inhabitants of the earth. Isaiah also looked forward to this day:

> [1]*Arise! Shine! Your light has come, and the glory of the* LORD *has dawned.* [2]*Darkness now covers the earth, and thick darkness covers the nations. But the Lord dawns, and his glory appears*

over you. ³Nations will come to your light, and kings will come
to the brightness of your dawn. (Isaiah 60:1–3)

Some, who were once kings on the earth, will also be numbered among the redeemed. Even here, the message of God's salvation had broken the pride of some of the world's leaders and brought them to His throne of grace and mercy. This is simply an example of what God had done in the hearts of people from all levels of the earth's social strata. God's work among people has saved both rich and poor, kings and slaves. Whatever glory these men possessed on earth will be thoroughly diminished by the superior brightness of Christ's glory as He dwells among His redeemed people.

21:25 *Its gates will be open all day. They will never close because there won't be any night there.*

No gate of the city wall would ever be closed. Now aware of the Source of light in this glorious city, John knows there will be no more night. Furthermore, God has wiped out all of His enemies. The purpose of city gates in ancient times was to provide protection from invaders at night. Now, since God dwells in the midst of His people, providing eternal light driving darkness completely away from His new creation, John realizes that the gates of this new city will always remain open. God has brought His people through tremendous persecution and provided a safe haven where they can live in peace and security in an environment where gates will never have to be closed again.

21:26 *They will bring the glory and wealth of the nations into the holy city.*

Again, the word *nations* used here simply denotes a vast assembly of people. Matthew Henry aptly described this multitude as "whole nations of saved souls; some out of all nations, and many out of some nations. All those multitudes that were sealed on earth are saved in heaven."⁶ This would be the entire sum of God's elect which completed the population of the New Jerusalem.

As if to accentuate the implication of the previous verse, this statement confirms that it would not only be kings of the earth who would bring glory and honor unto the throne of God and the Lamb. The inhabitants of God's new creation were not offering things of a material nature but something that was intangible and far more precious to God—they offered their fullest expressions of praise, honor, and worship.

21:27 *Nothing unclean, no one who does anything detestable, and no liars will ever enter it. Only those whose names are written in the Lamb's Book of Life will enter it.*

As we have already read, the gates of the new city will never be closed because there will be no threat from which the city needed protection. This verse does not suggest that defilement and abominations would be kept from entering into God's eternal Kingdom but that such things would not even exist in the new heaven and new earth.[7] In truth, all such people have already been condemned to their eternal destiny in the lake of fire. God will do this because He has reserved this Holy City only for those whose names are written in the Lamb's Book of Life. No one will escape God's judgment that He has imposed, thus guaranteeing, not only safety and security to its inhabitants, but also purity and unity.

DIG DEEPER: *Book of Life*

The Book of Life is referred to seven times in the Book of Revelation, but this is the only occurrence where ownership of that book is defined. This book is owned by the *"Lamb slain before the foundation of the world" (Revelation 13:8; Philippians 4:3).* Again, the focus of Revelation turns our attention back to Jesus Christ, the only one to Whom all praise and honor, glory and power is due, and Who owns the Book of Life and preserves the names of His saints by the power of His blood (Acts 20:28).

Notes/Applications

Renowned commentator Matthew Henry observed: "There is nothing magnificent enough in this world fully to set forth the glory of heaven. Could we, in the glass of a strong imagination, contemplate such a city as is here described, even as to the exterior part of it, such a wall, and such gates, how amazing, how glorious would the prospect be! And yet this is a faint and dim representation of what heaven is in itself."[8]

When we look at the beauty of God's creation as we make our earthly pilgrimage, we exclaim with the psalmist: "The heavens declare the glory of God; and the firmament shows His handiwork" (*Psalm 19:1*, NKJV). We agree with Paul: "From the creation of the world, God's invisible qualities, his eternal power and divine nature, have been clearly observed in what he made" (*Romans 1:20*). Whether we look at the stellar display of stars at night or look at the intricate nature of a single cell, we are astounded at the beauty and reliability of the world that God has created. As humans, we stand in awe of the majesty of the world around us.

Yet nothing in this world compares to the magnificence of the new heaven and earth that God has prepared for those He has redeemed. With John, we stand on the mountaintop and look at the New Jerusalem coming down from heaven. What we see dazzles the imagination and silences our voices. It is virtually impossible to describe in human terms the glowing radiance of a city that is made of gold as clear as glass. To our minds, this seems like a physical impossibility. Yet, God is certainly capable of creating materials that we have never dreamed of.

Perhaps the most important aspect of God's new world is the absence of sin and evil. The new city will never be tainted by the stain of human rebellion. God's provision of salvation and security for those He has saved comes to the saints on the sure justice of His judgment on Satan, the beast, the false prophet, and the host of people who follow them into the lake of fire. Thus, God's people rest securely in the protected environment of the New Jerusalem, living in unity and purity with the One Who has saved them.

If we marvel at the beauty of this present universe, then the beauty of God's new creation will overwhelm us. More important than the physical beauty and security of this new world is the fact that God and His Lamb will dwell in the midst of His people. This will be the most beautiful aspect of the world that God gives to His people. No longer looking through the lens of human sin, basking in the radiance of His matchless glory, God's people will praise His Name forever, never tiring, always singing His praise for the gift of life eternal that God has bestowed on them.

REVELATION 22

Revelation 22:1–6

22:1 *The angel showed me a river filled with the water of life, as clear as crystal. It was flowing from the throne of God and the Lamb.*

The angel introduced in Revelation 19:9 continued to show John additional features of the New Jerusalem. John is now inside the walls of God's eternal city, and the angel shows him a river. This river is absolutely clear, so clear that it seems to be pure crystal. The major property of this water is the life that it provides to those who drink from it. The reason for the clarity of the water and the life that it bestows and sustains is simple to understand—the source of the water is the very throne of God and the Lamb.

When John sees this river of life, he must certainly have remembered a time when he walked with Jesus during His earthly ministry. When Jesus traveled from Judea through Samaria, He met a woman at Jacob's well. In their conversation, Jesus told the woman: *"If you only knew what God's gift is and who is asking you for a drink, you would have asked him for a drink. He would have given you living water"* (John

4:10). From the time of Jesus' incarnation to this time when John sees the river of life, the Word of God has consistently offered living water to those who have been enslaved to sin. Now John sees the physical manifestation of God's promise to His people—a river of life whose source is the throne of God and the Lamb Who was sacrificed for the sins of the world.

22:2 *Between the street of the city and the river there was a tree of life visible from both sides. It produced 12 kinds of fruit. Each month had its own fruit. The leaves of the tree will heal the nations.*

Like the river of life, John also sees a tree of life. This tree is nourished from the river that runs by it. The tree was visible from both sides of the river, leading some commentators to conclude that there appeared to be a tree on each side of the river. If this is accurate, then it is certain that both trees come from the same root structure. From the crystal clear water, nourishment flows through the root structure of this tree into its branches and ultimately to its leaves.

One of the interpretive difficulties of this verse comes from the last phrase: "The leaves of the tree will heal the nations." It is difficult to understand why there is any need for healing in the perfect environment of the New Jerusalem. We have already said that the nations represent, not political structures with geographical boundaries, but the wide range of cultures and people groups that make up the great host of God's redeemed people. However, the question of the need for healing comes quickly to mind. Since the river nourishes the leaves of this tree, it is easy to understand that the healing properties of the leaves comes, not from the river itself, but from the source of the river, the throne of God and the Lamb. Kenneth Wuest translates this phrase: "And the leaves of the tree were for the health of the nations."[1] This translation provides a slightly different perspective in which the leaves maintain the health of the culturally diverse people that make up the saints of God rather than working among the nations to heal some rift that does not and can not exist in the environment of God's new creation.

> ## DIG DEEPER: *Tree of Life*
>
> The tree of life was first introduced in the Book of Genesis as the means by which one could live forever (*Genesis 2:8–3:24*). Adam and Eve were invited to partake of its fruit but were forbidden from eating of the tree of the knowledge of good and evil. They disobeyed God, sin entered the world, and so did the consequence of sin— death (*Romans 6:23*). When the curse of death is lifted, all of God's redeemed will once again be permitted to partake of the tree of life, the privilege forfeited at the dawn of creation and restored at the end of it (*Revelation 22*).

22:3–4 *³There will no longer be any curse. The throne of God and the Lamb will be in the city. His servants will worship him ⁴and see his face. His name will be on their foreheads.*

Because of the "river of life" and the "tree of life," the saints dwell securely in the purity and unity provided through the protection of God's salvation as well as His judgment. It should be obvious by now that God has eradicated sin when He threw hell and death into the lake of fire. In this newly created city, the curse of sin no longer exists. It no longer exists, not only because God has removed sin and death from the city, but because God and the Lamb dwell within the walls of the city, sustaining the saints by the nourishment He provides from the "river of life" and the "tree of life." As a result, His servants will worship Him continually, rejoicing in the gift of His mercy through Jesus that brought them to this glorious destination where they will live and worship before His face forever.

It is certain that everyone in this city will have this mark on their foreheads. These people have belonged to God since they were sealed by the Holy Spirit for their salvation (*Ephesians 4:30*). This will be the mark of Christ's ownership placed on the foreheads of God's servants by the very One Who purchased their redemption through His grace with His blood and secured their eternity in His presence by the determination of His sovereign will.

22:5 *There will be no more night, and they will not need any light from lamps or the sun because the Lord God will shine on them. They will rule as kings forever and ever.*

This feature of the New Jerusalem was shown to John before (*Revelation 21:23, 25*). John's repetition of this aspect of the New Jerusalem displays an emphasis that lies at the heart of God's new creation. In the framework of the preceding verses, revealing the "river of life" and the "tree of life" and restating that the curse of sin no longer impacts the new world, it seems wise to interpret this both literally and symbolically. Literally, God dwells in the midst of the city and His very presence will provide all the light needed to illuminate the entire city. Symbolically, the same presence of the Lord God Who has eradicated sin and condemned it to the lake of fire creates a spiritual atmosphere that eliminates the darkness of sin and evil.

The last phrase of this verse has caused quite a bit of debate among Christians. The pronoun *they* certainly refers to those servants John described in verse three. These servants will *rule* as kings forever. The word *rule* indicates that all the saints will have some political or administrative duties to perform. But this raises the question: Why is there a need for such a function in the sin-free environment of the new world where God and the Lamb are eternally present with the saints? In the new city there are only two levels of administrative hierarchy: the Lord God Who sits on the throne and His redeemed people who continually sing the song of God's salvation though the sacrifice of the Lamb. Thus, the word *reign* as used in most other translations is probably a better description. In that sense, all the saints reign as though they were kings in the company and service of their Lord. The prophecy of Daniel lends support to this idea: *"But the holy people of the Most High will take possession of the kingdom and keep it forever and* ever" (Daniel 7:18). At the beginning of this book, John quotes Jesus' promise: "The one who conquers, I will grant him to sit with me on my throne, as I also conquered and sat down with my Father on his throne" (Revelation 3:21, ESV). In light of Jesus' promise, it seems best to interpret this phrase as the fulfillment of that promise, where all the saints share with Jesus as His redeemed royalty.

22:6 *He said to me, "These words are trustworthy and true. The Lord God of the spirits of the prophets has sent his angel to show his servants the things that must happen soon.*

Jesus Christ Himself is the author of this revelation that has been given to John. Coming from the mouth of the Holy One of Israel, God's promised Messiah, and now God's conquering Son, God's servants can be absolutely certain of the reliability of this portrayal of the things which will happen at the end of days. The truth of this revelation from the opening words to its closing "Amen" are incontestable, since God Himself is the One Who reveals these scenes to John. The angel hereby establishes and affirms the authenticity of the prophecies contained within the book. All of these visions that John witnessed are the preordained plan of God in the execution of His salvation and His judgment. Precisely at their appointed times, these events will occur swiftly. When these events that will turn the world upside down begin to occur, they will do so suddenly and rapidly without opportunity for reflection or repentance.

The angel tells John that he has seen these visions in the same way that the prophets of old had received their prophecies. The same Spirit that inspired Ezekiel, Daniel, Isaiah, Jeremiah, and the rest of His anointed messengers is the same Spirit that has shown John the things that must come to pass.

Notes/Applications

In Exodus 33:18–23, God told Moses that no man could look upon the face of God and live. Nevertheless, God allowed Moses to view His back, but He hid His face, which reflected the glory of the eternal God. In this way God protected His servant so that he would not be killed by His transcendent glory.

Now in this passage we read: "They shall see His face, and His name shall be on their foreheads." Here God reveals through His servant John the reality that in God's holy city God's saints will no longer be subject to normal human limitations. Revelation 22:4 affirms Revelation 21:3, which states, "God lives with humans! God will make his home with them, and they will be his people. God himself will be with them and be their God." Both verses explain clearly the certain destiny awaiting the redeemed beyond eternity's threshold. First, heaven will be the everlasting home of God, and second, His children will see Him face-to-face and will be sealed with His name forevermore.

In heaven, there will be no more curse. The physical and spiritual barriers, which once veiled God's glory from human eyes, are completely dismantled. Like Moses, we cannot look at the glory of God in our human frames, but in that glorious city, those adorned with His seal of ownership will share in the birthright given to every child of His family. God's presence will envelop His people in His redeeming love, in safety and security, and they will look at Him face-to-face in all of His majesty.

Only by Christ's righteousness that removes the scales of sin from our eyes and cleanses us can we, once members of a fallen race, behold the glory of the Holy God. Only by the blood of the sacrificial Lamb can we, once the world's reprobate, become sanctified vessels who are holy as He is holy. Only by His extended grace, incomprehensible mercy, and immeasurable love will we, who are marked with His name on our foreheads, enter the eternal tabernacle of God and worship Him face-to-face and bask in the glory of His eternal presence.

Revelation 22:7–14

22:7 *I'm coming soon! Blessed is the one who follows the words of the prophecy in this book."*

It seems that the angel reminds John of Jesus' words. Through the angel, John heard the voice of Jesus Christ in which He speaks of His return to the earth, arrayed in all His glory and with the armies of His saints following Him into battle. Jesus then emphasizes the importance of this book when He encourages His people to follow the words of the prophecy unveiled within its pages. There is blessing when one of God's saints reads this book and discovers within its revelation both the glory of the salvation He gives to His saints and the horror that awaits those who are destined for His judgment.

22:8 *I, John, heard and saw these things. When I had heard and seen them, I bowed to worship at the feet of the angel who had been showing me these things.*

After the visions of revelation were finished, John was so overwhelmed by the incredible things that he had seen, heard, and understood that he fell down prostrate before the angel who showed him these things that would come to pass. John was completely awestruck, and after observing all of these coming events, he instinctively fell to the ground in a gesture of humility and worship. Earlier in the revelation, he had reacted similarly to the angel who had shown him the vision of Christ's return, and the response of the angel then was the same as it is now.

22:9 *He told me, "Don't do that! I am your coworker. I work with other Christians, the prophets, and those who follow the words in this book. Worship God!"*

As on that earlier occasion, the angel urged John not to worship him because he, too, was a "coworker" (*Revelation 19:10*). The angel considered himself John's equal, not God's. In the eternal presence of God, the angels are no different than the prophets and every other believer who has read, learned, and committed themselves to the writings of this book. Accordingly, the angel gently reminded John to focus all of his worship on God, the only One truly worthy of all glory and praise.

22:10 *Then the angel said to me, "Don't seal up the words of the prophecy in this book because the time is near.*

The angel directed John to record all that he had witnessed and not to seal the prophecies revealed to him. This is the opposite of what the prophet Daniel was told to do after receiving similar visions. *"He replied, 'Go, Daniel. These words are to be kept secret and sealed until the end times'" (Daniel 12:9).* The difference between the two prophecies was the time in which the revelations were given. Daniel's visions and prophecies were given hundreds of years before the birth of the Messiah. John, on the other hand, was told that the "time is near." This statement should not be interpreted in such a way that Christ's return is imminent, though Christians await Christ's coming with eager anticipation *(Matthew 24:42–44; Revelation 3:3).* Rather, it means only that the time for John to reveal these prophecies was immediate. Regardless of the timing of the Lord's return, the call for response is always pressing. Since these visions were undoubtedly true (v. 6), those who continue in rebellion against God must understand the precariousness of their complacency and disobedience.

22:11 *Let those who don't have God's approval go without it, and let filthy people continue to be filthy. Let those who have God's approval continue to have it, and let holy people continue to be holy."*

In the context of the visions John witnessed during this revelation, the angel provides John with the ultimate conclusion of God's predetermined plan for the end of days. Those who will be condemned will remain in their condemnation. Those who have been saved by the blood of the Lamb will remain in the security of the salvation Christ has purchased for them. Thus, unrighteous and filthy people will continue in their waywardness and rebellion. Those who have been justified by the Cross of Christ and the work of the Holy Spirit will continue on their journey to their eternal home.

22:12–13 *12"I'm coming soon! I will bring my reward with me to pay all people based on what they have done. 13I am the A and the Z, the first and the last, the beginning and the end.*

Again, the angel speaks for Jesus telling John that Jesus is coming *soon*. This time Jesus will bring His reward with Him, giving to each person the judgment that is determined by the things they have done. In this case, reward should not be understood as something given in appreciation for something done. Rather, when Jesus comes again He will come with judgment, executing His justice in righteousness and truth.

The reliability of John's prophecy as given to him by Jesus Christ is again affirmed with the reminder that these visions are authored by the one, true, eternal Christ. He is the One, the only One Who knows the beginning from the ending. Indeed, He is the One, the only One Who has ordained all things from the time before the foundation of the world to the time when this world will no longer exist. Therefore, no finite, sin-infested human being should ever take the words of this book lightly. They are given by Jesus to inform His people of the consequences of both faith and unbelief.

22:14 *"Blessed are those who wash their robes so that they may have the right to the tree of life and may go through the gates into the city.*

Like those who keep the words of this prophecy (*v. 7*), those whose robes are washed in the blood of the Lamb will have access to the tree of life in the New Jerusalem. "Those who wash their robes" describes those who have received forgiveness for their sins through the atonement provided by Jesus Christ's death on the Cross. Only those who receive the salvation the Lord Jesus Christ offers will be granted the reward of eternal life and be ushered into God's new creation, dwelling in the glorious city of God where God Himself dwells with the people He has redeemed.

Notes/Applications

Jesus tells readers of this revelation three times that He is coming soon. Other translations say that Jesus is coming quickly. These words do not necessarily come from the same perspective. The word *soon* falls within the framework of a timeline. *Quickly* denotes the speed at which an event happens. The problem in understanding these words within the context of some specific timeline negates the biblical revelation that God exists above and beyond time as understood from our human perspectives (2 Peter 3:8). The real emphasis of this chapter is not the timeline, but the certainty of the events portrayed in this book.

John's record of the events which will occur at the end of days is often interrupted with Jesus' assurance that what He has said, He will do. Thus Jesus follows His declaration that He is coming soon with a statement that clearly reminds believers that the One Who is saying this is the eternal God, the One Who existed before time began and will still be present with the people He has redeemed when time and history are no more.

Therefore, God's people can believe what the eternal One has said. They can look beyond the difficulties and trials of this life even as they endure persecution and ridicule and see the New Jerusalem on the far horizon. What God has promised His people is far more important than the immediate circumstances that attempt to threaten the proclamation of the Gospel of Jesus Christ. The very idea of living within the walls of that glorious city in the presence of the One Who has created them and then redeemed them is food for the soul, strengthening the resolve of God's saints to endure to the end. Death and hell have no hold over them. Rather, they look forward to that day when they look on their Savior face-to-face and praise His Name in everlasting song.

Just as God's blessing rests certainly on the people He has redeemed, so God's judgment is imposed on those who have rejected

His salvation. God's judgment on unbelievers is as certain as His salvation for those He has saved. Though frightening to witness those scenes of torment and torture revealed in this book, we are convinced that God is absolutely righteous in His justice. There is a sense in which the rebellion of the unsaved is an affirmation by which such people acknowledge God's existence and authority, but willingly and with knowledge shake their fists in His face, turn their backs on Him, and go their own way, rushing headlong to their own destruction.

Thus, the angel says to John, "Let the evildoer still do evil, and the filthy still be filthy, and the righteous still do right, and the holy still be holy" (*Revelation 22:11,* ESV). God is in His heaven. He still sits on His throne. God will do what He says He will do. The fear of the Lord rests on those who refuse to believe in God's only Son. The redeemed of the Lord rejoice as they anticipate the consummation of their salvation, living forever in the presence of the eternal God, Who has prepared this new city for their eternal dwelling place.

Revelation 22:15–21

22:15 *Outside are dogs, sorcerers, sexual sinners, murderers, idolaters, and all who lie in what they say and what they do.*

Outside the pale of Christ's salvation are those who have rejected the salvation offered to them. Instead, they have invested in their own selfish pursuits and in that foolishness have lost their eternal souls. Like the earlier description John received from the angel *(Revelation 21:8)*, this is not a summary of sins that God will not or cannot forgive. Rather, it is a representation of the sins committed by those who absolutely hate God and everything that He has revealed to them. In that rebellion, they demonstrate the rightness of God's punishment that He imposes on them.

22:16 *"I, Jesus, have sent my angel to give this testimony to you for the churches. I am the root and descendant of David. I am the bright morning star."*

Jesus now personally verifies that He Himself has been the source of this revelation and that He has sent the angels that escorted John throughout these visions. The purpose of the visions is not a private matter intended solely for John's benefit but for all churches and believers throughout history.[2]

Drawing on the words of His prophets, Jesus then confirmed His identity by calling Himself the *"Root and the Descendant of David."* "Then a shoot will come out from the stump of Jesse, and a branch from its roots will bear fruit" *(Isaiah 11:1)*. This also is a repetition of the angel's description of Jesus earlier in this book: "Then one of the leaders said to me, 'Stop crying! The Lion from the tribe of Judah, the Root of David, has won the victory. He can open the scroll and the seven seals on it'" *(Revelation 5:5)*. Jesus also referred to Himself as the Morning Star. "I will also give them the morning star" *(Revelation 2:28)*. Jesus was both the spiritual foundation Who eternally preexisted David and also the physical descendant of the line of

David. Jesus has always existed, even before the creation of the world. The opening preface of John's Gospel identifies Jesus as the eternal Creator: "[1]In the beginning the Word already existed. The Word was with God, and the Word was God. [2]He was already with God in the beginning" *(John 1:1-2)*. It is this same bright glory of God the Father and of Jesus Christ that will illuminate the new heaven and new earth throughout eternity.

22:17 *The Spirit and the bride say, "Come!" Let those who hear this say, "Come!" Let those who are thirsty come! Let those who want the water of life take it as a gift.*

Through the apostle John, Jesus gives this revelation to His churches still on earth *(v. 16)*. This letter is not given to the world, to those who rebel against Christ and His people. It is the Holy Spirit that works in the hearts of unbelievers and brings them to repentance and salvation *(John 16:8-10)*. The Bride includes all people that have been redeemed through the work of the Holy Spirit, showing people their need for salvation and pointing to the Cross of Christ as the remedy for their sin.

With this in mind, it seems that the Holy Spirit and the Bride, Christ's Church, join their voices in an invitation to unbelievers to come. The church, still on earth and still engaged in the battle for unbelieving souls on behalf of their Savior and King, issues this invitation at the prompting of the Spirit that dwells within her. The urgency of the invitation increases when one reads the words of this book. Here the church invites others to drink from the water of life, partaking of the same salvation that has brought them to the very throne of God.

22:18 *[18]I warn everyone who hears the words of the prophecy in this book: If anyone adds anything to this, God will strike him with the plagues that are written in this book. [19]If anyone takes away any words from this book of prophecy, God will take*

away his portion of the tree of life and the holy city that are
described in this book.

Jesus then personally warned His churches about the serious nature
in which this book was given to His Church. It is a matter of significant consequence should anyone alter the words of this revelation.
The scenes that the Spirit has shown to John represent the absolutely
unchangeable truth of God's plan during the last days. As such, the
visions of God's gift of the New Jerusalem to His Bride is as certain
as the Word of the eternal God. The visions of judgment, plague, and
eternal condemnation are equally trustworthy. Thus, the penalties for
changing the words of God's unchangeable plan are severe. The only
individuals who would dare try to change the words of this revelation would be people who were already condemned. God's redeemed
people would never presume to change anything God has said or done.

DIG DEEPER: *The Book*

Readers are admonished in verses eighteen and nineteen not to
add to or take from any part of "this book," referring to the Book of
Revelation, which is called this "prophecy." The same warning holds
true for the entire Bible (*Deuteronomy 4:2; Proverbs 30:6*). God's
Word is complete as intended and inerrant as presented.

22:20 *The one who is testifying to these things says, "Yes, I'm*
coming soon!" Amen! Come, Lord Jesus!

This verse marks the third and final time that the Lord declared, "I'm
coming soon." This phrase could be considered a theme for this final
chapter of Revelation. Though the significance of this repeated message has already been studied, John added his own commentary to
this particular passage: "Amen. Come, Lord Jesus!" This should be the
attitude of every believer until the Lord returns.

There are many positions regarding the return of the Lord Jesus
Christ, and each has been adamantly defended with Scripture.

However, regardless of any believer's particular position, there should be nothing that keeps us from anticipating the Lord's glorious return. The promise of the magnificent eternity that God Almighty has prepared for His elect should far outshine even the most ominous and terrifying events that must also come to pass. This glorious hope we have in Jesus Christ should join our hearts with John's urgent cry: *"Come, Lord Jesus!"*

22:21 *The good will of the Lord Jesus be with all of you. Amen!*

After expressing his fervent desire for Jesus to come and usher in His new Kingdom, John closes his book with a simple benediction. John expressed his sincere desire for the grace of the Lord Jesus to rest upon God's saints. In the light of everything that he has witnessed, John prays that God's grace would strengthen and sustain the Church of Jesus Christ, even at this time when the Church still struggled with persecution and conflict in a world reeling with sin and chaos. The grace of Jesus Christ also gives comfort and hope to God's redeemed people, knowing that one day they will dwell eternally with the Lord (*1 Thessalonians 4:13–17*).

Notes/Applications

How does one summarize what is one of the most sobering books of the Holy Bible? There is probably no other biblical book that so vividly reveals that there is indeed a hell to be feared and a heaven to be anticipated. Every individual that has ever lived is subject to an eternity either in the tormenting lake of fire or in the glorious presence of God Almighty and the Lord Jesus Christ.

As the record of the end of days draws to a close, Jesus makes one final appeal to the inhabitants of this broken, sin-infested world. "The Spirit and the bride say come." The Church of Jesus Christ, Christ's Bride, is the earthly witness to the lost race of mankind, urging them to fear the lake of fire and embrace Jesus Christ. While the glories awaiting God's saints and the horrors awaiting the Satan's armies are absolutely certain, Jesus nevertheless encourages people to consider the salvation that He has purchased for them on Calvary's Cross.

We said at the beginning and we emphasize here at the end that this book is not the revelation of John, but the revelation of Jesus Christ given to John when he was exiled on Patmos. Thus, Jesus Christ Himself is the One Who unveils the truth about His salvation and His judgment. He is the One Who shows John the radiant beauty of the New Jerusalem and the frightening torment of those destined for the lake of fire.

Thus, at the close of this book, we see that it is not really difficult to understand the message of Jesus' revelation to His churches. We do not have to work hard to decode what Jesus is saying here in these pages. In fact, the message is only too clear. To avoid or delay consideration of the message of this revelation given directly from Jesus Christ is to play with fire. Nevertheless, God's people can be confident of God's trustworthiness both in His judgment and His redemption, and that confidence should encourage and strengthen their faith.

The Church of Jesus Christ throughout the ages should never forget that Jesus is both the root and the offspring of David. Physically, Jesus is the descendent of David and, as God incarnate, He is David's predecessor. He is the only One fully and absolutely in control of all aspects of His Creation before, during, and after all the days of time and history. That truth must sustain, motivate, and encourage God's people as they fulfill the great commission, proclaiming the Gospel to the ends of the earth. Even as the Spirit and the Bride are calling the thirsty to refreshing water, saints are individually appointed to be the agents of this commission both in life and in word.

As depicted in a German hymn from the nineteenth century, no matter what may happen in the physical realm of this life, our souls are protected by Him and preserved in Him:

> *Whate'er my God ordains is right:*
> *He is my Friend and Father;*
> *He suffers naught to do me harm,*

though many storms may gather,
Now I may know both joy and woe,
some day I shall see clearly
that He hath loved me dearly.

Whate'er my God ordains is right:
though now this cup, in drinking,
may bitter seem to my faint heart,
I take it, all unshrinking.
My God is true; each morn new
sweet comfort yet shall fill my heart,
and pain and sorrow shall depart.

Whate'er my God ordains is right:
here shall my stand be taken;
Though sorrow, need, or death be mine,
yet I am not forsaken.
My Father's care is round me there;
He holds me that I shall not fall:
and so to Him I leave it all.[3]

Amen! Come, Lord Jesus!

TEXT NOTES

Introduction

1. J. D. Douglas, ed., *New Bible Dictionary*, 2nd ed. (Wheaton, IL: Tyndale House Publishers, 1962), 1024.

2. Merrill C. Tenney, *Interpreting Revelation: A Reasonable Guide to Understanding the Last Book in the Bible* (1957; reprint, Peabody, Massachusetts: Hendrickson Publishers, 2001), 135-146.

3. R.C. Sproul, *The Last Days According to Jesus* (Grand Rapids: Baker Books, 1998), 153-159.

4. Bruce B. Barton et al., *Life Application Bible Commentary: Revelation* (Wheaton: Tyndale House Publishers, 2000), xi-xii.

5. Steve Gregg, ed., *Revelation: Four Views, A Parallel Commentary* (Nashville: Thomas Nelson Publishers, 1997), 13.

6. Barton et al., *Life Application Bible Commentary: Revelation*, xiii.

7. Albert Barnes, *Revelation, of Barnes' Notes on the New Testament* (1884; reprint, Grand Rapids: Baker Books, 2001), xlvi-xlix.

8. Robert H. Mounce, *The Book of Revelation, of The New International*

Commentary on the New Testament, 2nd ed. (Grand Rapids: Eerdmans Publishing Company, 1998), 19.

9. Vern S. Poythress, *The Returning King: A Guide to the Book of Revelation* (Phillipsburg, New Jersey: P & R Publishing, 2000), 11–13.

Chapter One

1. D. A. Carson, New Bible Commentary: 21st Century Edition, 4th ed. (Leicester, England; Downers Grove, Ill., USA: Inter-Varsity Press, 1994), Revelation 1:1.

2. George Ricker Berry, *Greek to English Interlinear New Testament (KJV)* (Grand Rapids: World Publishing, 1981), 623.

3. John Gill, *Exposition of the Old and New Testaments,* vol. 9 (1810; reprint, Paris, Arkansas: The Baptist Standard Bearer, 1989), 683–684.

4. Kenneth L. Barker and John R. Kohlenberger III, ed., *Zondervan NIV Bible Commentary,* vol. 2 (Grand Rapids: Zondervan Publishing House, 1994), 1132.

5. Barker and Kohlenberger, *Zondervan NIV Bible Commentary,* 1132.

6. D. A. Carson, New Bible Commentary: 21st Century Edition, 4th ed. (Leicester, England; Downers Grove, Ill., USA: Inter-Varsity Press, 1994), Revelation 1:1.

7. Joseph A. Seiss, *The Apocalypse: Exposition of the Book of Revelation* (Grand Rapids: Kregel Publications, 1987), 31.

8. Seiss, *The Apocalypse,* 31.

9. Gill, *Exposition of the Old and New Testaments,* vol. 9, 686.

10. Barker and Kohlenberger, *Zondervan NIV Bible Commentary,* 1135.

11. Gill, *Exposition of the Old and New Testaments,* vol. 9, 688.

12. William MacDonald, *Believer's Bible Commentary,* ed. Art Farstad (Nashville: Thomas Nelson Publishers, 1995), 2353.

13. W. E. Vine, *Vine's Expository Dictionary of Old and New Testament Words* (Nashville: Thomas Nelson Publishers, 1997), 75-76.

14. Excerpt from "O Christ, the Heavens' Eternal King," author unknown (ca. 6th century).

15. Matthew Henry, *Matthew Henry's Commentary on the Whole Bible* (Peabody, Massachusetts: Hendrickson Publishers, 1991), 2465.

16. Charles F. Pfeiffer and Everett F. Harrison, *The Wycliffe Bible Commentary* (Chicago: Moody Press, 1962), 1502.

17. George Eldon Ladd, *A Commentary on the Revelation of John* (Grand Rapids: Eerdmans Publishing Company, 1972), 33.

Chapter Two

1. Robert H. Mounce, *The Book of Revelation, The New International Commentary on the New Testament*, 2nd ed. (Grand Rapids: Eerdmans Publishing Company, 1998), 66-67.

2. Kenneth L. Barker and John R. Kohlenberger III, ed., *Zondervan NIV Bible Commentary*, vol. 2 (Grand Rapids: Zondervan Publishing House, 1994), 1140.

3. Mounce, *The Book of Revelation*, 67.

4. Matthew Henry, *Matthew Henry's Commentary on the Whole Bible* (Peabody, Massachusetts: Hendrickson Publishers, 1991), 2465.

5. W. E. Vine, *Vine's Expository Dictionary of Old and New Testament Words* (Nashville: Thomas Nelson Publishers, 1997), 951-952.

6. Barker and Kohlenberger, *Zondervan NIV Bible Commentary*, 1142.

7. Frank S. Mead, ed., *12,000 Religious Quotations* (1965; reprint, Grand Rapids: Baker Book House, 1989), 258.

8. Barker and Kohlenberger, *Zondervan NIV Bible Commentary*, 1142.

9. Mounce, *The Book of Revelation*, 73.

10. Gill, *Exposition of the Old and New Testaments*, vol. 9, 697.

11. Joseph A. Seiss, *The Apocalypse: Exposition of the Book of Revelation* (Grand Rapids: Kregel Publications, 1987), 70.

12. William MacDonald, *Believer's Bible Commentary*, ed. Art Farstad (Nashville: Thomas Nelson Publishers, 1995), 2356.

13. Gill, *Exposition of the Old and New Testaments*, vol. 9, 698.

14. Henry, *Matthew Henry's Commentary on the Whole Bible*, 2466.

15. G. R. Beasley-Murray, *The Book of Revelation*, of *The New Century Bible Commentary* (Grand Rapids: Eerdmans Publishing Company, 1974), 84.

16. Barker and Kohlenberger, *Zondervan NIV Bible Commentary*, 1144.

17. Mounce, *The Book of Revelation*, 78.

18. Henry, *Matthew Henry's Commentary on the Whole Bible*, 2466–2467.

19. Gill, *Exposition of the Old and New Testaments*, vol. 9, 699.

20. J. Vernon McGee, *Thru the Bible*, vol. 5 (Nashville: Thomas Nelson Publishers, 1982), 906.

21. John R. W. Stott, *What Christ Thinks of the Church*, of *Expository Addresses on the First Three Chapters of the Book of Revelation* (Grand Rapids: Eerdmans Publishing Company, 1958), 54.

22. Seiss, *The Apocalypse*, 71.

23. Mounce, *The Book of Revelation*, 81; Barker and Kohlenberger, *Zondervan NIV Bible Commentary*, 1144.

24. Stott, *What Christ Thinks of the Church*, 66.

25. Thomas à Kempis, *The Imitation of Christ*, trans. Harold Bolton and Aloysius Croft (Milwaukee, Wisconsin: Bruce Publishing Company, 1940), 106.

26. *The Valley of Vision* (Banner of Truth Trust, Edinburgh, UK, 2005), 33.

27. Barker and Kohlenberger, *Zondervan NIV Bible Commentary*, 1145.

28. Cleon L. Rogers, Jr. and Cleon L. Rogers III, *The New Linguistic and Exegetical Key to the Greek New Testament* (Grand Rapids: Zondervan Publishing House, 1998), 618.

29. *Antiquities of the Jews*, in *The Complete Works of Flavius Josephus*,

trans. William Whiston (Grand Rapids: Kregel Publications, 1960), 245.

30. Mounce, *The Book of Revelation*, 84–85.

31. Gill, *Exposition of the Old and New Testaments*, vol. 9, 703.

32. *New Geneva Study Bible*, ed. R.C. Sproul (Nashville: Thomas Nelson Publishers, 1995), 502.

33. Barker and Kohlenberger, *Zondervan NIV Bible Commentary*, 1145.

34. Barker and Kohlenberger, *Zondervan NIV Bible Commentary*, 1146.

35. Mounce, *The Book of Revelation*, 88.

36. Henry, *Matthew Henry's Commentary on the Whole Bible*, 2467.

37. James Moffatt, *The Revelation of St. John the Divine*, vol. 5 of *The Expositor's Greek Testament* (Grand Rapids: Eerdmans Publishing Company, 1951), 361.

38. Mounce, *The Book of Revelation*, 90.

39. Henry, *Matthew Henry's Commentary on the Whole Bible*, 2469.

Chapter Three

1. Kenneth L. Barker and John R. Kohlenberger III, ed., *Zondervan NIV Bible Commentary*, vol. 2 (Grand Rapids: Zondervan Publishing House, 1994), 1147.

2. John Gill, *Exposition of the Old and New Testaments*, vol. 9 (1810; reprint, Paris, Arkansas: The Baptist Standard Bearer, 1989), 706.

3. J.D. Douglas, ed., *New Bible Dictionary*, 2nd ed. (Wheaton, IL: Tyndale House Publishers, 1962), 88.

4. Robert H. Mounce, *The Book of Revelation, of The New International Commentary on the New Testament*, 2nd ed. (Grand Rapids: Eerdmans Publishing Company, 1998), 91–92.

5. Barker and Kohlenberger, *Zondervan NIV Bible Commentary*, 1148.

6. Gill, *Exposition of the Old and New Testaments*, vol. 9, 707.

7. William MacDonald, *Believer's Bible Commentary*, ed. Art Farstad (Nashville: Thomas Nelson Publishers, 1995), 2358.

8. Mounce, *The Book of Revelation*, 98–99.

9. Steve Gregg, ed., *Revelation: Four Views, A Parallel Commentary* (Nashville: Thomas Nelson Publishers, 1997), 75.

10. G. R. Beasley-Murray, *The Book of Revelation, of The New Century Bible Commentary* (Grand Rapids: Eerdmans Publishing Company, 1974), 100.

11. George Eldon Ladd, *A Commentary on the Revelation of John* (Grand Rapids: Eerdmans Publishing Company, 1972), 59.

12. Simon J. Kistemaker, *Revelation, of New Testament Commentary* (Grand Rapids: Baker Books, 2001), 161.

13. Beasley-Murray, *The Book of Revelation*, 100–101.

14. Kistemaker, *Revelation*, 162–163.

15. Cleon L. Rogers, Jr. and Cleon L. Rogers III, *The New Linguistic and Exegetical Key to the Greek New Testament* (Grand Rapids: Zondervan Publishing House, 1998), 621.

16. Matthew Henry, *Matthew Henry's Commentary on the Whole Bible* (Peabody, Massachusetts: Hendrickson Publishers, 1991), 2469.

17. Excerpt from "Thus Saith the Holy One, and True," words by John Newton, in *Olney Hymns*, Book 1, 1779.

18. Bruce B. Barton et al., *Life Application Bible Commentary: Revelation* (Wheaton: Tyndale House Publishers, 2000), 46.

19. M.G. Easton, *Illustrated Bible Dictionary* (New York: Harper and Brothers, 1897), 415.

20. Gregg, *Revelation: Four Views*, 78.

21. Mounce, *The Book of Revelation*, 107.

22. Ladd, *A Commentary on the Revelation of John*, 64.

23. Barton et al., *Life Application Bible Commentary: Revelation*, 48.

24. Kistemaker, *Revelation*, 169.

25. D. A. Carson, *New Bible Commentary: 21st Century Edition*, 4th ed. (Leicester, England; Downers Grove, Ill., USA: Inter-Varsity Press, 1994), Revelation 3:14.
26. MacDonald, *Believer's Bible Commentary*, 2360.
27. Robert Jamieson, Andrew R. Fausset, and David Brown, *Jamieson, Fausset, and Brown's Commentary* (Grand Rapids: Zondervan Publishing House, 1961), 1540.

Chapter Four

1. John Gill, *Exposition of the Old and New Testaments*, vol. 9 (1810; reprint, Paris, Arkansas: The Baptist Standard Bearer, 1989), 716; Bruce B. Barton et al., *Life Application Bible Commentary: Revelation* (Wheaton: Tyndale House Publishers, 2000), 53; William MacDonald, *Believer's Bible Commentary*, ed. Art Farstad (Nashville: Thomas Nelson Publishers, 1995), 2361.
2. Joseph A. Seiss, *The Apocalypse: Exposition of the Book of Revelation* (Grand Rapids: Kregel Publications, 1987), 95-97; Steve Gregg, ed., *Revelation: Four Views, A Parallel Commentary* (Nashville: Thomas Nelson Publishers, 1997), 85.
3. Merrill C. Tenney, *Interpreting Revelation: A Reasonable Guide to Understanding the Last Book in the Bible* (1957; reprint, Peabody, Massachusetts: Hendrickson Publishers, 2001), 141.
4. Seiss, *The Apocalypse*, 99.
5. Robert H. Mounce, *The Book of Revelation, of The New International Commentary on the New Testament*, 2nd ed. (Grand Rapids: Eerdmans Publishing Company, 1998), 119.
6. Gregg, *Revelation: Four Views*, 87-89.
7. Mounce, *The Book of Revelation*, 121-122.
8. J. Vernon McGee, *Thru the Bible*, vol. 5 (Nashville: Thomas Nelson Publishers, 1982), 930-931.
9. Pfeiffer and Harrison, *The Wycliffe Bible Commentary*, 1505.

10. Seiss, *The Apocalypse*, 102.

11. George Ricker Berry, *Greek to English Interlinear New Testament (KJV)* (Grand Rapids: World Publishing, 1981), 631.

12. Kenneth L. Barker and John R. Kohlenberger III, ed., *Zondervan NIV Bible Commentary*, vol. 2 (Grand Rapids: Zondervan Publishing House, 1994), 1156.

13. MacDonald, *Believer's Bible Commentary*, 2362.

14. Henry, *Matthew Henry's Commentary on the Whole Bible*, 2470–2471.

Chapter Five

1. W. A. Criswell, *Expository Sermons on Revelation* (Grand Rapids: Zondervan Publishing House, 1962), 56.

2. Merrill C. Tenney, *Interpreting Revelation: A Reasonable Guide to Understanding the Last Book in the Bible* (1957; reprint, Peabody, Massachusetts: Hendrickson Publishers, 2001), 126.

3. Kenneth L. Barker and John R. Kohlenberger III, ed., *Zondervan NIV Bible Commentary*, vol. 2 (Grand Rapids: Zondervan Publishing House, 1994), 1157.

4. Bruce B. Barton et al., *Life Application Bible Commentary: Revelation* (Wheaton: Tyndale House Publishers, 2000), 59; Robert H. Mounce, *The Book of Revelation*, of *The New International Commentary on the New Testament*, 2nd ed. (Grand Rapids: Eerdmans Publishing Company, 1998), 129.

5. John Gill, *Exposition of the Old and New Testaments*, vol. 9 (1810; reprint, Paris, Arkansas: The Baptist Standard Bearer, 1989), 723.

6. Matthew Henry, *Matthew Henry's Commentary on the Whole Bible* (Peabody, Massachusetts: Hendrickson Publishers, 1991), 2471; Barker and Kohlenberger, *Zondervan NIV Bible Commentary*, 1158.

7. Joseph A. Seiss, *The Apocalypse: Exposition of the Book of Revelation* (Grand Rapids: Kregel Publications, 1987), 114.

8. Mounce, *The Book of Revelation*, 131.

9. Barton et al., *Life Application Bible Commentary: Revelation*, 60; Mounce, *The Book of Revelation*, 144; Henry, *Matthew Henry's Commentary on the Whole Bible*, 2471.

10. Gill, *Exposition of the Old and New Testaments*, vol. 9, 727–728.

11. Barton et al., *Life Application Bible Commentary: Revelation*, 66.

12. Isaac Watts, "What Equal Honors Shall We Bring," in *Hymns and Spiritual Songs*, 1707–1709. Public Domain.

Chapter Six

1. Bruce B. Barton et al., *Life Application Bible Commentary: Revelation* (Wheaton: Tyndale House Publishers, 2000), 71.

2. Matthew Henry, *Matthew Henry's Commentary on the Whole Bible* (Peabody, Massachusetts: Hendrickson Publishers, 1991), 2472.

3. Kenneth L. Barker and John R. Kohlenberger III, ed., *Zondervan NIV Bible Commentary*, vol. 2 (Grand Rapids: Zondervan Publishing House, 1994), 1160–1161.

4. Barker and Kohlenberger, *Zondervan NIV Bible Commentary*, 1161.

5. Robert H. Mounce, *The Book of Revelation*, of *The New International Commentary on the New Testament*, 2nd ed. (Grand Rapids: Eerdmans Publishing Company, 1998), 144.

6. Steve Gregg, ed., *Revelation: Four Views, A Parallel Commentary* (Nashville: Thomas Nelson Publishers, 1997), 111.

7. M. Eugene Boring, *Revelation* (Louisville: John Knox Publishers, 1989), 122.

8. R. C. H. Lenski, *The Interpretation of St. John's Revelation*, of *Commentary on the New Testament* (Columbus: Wartburg Press, 1943), 228.

9. D. A. Carson, *New Bible Commentary: 21st Century Edition*, 4th ed. (Leicester, England; Downers Grove, Ill., USA: Inter-Varsity Press, 1994), Revelation 6:5.

10. William MacDonald, *Believer's Bible Commentary*, ed. Art Farstad (Nashville: Thomas Nelson Publishers, 1995), 2364.

11. Simon J. Kistemaker, *Revelation*, of *New Testament Commentary* (Grand Rapids: Baker Books, 2001), 237.

12. W. E. Vine, *Vine's Expository Dictionary of Old and New Testament Words* (Nashville: Thomas Nelson Publishers, 1997), 984.

Chapter Seven

1. Gleason L. Archer, *Encyclopedia of Bible Difficulties* (Grand Rapids: Zondervan Publishing House, 1982), 432–444; Michael Wilcock, *The Message of Revelation* (Downers Grove: Inter-Varsity Press, 1975), 80.

2. Joseph A. Seiss, *The Apocalypse: Exposition of the Book of Revelation* (Grand Rapids: Kregel Publications, 1987), 162.

3. Kenneth L. Barker and John R. Kohlenberger III, ed., *Zondervan NIV Bible Commentary*, vol. 2 (Grand Rapids: Zondervan Publishing House, 1994), 1165.

4. J. B. Jackson, *A Dictionary of Scripture Proper Names* (Neptune, New Jersey: Loizeaux Brothers, 1909), 55.

5. Ibid., 79, 32.

6. Ibid., 11, 68.

7. Ibid., 62.

8. Ibid., 89.

9. Ibid., 58.

10. Ibid., 46.

11. Ibid., 97, 54, 17.

12. William MacDonald, *Believer's Bible Commentary*, ed. Art Farstad (Nashville: Thomas Nelson Publishers, 1995), 2364.

13. Robert H. Mounce, *The Book of Revelation*, of *The New International Commentary on the New Testament*, 2nd ed. (Grand Rapids: Eerdmans Publishing Company, 1998), 163.

14. Robert W. Wall, *Revelation, of New International Biblical Commentary* (Peabody, Massachusetts: Hendrickson Publishers, 1991), 120.

15. John Peter. Lange, Philip. Schaff, Evelina. Moore, E. R. Craven and John H. Woods, *A Commentary on the Holy Scriptures: Revelation* (Bellingham, WA: Logos Research Systems, Inc., 2008). 191.

16. Bruce B. Barton et al., *Life Application Bible Commentary: Revelation* (Wheaton: Tyndale House Publishers, 2000), 89-90.

Chapter Eight

1. Steve Gregg, ed., *Revelation: Four Views, A Parallel Commentary* (Nashville: Thomas Nelson Publishers, 1997), 139.

2. George T. Montague, *The Apocalypse* (Ann Arbor: Servant Publications, 1992), 116-117.

3. Bruce B. Barton et al., *Life Application Bible Commentary: Revelation* (Wheaton: Tyndale House Publishers, 2000), 89-90.

4. Robert H. Mounce, *The Book of Revelation, of The New International Commentary on the New Testament*, 2nd ed. (Grand Rapids: Eerdmans Publishing Company, 1998), 174-175.

5. Joseph A. Seiss, *The Apocalypse: Exposition of the Book of Revelation* (Grand Rapids: Kregel Publications, 1987), 190-192.

6. Albert Barnes, *Revelation, of Barnes' Notes on the New Testament* (1884; reprint, Grand Rapids: Baker Books, 2001), 199-200.

7. Barton et al., *Life Application Bible Commentary: Revelation*, 96.

8. W. E. Vine, *Vine's Expository Dictionary of Old and New Testament Words* (Nashville: Thomas Nelson Publishers, 1997), 1246.

9. Mounce, *The Book of Revelation*, 181.

10. Cleon L. Rogers, Jr. and Cleon L. Rogers III, *The New Linguistic and Exegetical Key to the Greek New Testament* (Grand Rapids: Zondervan Publishing House, 1998), 630.

11. R. C. H. Lenski, *The Interpretation of St. John's Revelation, of*

Commentary on the New Testament (Columbus: Wartburg Press, 1943), 283.

Chapter Nine

1. Joseph A. Seiss, *The Apocalypse: Exposition of the Book of Revelation* (Grand Rapids: Kregel Publications, 1987), 204; William MacDonald, *Believer's Bible Commentary*, ed. Art Farstad (Nashville: Thomas Nelson Publishers, 1995), 2366.

2. Albert Barnes, *Revelation*, of *Barnes' Notes on the New Testament* (1884; reprint, Grand Rapids: Baker Books, 2001), 210.

3. Robert H. Mounce, *The Book of Revelation*, of *The New International Commentary on the New Testament*, 2nd ed. (Grand Rapids: Eerdmans Publishing Company, 1998), 187.

4. J.B. Jackson, *A Dictionary of Scripture Proper Names* (Neptune, New Jersey: Loizeaux Brothers, 1909), 1, 9.

5. Barnes, *Revelation*, 226.

6. R. C. H. Lenski, *The Interpretation of St. John's Revelation*, of *Commentary on the New Testament* (Columbus: Wartburg Press, 1943), 301.

7. Barnes, *Revelation*, 227.

8. Robert Jamieson, Andrew R. Fausset, and David Brown, *Jamieson, Fausset, and Brown's Commentary* (Grand Rapids: Zondervan Publishing House, 1961), 1553.

9. Simon J. Kistemaker, *Revelation*, of *New Testament Commentary* (Grand Rapids: Baker Books, 2001), 298; Mounce, *The Book of Revelation*, 196.

10. Barnes, *Revelation*, 229–230.

11. John Milton, *Samson Agonistes*, 1671 (public domain).

Chapter Ten

1. R. H. Charles, *The Revelation of St. John*, vol. 1, of *The International Critical Commentary* (Edinburgh: T & T Clark, 1920), 258–259.

2. R. C. H. Lenski, *The Interpretation of St. John's Revelation*, of *Commentary on the New Testament* (Columbus: Wartburg Press, 1943), 311.

3. Donald W. Richardson, *The Revelation of Jesus Christ* (Louisville: John Knox Publishers, 1964), 101; Matthew Henry, *Matthew Henry's Commentary on the Whole Bible* (Peabody, Massachusetts: Hendrickson Publishers, 1991), 2475.

4. Robert H. Mounce, *The Book of Revelation*, of *The New International Commentary on the New Testament*, 2nd ed. (Grand Rapids: Eerdmans Publishing Company, 1998), 201.

5. Joseph A. Seiss, *The Apocalypse: Exposition of the Book of Revelation* (Grand Rapids: Kregel Publications, 1987), 223-224.

6. Bruce B. Barton et al., *Life Application Bible Commentary: Revelation* (Wheaton: Tyndale House Publishers, 2000), 111.

7. Mounce, *The Book of Revelation*, 204.

8. George T. Montague, *The Apocalypse* (Ann Arbor: Servant Publications, 1992), 128.

9. Mounce, *The Book of Revelation*, 208.

10. William MacDonald, *Believer's Bible Commentary*, ed. Art Farstad (Nashville: Thomas Nelson Publishers, 1995), 2367.

11. William Hendrickson, *More Than Conquerors* (Grand Rapids: Baker Books, 1944), 151; Kenneth L. Barker and John R. Kohlenberger III, ed., *Zondervan NIV Bible Commentary*, vol. 2 (Grand Rapids: Zondervan Publishing House, 1994), 1174; Lenski, *The Interpretation of St. John's Revelation*, 323-324.

12. Mounce, *The Book of Revelation*, 209.

13. Simon J. Kistemaker, *Revelation*, of *New Testament Commentary* (Grand Rapids: Baker Books, 2001), 317.

14. "Come, Divine Interpreter," words by Charles Wesley, in *Short Hymns on Select Passages of Holy Scripture*, 1762 (public domain).

Chapter Eleven

1. Gerhard A. Krodel, *Revelation*, of *The Augsburg Commentary on the New Testament* (Minneapolis: Augsburg Publishing House, 1989), 221.

2. Cleon L. Rogers, Jr. and Cleon L. Rogers III, *The New Linguistic and Exegetical Key to the Greek New Testament* (Grand Rapids: Zondervan Publishing House, 1998), 633.

3. Bruce B. Barton et al., *Life Application Bible Commentary: Revelation* (Wheaton: Tyndale House Publishers, 2000), 116.

4. Steve Gregg, ed., *Revelation: Four Views, A Parallel Commentary* (Nashville: Thomas Nelson Publishers, 1997), 222.

5. Albert Barnes, *Revelation*, of *Barnes' Notes on the New Testament* (1884; reprint, Grand Rapids: Baker Books, 2001), 268.

6. *Gregg, Revelation: Four Views*, 220.

7. R. C. H. Lenski, *The Interpretation of St. John's Revelation*, of *Commentary on the New Testament* (Columbus: Wartburg Press, 1943), 328; M. Eugene Boring, *Revelation* (Louisville: John Knox Publishers, 1989), 143.

8. Michael. Wilcock, *The Message of Revelation: I Saw Heaven Opened, The Bible Speaks Today* (Leicester, England; Downers Grove, Ill., U.S.A.: Inter-Varsity Press, 1986], c1975). 104.

9. Joseph A. Seiss, *The Apocalypse: Exposition of the Book of Revelation* (Grand Rapids: Kregel Publications, 1987), 236.

10. Robert H. Mounce, *The Book of Revelation*, of *The New International Commentary on the New Testament*, 2nd ed. (Grand Rapids: Eerdmans Publishing Company, 1998), 213.

11. Martin Kiddle, *The Revelation of St. John*, of *The Moffatt New Testament Commentary* (London: Hodder and Stoughton, 1940), 189.

12. J. P. M. Sweet, *Revelation*, of *Westminster Pelican Commentaries* (Philadelphia: Westminster, 1979), 182.

13. Kenneth L. Barker and John R. Kohlenberger III, ed., *Zondervan NIV Bible Commentary*, vol. 2 (Grand Rapids: Zondervan Publishing House, 1994), 1176.

14. Alfred Marshall, *The Interlinear NKJ-NIV Parallel New Testament in Greek and English* (Grand Rapids: Zondervan Publishing House, 1975), 747.

15. Barnes, *Revelation*, 271–273.

16. Mounce, *The Book of Revelation*, 215.

17. Matthew Henry, *Matthew Henry's Commentary on the Whole Bible* (Peabody, Massachusetts: Hendrickson Publishers, 1991), 2476.

18. Mounce, *The Book of Revelation*, 217.

19. Lenski, *The Interpretation of St. John's Revelation*, 334–335.

20. Seiss, *The Apocalypse*, 242–243.

21. James M. Freeman, *The New Manners and Customs of the Bible*, ed. Harold J. Chadwick (North Brunswick, New Jersey: Bridge-Logos Publishers, 1998), 73.

22. Simon J. Kistemaker, *Revelation*, of *New Testament Commentary* (Grand Rapids: Baker Books, 2001), 330.

23. Barton et al., *Life Application Bible Commentary: Revelation*, 121; Mounce, *The Book of Revelation*, 216.

24. Seiss, *The Apocalypse*, 250.

25. Henry, *Commentary on the Whole Bible*, 2476.

26. Barton et al., *Life Application Bible Commentary: Revelation*, 125.

27. Seiss, *The Apocalypse*, 264.

28. George T. Montague, *The Apocalypse: Understanding the Book of Revelation & the End of the World* (Ann Arbor: Servant Publications, 1992), 138.

29. Sweet, *Revelation*, 187.

30. Mounce, *The Book of Revelation*, 226.

31. Barton et al., *Life Application Bible Commentary: Revelation*, 134.

Chapter Twelve

1. Steve Gregg, ed., *Revelation: Four Views, A Parallel Commentary* (Nashville: Thomas Nelson Publishers, 1997), 252–257.

2. William MacDonald, *Believer's Bible Commentary*, ed. Art Farstad (Nashville: Thomas Nelson Publishers, 1995), 2369; Joseph A. Seiss, *The Apocalypse: Exposition of the Book of Revelation* (Grand Rapids: Kregel Publications, 1987), 279–280.

3. Seiss, *The Apocalypse*, 310.

4. Barnes, *Revelation*, 312; Kenneth L. Barker and John R. Kohlenberger III, ed., *Zondervan NIV Bible Commentary*, vol. 2 (Grand Rapids: Zondervan Publishing House, 1994), 1185; Lenski, *The Interpretation of St. John's Revelation*, 380.

5. Barton et al., *Life Application Bible Commentary: Revelation*, 143; Gregg, *Revelation: Four Views*, 269.

6. Robert H. Mounce, *The Book of Revelation*, of *The New International Commentary on the New Testament*, 2nd ed. (Grand Rapids: Eerdmans Publishing Company, 1998), 239.

7. Mounce, *The Book of Revelation*, 242; Tenney, *Interpreting Revelation*, 77.

Chapter Thirteen

1. *The King James Version, New King James Version, Young's Literal Translation, and Darby Bible* are among the major translations that render the subject standing on the seashore as John rather than the dragon. GOD'S WORD Translation, *The New American Standard Bible, New International Version, New Century Version,* and *New Living Translation* are among the major translations that render the subject standing on the seashore as the dragon rather than John.

2. Bruce B. Barton et al., *Life Application Bible Commentary: Revelation* (Wheaton: Tyndale House Publishers, 2000), 153.

3. W. E. Vine, *Vine's Expository Dictionary of Old and New Testament Words* (Nashville: Thomas Nelson Publishers, 1997), 1075, 229.

4. Robert H. Mounce, *The Book of Revelation*, of *The New International Commentary on the New Testament*, 2nd ed. (Grand Rapids: Eerdmans Publishing Company, 1998), 245.

5. Merrill C. Tenney, *Interpreting Revelation: A Reasonable Guide to Understanding the Last Book in the Bible* (1957; reprint, Peabody, Massachusetts: Hendrickson Publishers, 2001), 77-78.

6. Simon J. Kistemaker, *Revelation*, of *New Testament Commentary* (Grand Rapids: Baker Books, 2001), 392.

7. Mounce, *The Book of Revelation*, 245.

Chapter Fourteen

1. Albert Barnes, *Revelation*, of *Barnes' Notes on the New Testament* (1884; reprint, Grand Rapids: Baker Books, 2001), 340-341.

2. Bruce B. Barton et al., *Life Application Bible Commentary: Revelation* (Wheaton: Tyndale House Publishers, 2000), 163-166.

3. Ronald F. Youngblood, gen. ed.; F. F. Bruce and R. K. Harrison, eds., *Nelson's New Illustrated Bible Dictionary* (Nashville: Thomas Nelson Publishers, 1997).

4. Kenneth L. Barker and John R. Kohlenberger III, ed., *Zondervan NIV Bible Commentary*, vol. 2 (Grand Rapids: Zondervan Publishing House, 1994), 1197; Merrill C. Tenney, *Interpreting Revelation: A Reasonable Guide to Understanding the Last Book in the Bible* (1957; reprint, Peabody, Massachusetts: Hendrickson Publishers, 2001), 78.

5. George Eldon Ladd, *A Commentary on the Revelation of John* (Grand Rapids: Eerdmans Publishing Company, 1972), 193.

6. R. C. H. Lenski, *The Interpretation of St. John's Revelation*, of *Commentary on the New Testament* (Columbus: Wartburg Press, 1943), 432.

7. Robert H. Mounce, *The Book of Revelation*, of *The New International*

Commentary on the New Testament, 2nd ed. (Grand Rapids: Eerdmans Publishing Company, 1998), 274–275.

8. W. E. Vine, *Vine's Expository Dictionary of Old and New Testament Words* (Nashville: Thomas Nelson Publishers, 1997), 923.

9. Merrill C. Tenney, *Interpreting Revelation: A Reasonable Guide to Understanding the Last Book in the Bible* (1957; reprint, Peabody, Massachusetts: Hendrickson Publishers, 2001), 79; *New Geneva Study Bible*, ed. R.C. Sproul (Nashville: Thomas Nelson Publishers, 1995), 2024.

10. Gleason L. Archer, Jr., Paul D. Feinberg, Douglas J. Moo, Richard R. Reiter, *Three Views on the Rapture: Pre; Mid; or Post-Tribulation?* (Grand Rapids: Zondervan Publishing House, 1996), 200.

11. Walter A. Elwell, ed., *Baker Commentary on the Bible* (Grand Rapids: Bakers Books, 1989), 1219; Matthew Henry, *Matthew Henry's Commentary on the Whole Bible* (Peabody, Massachusetts: Hendrickson Publishers, 1991), 2479.

12. Youngblood, *Nelson's New Illustrated Bible Dictionary.*

Chapter Fifteen

1. Robert H. Mounce, *The Book of Revelation*, of *The New International Commentary on the New Testament*, 2nd ed. (Grand Rapids: Eerdmans Publishing Company, 1998), 285.

2. George Ricker Berry, *Lexicon of Greek to English Interlinear New Testament (KJV)* (Grand Rapids: World Publishing, 1981), 105.

Chapter Sixteen

1. Gregory K. Beale, *The Book of Revelation: A Commentary on the Greek Text*, of *New International Greek Testament Commentary* (Grand Rapids: Eerdmans Publishing Company, 1998), 818.

2. Excerpt from "While Men Grow Bold in Wicked Ways," words by Isaac Watts, in *The Psalms of David*, 1719 (public domain).

3. J. B. Jackson, *A Dictionary of Scripture Proper Names* (Neptune, New Jersey: Loizeaux Brothers, 1909), 10.

4. R. C. H. Lenski, *The Interpretation of St. John's Revelation*, of *Commentary on the New Testament* (Columbus: Wartburg Press, 1943), 481.

5. Robert L. Thomas, *Revelation 8–22: An Exegetical Commentary* (Chicago: Moody Press, 1995), 207.

6. Simon J. Kistemaker, *Revelation*, of *New Testament Commentary* (Grand Rapids: Baker Books, 2001), 456.

Chapter Seventeen

1. W. E. Vine, *Vine's Expository Dictionary of Old and New Testament Words* (Nashville: Thomas Nelson Publishers, 1997), 455.

2. Warren W. Wiersbe, *Wiersbe's Expository Outlines on the New Testament* (Colorado Springs: Victor Books, 1992) 845; Robert Jamieson, Andrew R. Fausset, and David Brown, *Jamieson, Fausset, and Brown's Commentary* (Grand Rapids: Zondervan Publishing House, 1961), 1540.

3. Robert H. Mounce, *The Book of Revelation*, of *The New International Commentary on the New Testament*, 2nd ed. (Grand Rapids: Eerdmans Publishing Company, 1998), 311; John F. Walvoord and Roy B. Zuck, *Bible Knowledge Commentary* (Colorado Springs: Chariot Victor Publishing, 1983), 970.

4. Merrill C. Tenney, *Interpreting Revelation: A Reasonable Guide to Understanding the Last Book in the Bible* (1957; reprint, Peabody, Massachusetts: Hendrickson Publishers, 2001), 83.

5. John Knox, *The Second Volume of the Ecclesiastical History: containing the Acts and Monuments of History* (reprint, Columbus, Ohio: Lazarus Ministry Press, 2000), 257-259.

6. Beasley-Murray, *The Book of Revelation*, 256; J.D. Douglas, ed., *New Bible Dictionary*, 1038-1039.

7. John MacArthur, *MacArthur Study Bible* (Nashville: Thomas

Nelson Bibles, 1997), 2016; Barton et al., *Life Application Bible Commentary: Revelation,* 202-203; Kistemaker, *Revelation,* 470-471; Walvoord and Zuck, *Bible Knowledge Commentary,* 971.

8. Mounce, *The Book of Revelation,* 316-317; Kistemaker, *Revelation,* 472.

Chapter Eighteen

1. Kenneth S. Wuest, *The New Testament: An Expanded Translation* (Grand Rapids, MI: Eerdmans, 1997, c1961), Revelation 18:1.

2. Vern S. Poythress, *The Returning King: A Guide to the Book of Revelation* (Phillipsburg, New Jersey: P & R Publishing, 2000), 159-160.

3. Poythress, *The Returning King,* 171.

Chapter Nineteen

1. Simon J. Kistemaker, *Revelation,* of *New Testament Commentary* (Grand Rapids: Baker Books, 2001), 517-518.

2. Joseph A. Seiss, *The Apocalypse: Exposition of the Book of Revelation* (Grand Rapids: Kregel Publications, 1987), 436.

3. Robert H. Mounce, *The Book of Revelation,* of *The New International Commentary on the New Testament,* 2nd ed. (Grand Rapids: Eerdmans Publishing Company, 1998), 353.

4. Vern S. Poythress, *The Returning King: A Guide to the Book of Revelation* (Phillipsburg, New Jersey: P & R Publishing, 2000), 174.

5. Matthew Henry, *Matthew Henry's Commentary on the Whole Bible* (Peabody, Massachusetts: Hendrickson Publishers, 1991), 1915.

Chapter Twenty

1. Steve Gregg, ed., *Revelation: Four Views, A Parallel Commentary* (Nashville: Thomas Nelson Publishers, 1997), 458-459.

2. Robert H. Mounce, *The Book of Revelation,* of *The New International*

Commentary on the New Testament, 2nd ed. (Grand Rapids: Eerdmans Publishing Company, 1998), 360.

3. Gregg, Revelation: Four Views, 460–464.

4. Wayne Grudem, Systematic Theology (Grand Rapids: Zondervan Publishing House, 1994), 1127–1129.

5. John F. Walvoord and Roy B. Zuck, Bible Knowledge Commentary (Colorado Springs: Chariot Victor Publishing, 1983), 981; Barton et al., Life Application Bible Commentary: Revelation, 244; MacArthur, MacArthur Study Bible, 2021.

6. F. F. Bruce, The Revelation to John, of A New Testament Commentary (London: Pickering & Inglis, 1969), 662; Simon J. Kistemaker, Revelation, of New Testament Commentary (Grand Rapids: Baker Books, 2001), 543.

7. Robert A. Peterson, Hell on Trial: The Case for Eternal Punishment (Phillipsburg, New Jersey: P & R Publishing, 1995), 89–90.

8. G. R. Beasley-Murray, The Book of Revelation, of The New Century Bible Commentary (Grand Rapids: Eerdmans Publishing Company, 1974), 301; Barton et al., Life Application Bible Commentary: Revelation, 248–249; Lenski, The Interpretation of St. John's Revelation, 604–605.

9. MacArthur, MacArthur Study Bible, 2022; MacDonald, Believer's Bible Commentary, 2378.

10. Mounce, The Book of Revelation, 377; Ladd, A Commentary on the Revelation of John, 273.

11. R. C. H. Lenski, The Interpretation of St. John's Revelation, of Commentary on the New Testament (Columbus: Wartburg Press, 1943), 608.

12. Simon J. Kistemaker, Revelation, of New Testament Commentary (Grand Rapids: Baker Books, 2001), 548

Chapter Twenty-one

1. Simon J. Kistemaker, *Revelation*, of *New Testament Commentary* (Grand Rapids: Baker Books, 2001), 565.

3. *Nelson's Three-in-One Bible Reference Companion* (Nashville: Thomas Nelson, 1982), 161.

4. Bruce B. Barton et al., *Life Application Bible Commentary: Revelation* (Wheaton: Tyndale House Publishers, 2000), 261.

5. W. E. Vine, *Vine's Expository Dictionary of Old and New Testament Words* (Nashville: Thomas Nelson Publishers, 1997), 774.

6. Matthew Henry, *Matthew Henry's Commentary on the Whole Bible* (Peabody, Massachusetts: Hendrickson Publishers, 1991), 2484.

7. George Eldon Ladd, *A Commentary on the Revelation of John* (Grand Rapids: Eerdmans Publishing Company, 1972), 285.

8. Matthew Henry, *Matthew Henry's Commentary on the Whole Bible* (Peabody, Massachusetts: Hendrickson Publishers, 1991), 2484.

Chapter Twenty-two

1. Kenneth S. Wuest, *The New Testament: An Expanded Translation* (Grand Rapids, MI: Eerdmans, 1997, c1961), Revelation 22:1.

2. Robert H. Mounce, *The Book of Revelation*, of *The New International Commentary on the New Testament*, 2nd ed. (Grand Rapids: Eerdmans Publishing Company, 1998), 408.

3. Excerpt from "Whate'er My God Ordains Is Right," words by Samuel Rodigast, 1676, trans. Catherine Winkworth, 1863 (public domain).

Contact Information

Practical Christianity Foundation
2514 Aloha Place
Holiday, Florida 34691
www.practicalchristianityfoundation.com

Study Notes

Study Notes

Study Notes

Study Notes

Study Notes

Study Notes